THE PHILADELPHIA PRESS

ROWAN
guide to
PUBLIC SPEAKING

FOURTH EDITION

Philadelphia Press is an eco-friendly, environmentally conscious company.
We strive to keep our carbon footprint to an absolute minimum,
and to deliver non-paper products whenever possible.

All rights reserved. No part of this book may be reproduced or utilized in
any form or by any means, electronic or mechanical, including photocopying
and recording, or by any information storage and retrieval system
without written permission from the publisher.
Books may be purchased for educational purposes.
For information, please call or write: (888) 851-3367

Philadelphia Press
Website: www.philadelphiapress.com
Email: info@philadelphiapress.com
ISBN: 978-1-956331-13-4
Printed in the United States of America

Contents

1. The Role of Public Speaking 1
What's the Big Deal about Public Speaking? 1
The Traditions of Public Speaking 2
Approaches to Public Speaking: Ancient Egypt 4
Critical Thinking and Listening as Communication Skills 6
The Speech Communication Process 8
The Gettysburg Address 11

2. Ethics in Public Speaking 13
NCA Credo for Ethical Communication 13
The Practice of Ethics in Public Speaking 15
The Practice of Ethics in the Digital World 16
Plagiarism 18
Be Inclusive: Speaker, Message, Audience Cycle 22
Respect Your Audience 23
Logical Fallacies 23
Ethical Listening 27

3. Speech Anxiety: Problems and Solutions 33
Glossophobia, Social Phobia and Social Anxiety 34
The Betrayal and Benefit of Biology 35
Managing Communication App 38
Practice 39
Breathe 40
Use Your Body (Release, Redirect, Reframe) 40
Exercise 41
Use Your Thinking Brain (Relabel and Rename) 42

4. Audience Analysis 49
What Does it Mean to be Audience Centered 50
Why am I Speaking to this Audience 51
Who Specifically is in My Audience 51
What are the Motivations and Expectations of the Audience 52
In What Context is this Speech Being Made 53
In What Environment is this Speech Being Made 53
How is the Topic I Choose Audience-Centered 53
Different Types of Audiences 55
Situational Audience Analysis 57
Speech Adaptation with Specific Audiences 59
Audience Relationship with the Speaker 61
Challenges Faced in the Speaker/Audience Relationship 62
Strategies to Improve Speaker Dialogue 63

5. Selecting a Topic and Purpose 65
What Do I Already Know That I Can Share with My Audience 65
Finding an Authentic Topic 66
What Do I Want to Know More About That The Audience Would Also 67
Overall Questions to Consider When Selecting a Topic 68
Your General and Specific Purpose 69
Specific Purpose 70
Central Idea 71

6. Research for Effective Communication 75
- Gathering Information 76
- Choose Your Search terms Carefully 77
- Use the Best Available Search Tools 78
- Use Your results to Refine Your Search Further 80
- Assessing information 82
- Placing Information 89

7. Outlining 93
- The Preparation Outline 94
- Criteria For Creating and Effective Preparation outline 95
- Converting the Preparation outline into the Speaking Outline 98
- Benefits to Using a Speaking Outline 99
- Sample Outline Structure 100
- Sample Preparation Outline 101
- Sample Speaking Outline 103
- References 104

8. Speech Structure 107
- Speech Body: A Review of Organizational Models with examples 108
- Chronological 109
- Spatial 110
- Problem-Solution 112
- Topical 112
- Introductions-The Beginning 114
- Conclusions 120
- Connectives 122

9. Rehearsal and Delivery 127
- Delivering Your Speech 130
- Using Your Body Movement 131
- Using Your Voice 137
- The Three 'C's' of Language 142
- Practicing Your Speech 144

10. Visual Aids for Effective Communication 149
- Graphs 150
- Charts 150
- Drawings and Photographs 151
- Presentation Technology (PowerPoint) 151
- Video 152
- Objects 152
- Developing S.M.A.R.T. VisualAids- Five Rules 153
- Things to Keep In Mind When Using Visual Aids 156
- Have a Clear Message 157
- Be Selective 157
- Use Variety 158
- Explain and Display 159
- Don't Talk to Your Visual Aid 160

11. Listening and Evaluating 171
- Types of Listening 172
- The Stages of Listening 172
- Barriers to Effective Listening 173
- Listening Styles 176
- Effective Listening: A Plan for Improvement 178
- Active Listening Activities 180

12. Informative Speaking ... 185
- The Function, Purpose, and Goal of the Informative Speech ... 185
- Types of Informative Speeches ... 185
- Description ... 186
- Explanation ... 187
- Report Speeches ... 188
- Other Types of Report Speech ... 191
- Speeches of Instruction ... 191
- Method of Organization ... 196

13. Technical Speaking ... 199
- Is a Technical Speech a Speech to Inform ... 200
- The Key Questions of Technical Speaking ... 201
- Methods of Organization for Technical Speaking ... 202
- Technical Language ... 204
- Analogies and Imagery ... 205
- Tips for Technical Speeches ... 206
- Purpose Statements for Technical Speeches ... 207
- Technical Visuals ... 208
- Technical Speech Outline Sample ... 213
- Sample Outline-Process- APA Format ... 219
- Sample Outline-Process-MLA Format ... 225

14. Persuasive Speaking ... 235
- Ethos/Pathos/Logos/Mythos ... 235
- Ethos ... 235
- Pathos ... 238
- Logos ... 239
- Mythos ... 240
- Informal Fallacies ... 241
- Types of Persuasive Speech ... 245
- Methods of Organization ... 249

15. Speaking on Special Occasions or Ceremonial Speaking ... 253
- Public Speaking Skills Application ... 254
- A Distinct Audience ... 255
- Reducing Apprehension ... 256
- Rules for Preparing a Ceremonial Speech ... 257
- Common Types of Ceremonial Speeches ... 262
- The Toast ... 262
- Speech of Introduction ... 264
- Speech of Presentation ... 265
- Speech of Acceptance ... 267
- Speech of Commemoration ... 270
- Eulogy ... 270

16. Small Group Presentation ... 275
- Characteristics of a Small Group ... 275
- Types of Small Group Presentations ... 277
- Small Group Presentational Formats ... 280
- Working Group Presentations: Preparation and Planning ... 285
- Working Group Decision Making ... 287
- Dewey's Six Steps for Decision Making ... 288
- Delivering Working Group Findings ... 294

The ability to communicate through public speaking can improve your life and your community

You may not realize it, but you are surrounded by public speaking every day. People employ the concepts that you will learn in this course to inform or persuade an audience or to commemorate a person, place, or event. In fact, whether you know it or not, you use many public speaking skills while talking to people in everyday life. You sculpt your stories, organize your arguments, and use a number of techniques intuitively that taking a course in public speaking can help you to improve.

Getting a Job and Advancing
Your abilities as a good public speaker can earn you more responsibility and higher pay in the workplace. In recent studies, employers cited the ability to communicate as one of the top qualities they look for in a job candidate. Whether you are working in a small group on a project, making a report in front of your colleagues and superiors, or speaking at a conference, the ability to comport yourself well and speak in a professional manner will set you apart from your peers.

Speaking to Inform, Persuade, or Commemorate
Public speaking skills can be used to inform an audience on important topics or persuade an audience to act on a certain issue. In fact, convincing someone of your abilities in a job interview is the quintessential persuasive public speaking setting. The skills learned in this course may also be employed when making a toast at a wedding, introducing a colleague, or accepting an award.

Civic Engagement
Being a good public speaker can help you to be an active member of your community, helping to ensure things like clean drinking water, equal rights, and better schools. Our system is set up to be used by the everyday people. When everyone participates in public discourse, there is nothing that can hold us back from achieving the highest goals. This course will help you learn how to get active and get involved.

The Role of Public Speaking

Dr. Tracey Quigley Holden
University of Delaware

What's the Big Deal about Public Speaking?

The big deal is that public speaking is an essential social and professional skill. The National Association of Colleges and Employers (NACE) periodically conducts surveys asking what key skills employers want in their staff. Year after year, the answer is public speaking, closely followed by good writing skills. In the 2016 surveys, verbal communication is ranked highest for job candidates (National Association of College and Employers Staff, 2016). It's not just job seekers who need public speaking. *The Wall Street Journal* reported that the "gift of gab" — effective public speaking skills – made the difference in professional achievement, from winning clients to closing sales (Haislip, 2010). Public speaking is recognized beyond the world of business as well, in settings ranging from major athletic programs (Cohen, 2015) to teaching (Silver, 2018).

One way to understand why public speaking is so highly valued is to break it down into its components. In order to speak well in public, you need to be well informed on a topic. You need to be able to discern quality information from the huge quantities that are available, and choose only the best and most relevant to craft your message. You need to be aware of the interests and attitudes of your listeners. You need to be organized in selecting what information to share with your listeners and the order in which you share particular pieces of information. You need to be loud enough to be heard, confident enough to engage with your listeners verbally and non-verbally, and you need to know when to stop. Each of these skills contributes to public speaking, and each is an important and valuable skills on its own. Added all together, they have a synergy that makes them far more powerful than any individual skill.

The anecdotal evidence is overwhelming - people with strong public speaking skills do better in interviews, are hired more often, get better reviews from their bosses, get more promotions and are more likely to ask for and get raises. Being able to speak effectively means you're more likely to be able to convince a client or a boss to buy your product or approve your project. Beyond the professional arena, effective communication can help you have better relationships, negotiate major purchases (think cars and houses) and understand the world around you with more clarity and competence.

In this course, we not only teach the presentation part of public speaking, but also the underlying skills that make it so powerful. We discuss both the long traditions of communication and their value to our contemporary world, and the innovations in communication that are bringing about huge changes in our channels and practices. Whether you are a public speaking aficionado or feel more fear than fun when thinking about giving a speech, you will come away from this class with tools you can use immediately to make your life better – now and in the future. You might not leave class being able to "Talk Like TED" (Gallo, 2014) but you'll gain confidence, knowledge, and the skills to communicate more effectively in every area of your life. Let's get started!

The Tradition of Public Speaking

Communication is a central characteristic of human beings; our brains are hardwired to develop language and seek social interaction. So it is not surprising that humans also have a long tradition of studying communication, how it works, what makes it more or less effective, and how we can improve our communication skills.

The ancient Greeks are credited with some of the earliest formal studies of communication. More than two thousand years ago, philosophers you have probably heard of - Socrates, Plato, and Aristotle – spoke and wrote extensively about the rhetoric of public persuasion. Aristotle's book, *On Rhetoric: A Theory of Civic Discourse* (trans. 1991), is still considered the most important book on rhetoric ever written (Golden, 2007). The Sophists were teachers and practitioners of rhetoric who offered instruction and gave extended public orations to demonstrate their talents. It's important to remember that Greek society depended on oral communication in many essential functions, including government and the courts.

All citizens were expected to participate in public debates and discussions. A skilled speaker had a tremendous advantage. Alcidamas, an important Sophist, argued that public speaking was more challenging and more effective than written texts. Public speaking, he thought, required the speaker to effectively communicate with their audiences in the moment, rather than taking time to reflect on and edit their words (Alcidamas, trans. 2001). Alcidamas believed and taught his pupils that they needed to be fully prepared on their topics, and able to respond to the audience in the moment of speaking. In many ways, Alcidamas was advocating for what we call a "conversational tone" from the speaker. Although the speaker has significant knowledge and has thought carefully about what he wants to say on a given topic, he also recognizes the needs of the audience and respond to those needs. That sense of mutual participation is at the core of excellent speaking. If both the speaker and the audience are contributing and engaged in the communicative process, it's far more likely that an effective exchange will occur.

Roman scholars and statesmen also valued public speaking and continued its study. Cicero, a Roman Senator and contemporary of Julius Caesar, developed the five essential Canons of Rhetoric as a guide to effective speech. They are invention, arrangement, style, delivery, and memory. Invention is what goes into a speech – the content and information it contains. Arrangement is the organization, how the content is structured and in what order. Style is how the information is presented – formally or informally, with ornate or plain language. Cicero held beautifully crafted, graceful, and polished speeches in high esteem; he believed that elegant style was a distinctive mark of excellence in a speaker. Delivery is the physical act of speech, including gestures, movement, tone, pace, and inflection. Memory, which was added some time after the first four Canons, is the process of learning and memorizing a speech. The principles of the canons endure, with some adjustments for our contemporary usage.

The Five Canons of Rhetoric

Invention
Arrangement
Style
Delivery
Memory

The central role of communication in community life and in the pursuit of knowledge has been well established by the Greeks, as is the importance of teaching communication as an important life skill adaptable to changing times. The Romans kept communication at the center of public and political action and incorporated key aspects of ethics, public service, and the role of the citizen.

Approaches to Public Speaking: Ancient Egypt
Contributed by Dr. Sheena Howard

The origins of rhetoric, and by extension public speaking, are largely rooted in Western thought; however over the last two decades scholars have sought to incorporate recognition and understanding of classical rhetorical legacies outside of Greece and Rome. This is particularly important as we consider the rapid demographic shifts we are seeing in the United States, as it relates to an increase in students of color and the multiculturalism of the student population. *African American Rhetoric(s): Interdisciplinary Perspectives* by Ronald L. Jackson and Elaine B. Richardson (2007), states:

> As we enter a new century of scholarship in interdisciplinary fields, many of us have finally come to appreciate and to understand critical advantages in having theoretical frames that take into account achievements that may and may not resonate with European cultural traditions. In broadening our horizons with experiences and information from different geographical and cultural spaces, we extend our horizons and enrich our understanding, not just of peripheral people in knowledge-making arenas but of human potential.

Other scholars continue to expand the base of public communication studies by drawing from ancestral Africa. Early work, by Molefi Kete Asante, connects the symbols, motifs and language practices of ancient Egypt to the current practices of diverse cultures, such as African-Americans. Asante is the author of several books, including but not limited to, *Kemet, Afrocentricity* and, *Knowledge and Rhetoric, Race and Identity: The Architecton of Soul*. From these works, including the works of others, we know that the Egyptians valued reticence, believing that language should not be used carelessly, and that silence can and was used strategically. These concepts are laid out in ancient Egyptian texts called sebyt (sebait), which means "instructions". Thus, according to Fox (1983), the Five-Canons of Kemet (ancient Egyptian) rhetoric are as follows:

- **Silence:** The act of self control as a way to maintain your good reputation.
- **Good timing:** Be deliberate when you speak, so as to say distinguish yourself.
- **Restraint:** Be aware that the heart may contain words that should not be said aloud, as speaking is more dangerous than fighting.
- **Fluency:** You must give the impression of confidence, security and stability when you speak.
- **Truthfulness:** Honesty creates your character and is in itself persuasive.

For ancient Egyptian teachers, these Five-Canons together encompass what Western thought would call ethos (appeal to ethic and good character). The ethos created by the aforementioned canons of Egyptian rhetoric is that of harmony with divine justice. There is a fundamental association between the Egyptian instructions and those of Quintilian in their emphasis on the orator (person speaking) rather than on the oratory (what is being said). Egyptian rhetoric can be encapsulated in Quintilian's dictum that only a good man can speak well (Fox, 1983).

Ancient Egyptian rhetorical practices have been used in examining, understanding and studying African-American oratory, communication dynamics and practices. Outside of the Five Canons of Kemetic Rhetoric, African classical rhetoric values communalism, nommo (the power of the word), building community, dignity, and eloquence.

Critical Thinking and Listening as Communication Skills

Much of our discussion and instruction around communication focuses on messages and messengers. But if we return to the foundations of public speaking, the first canon is invention – careful consideration and evaluation of the content of our speeches. Knowing what facts to include and what to leave out is a key part of effective, ethical communication. Senator Daniel Moynihan (2010) is credited with the saying, "Everyone is entitled to their own opinion, but they are not entitled to their own facts." We live in a society swamped with information, with very little distinction made between fact, fiction, opinion, and fabrications. In 1982, Buckminster Fuller reported that human knowledge had doubled about every century prior to 1900. Since the beginning of the 20th century, that pace has rapidly increased and shows every sign of continuing to accelerate. Some estimates hold that human knowledge is doubling every 12 months and that the pace continues to increase; a decade ago, IBM scientists claimed that by the mid-21st century, the Internet of Things could be doubling our knowledge every 12 hours (IBM Global Technology Services, 2006).

As we try to manage life and make decisions in the midst of all of this information, two key but often underdeveloped and underused skills become essential – critical thinking and critical listening.

Critical thinking is the ability to thoughtfully and carefully gather, assess, and use information to improve understanding, refine our beliefs, and guide our actions.

Critical thinking is an active process, which requires self-reflection and assessment of our own tendencies, biases, and pre-conceptions along with assessment of the information we consider. With over 4.5 billion pages on the indexed Web, more than 500 direct broadcast channels, nearly 2,000 television stations, and over 1,000 newspapers in the U.S., access to information is almost unlimited, but the quality and accuracy of this information varies wildly. Developing our abilities to evaluate, interpret, analyze, explain, and regulate our preconceptions allow us to function more effectively (Tillius, 2012). The saying, "Knowledge is power" only holds true when the knowledge we hold is accurate and usable.

If critical thinking skills are underdeveloped and underused, the ability to listen critically is on the endangered list. Not only is listening rarely taught or practiced, but our culture values multi-tasking and multiple inputs in ways that diminish our capacity to listen. You probably know someone who does homework with a television on or can't seem to walk across campus without talking on his or her phone or listening to music.

Critical listening shares many qualities with critical thinking – the incorporation of careful attention, comprehension checking, and reasoning applied to what we hear.

If critical thinking poses significant challenges for us, critical listening adds another level. We have become accustomed to high levels of distraction and low levels of attention. Practicing good listening takes concentrated effort and focus. Not only do we need to use our critical thinking skills to discern the differences between facts and mere opinion, we also need to be able to check assumptions; does the speaker offer support for his or her claims, or merely make unfounded statements? Accepting claims without evidence makes for easier listening, but less reliable information. Finally, we need to maintain a reasonable level of openness to new ideas.

When we hear ideas or information that contradicts our existing knowledge, we experience cognitive dissonance. It takes effort to evaluate the new information, to then check to see if it can be connected to what we already know, and then to incorporate both into new, usable knowledge. Finally, along with openness to new ideas, critical listening requires that we refrain from prejudging a speaker. As with critical thinking, our own biases and pre-conceptions can cause us to reject accurate and valuable information from a speaker simply because they don't conform to our existing understanding. Critical thinking and critical listening set standards for speakers and listeners – both strive for accuracy, understanding, and increased knowledge. How that happens is the focus of the next section.

The Speech Communication Process

As much as history can (and should) inform our current understanding of the world we live in, it's an imperfect and often misdirected record. Early speech communication analysis was influenced by information processing models developed by engineers working for Bell Laboratories – the telephone company. Claude Shannon and Warren Weaver developed a model to determine the information capabilities of transmission equipment. The model offers an elegant and parsimonious view of the communication process, but leaves out nearly all of the confounding human factors. Shannon and Weaver didn't need to consider the faults and foibles of humans in their model. And from the most basic perspective, it provides some clarity about how communication happens, what can interfere with the communication process, and the idea of options for sending messages.

The sender has an idea, crafts a message into language (encoding), and sends

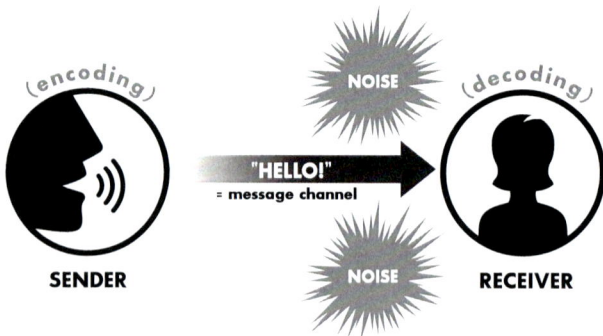

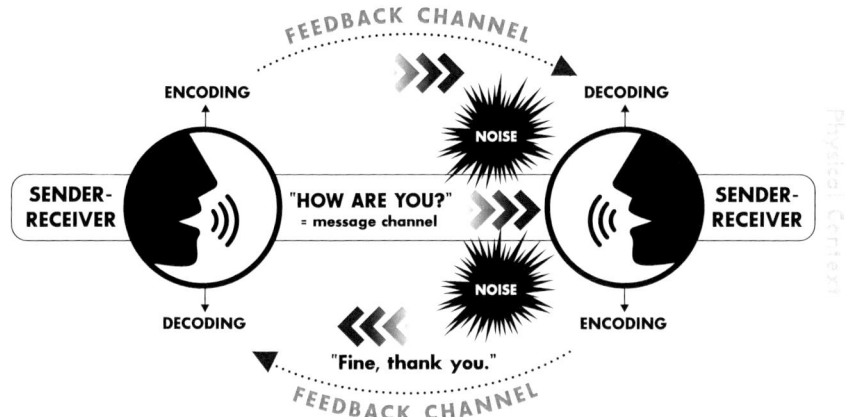

the message to a receiver. The receiver decodes the message, and then can send a response back to the sender. Noise is anything that interferes with the message transmission or receipt; it can be literal noise, distraction, lack of comprehension, or a host of other possibilities.

The problems with this basic model are significant. Communication simply doesn't occur in a neat, one-at-a-time, linear way. In many ways we are always communicating; we don't stop conveying meaning when we stop speaking. Perhaps more importantly, we bring our full selves into every communication situation or interaction. Our understanding of the context, the participants, the intentions for this particular interaction, the possible outcomes, and our own history and experience up to that very moment all influence how, what, and when we communicate. And it all happens at the same time!

Instead of a linear, transactional model, the actual communication process involves multiple potential contributing elements, including the participants seeking to share meaning. If you can imagine everything in the model above rolled into a ball and happening at the same time, you'd be close. The picture tries to incorporate more of the pieces and influences, but still falls well short of the complexity of human communication in progress.

If you're still wondering why you're taking a class in communication – just understanding the elements of the process should help justify the need. The more you understand how communication works, the more effective you can be when you communicate.

Conclusion

In this chapter we have covered a lot of ground, from the early traditions and foundations of communication, to key cognitive skills needed for effective communication and a first look at communication processes and models. Each of these elements connects to and informs the others. What we have learned from the ancient rhetoricians still holds currency today. Perhaps because communication is such a central aspect of humanity, perhaps because communication pervades our culture and society, the lessons learned thousands of years ago continue to teach us today.

References

Alcidamas. (2001). *Alcidamas: The works and fragments.* (J. Muir, Trans.) Briston: Bristol Classical Press.

Aristotle. (1991). *On rhetoric: a theory of civic discoursee.* (G. A. Kennedy, Trans.) Oxfort: Oxford University Press.

Everitt, A. (2001). Cicero: the life and times of Rome's greatest politician. New York: Random House.

Gallo, C. (2014). *Talk like TED.* New York City: St.Martin's Press.

Golden, J. L. (2007). The rhetoric of western thought: from the mediterranean world to the global setting. Dubuque, IA: Kendall Hunt.

Haislip, B. (2010, August 16). The gift of gab. The *Wall Street Journal*, retreived from https://www.wsj.com

IBM Global Technology Services. (2006). *The toxic terabyte.* London: IBM UK.

Moynihan, D. P. (2010). *Daniel Patrick Moynihan: A portrait in letter of an American visionary.* (S. R. Weisman, Ed.) New York: Public Affairs.

Tillius, G. (2012, June). *Six critical thinking skills you need to master now.* Retrieved from Rasmussen College: http://www.rasmussen.edu student-life/blogs/main/critical-thinking-skills-you-need-to-master-now/

Richardson, E. B., & Jackson, R. L. (2007). *African American rhetoric (s): interdisciplinary perspectives.* SIU Press Carbondale, IL.

Silver, F. (2018, February 20). Why is it important for teachers to have good public speaking skills? *The Chronicle of Higher Education* , retreived from https://www.wsj.com

Abraham Lincoln's Gettysburg Address is one of the most well-known and well-loved examples of American oratory.

The Gettysburg Address

"Fourscore and seven years ago our fathers brought forth on this continent a new nation, conceived in liberty and dedicated to the proposition that all men are created equal. Now we are engaged in a great civil war, testing whether that nation or any nation so conceived and so dedicated can long endure. We are met on a great battlefield of that war. We have come to dedicate a portion of that field as a final resting-place for those who here gave their lives that this nation might live. It is altogether fitting and proper that we should do this. But in a larger sense, we cannot dedicate, we cannot consecrate, we cannot hallow this ground. The brave men, living and dead who struggled here have consecrated it far above our poor power to add or detract. The world will little note nor long remember what we say here, but it can never forget what they did here. It is for us the living rather to be dedicated here to the unfinished work which they who fought here have thus far so nobly advanced. It is rather for us to be here dedicated to the great task remaining before us--that from these honored dead we take increased devotion to that cause for which they gave the last full measure of devotion--that we here highly resolve that these dead shall not have died in vain, that this nation under God shall have a new birth of freedom, and that government of the people, by the people, for the people shall not perish from the earth."

Considering The Ethics of Communication

The National Communication Association is the most influential communication group in the United States, with more than 8,000 communication scholars and practitioners (Abbott, Timmerman, McDorman, & Lamberton, 2016). Over the years, NCA has published documents defining and defending free, responsible, and ethical communication. In 1963, the association published a Credo For Free and Responsible Communication, outlining guiding principles for free speech. NCA reaffirmed its commitment to those principles in 2017 and 2019. (National Communication Association, 1963) With the rise of the "information society" and the advent of massive communication capabilities, the association saw the need to codify the ethics of communication. In 1999, the association published its credo that outlines ethical communicat[ion] behaviors in communication in the public and priv[ate] sphere and reaffirmed its commitment to the Cre[do] for Ethical Communication in 2017. We will a[lso] examine this credo relating to online communicati[on] providing us with an overview of the implications o[f] practices of ethics across the field of communicati[on].

Ethics in Public Speaking

With contributions from
DR. SHEENA HOWARD
Rider University

NCA Credo for Ethical Communication
(approved by the NCA Legislative Council, November 1999 reaffirmed 2017.)

Questions of right and wrong arise whenever people communicate. Ethical communication is fundamental to responsible thinking, decision making, and the development of relationships and communities within and across contexts, cultures, channels, and media. Moreover, ethical communication enhances human worth and dignity by fostering truthfulness, fairness, responsibility, personal integrity, and respect for self and others. We believe that unethical communication threatens the quality of all communication and consequently the well-being of individuals and the society in which we live. Therefore we, the members of the National Communication Association, endorse and are committed to practicing the following principles of ethical communication:

- We advocate truthfulness, accuracy, honesty, and reason as essential to the integrity of communication
- We endorse freedom of expression, diversity of perspective, and tolerance of dissent to achieve the informed and responsible decision-making fundamental to a civil society.
- We strive to understand and respect other communicators before evaluating and responding to their messages.
- We promote access to communication resources and opportunities as necessary to fulfill human potential and contribute to the well-being of families, communities, and society.
- We promote communication climates of caring and mutual understanding that respect the unique needs and characteristics of individual communicators.

- We condemn communication that degrades individuals and humanity through distortion, intimidation, coercion, and violence, and through the expression of intolerance and hatred.
- We are committed to the courageous expression of personal convictions in pursuit of fairness and justice.
- We advocate sharing information, opinions, and feelings when facing significant choices while also respecting privacy and confidentiality.
- We accept responsibility for the short- and long-term consequences for our own communication and expect the same of others.
- As you can identify in the qualities described by the National Communication Association credo, the following are important as it relates specifically to ethics and public speaking:
  - Honesty and accuracy
  - Actively and empathetically listening before responding
  - Access to communication resources
  - Positive contributions to the well-being of humanity through communication
  - Creating a climate of mutual understanding
  - Focus on unity and communalism, despite varying perspectives and viewpoints
  - Courage in expression
  - Accountability and responsibility for speech acts

The Ethics of Public Speaking

The aforementioned list may be helpful in understanding the nature of ethics and public speaking. Though it is not always clear how one can practice the ethics of communication as a student of public speaking, such a practice is often made more apparent by our pre-existing ethical standards. Ethical standards, or moral principles, are the set of rules we abide by that help us distinguish good from bad and right from wrong in our thinking and actions (Millner & Price, 2016).

In the next section, we will use the foundational criteria established here to provide concrete tactics for incorporating ethics into the process and delivery of public communication messages. Incorporating and understanding ethical practices of public speaking will not only make you a better speaker but also shield you from the possible embarrassment of the consequences related to unethical public communication. These consequences could include, removal from one's job, loss of friendships, being shamed and smeared via social media, and failing a college course.

The Practice of Ethics in Public Speaking

As a public speaker you should always be aware of the power, responsibilities, and consequences that come with addressing an audience. Below are some core ethical public speaking ideas and behaviors that you should consider.

The Law and Practice of Public Speaking: Respecting the First Amendment The First Amendment

Congress shall make no law respecting an establishment of religion, or prohibiting the free exercise thereof; or abridging the freedom of speech, or of the press; or the right of the people peaceably to assemble, and to petition the Government for a redress of grievances.

Under the First Amendment freedom of speech is guaranteed except in certain instances. These instances include hate speech, support of terror, slander, false threats, true threats, and false advertising among others. As a public speaker it is important to be aware of when you are crossing the line between legal and illegal speech.

Source: National Communication Association. Credo for Ethical Communication. 1999. https://www.natcom.org/uploadedFiles/About_NCA/Leadership_and_Governance/Public_Policy_Platform/PDF-PolicyPlatform-NCA_Credo_for_Ethical_Communication.pdf

The Practice of Ethics in the Digital World

Although National Communication Association doctrine is from the late 1990s, before the advent of the current online tools we now have available, communication principles are just as, if not more, relevant in the current digital sphere. Online communication allows us to exercise the option of anonymity, both as a speaker and as a receiver of communication. You can choose to deliver or receive a message in the digital sphere without disclosing your identity. With AI tools trained on ever-larger amounts of public data, you can ask ChatGPT to generate a response to nearly any prompt, including intentionally imitating someone else or even "deepfaking" another person's image or voice. It's already well known that AI and LLM models "hallucinate" incorrect information and are unable to differentiate between truth, misinformation and disinformation. (Stanford Report, 2023) (Marcus, 2022). All of these factors and others demonstrate how online communication can be used in different and sometimes more unethical ways than face-to-face communication.

Some might argue that the principles of the NCA credo are even more important in the digital space because we all have the potential to use our messages to reach a wider number of people and affect a larger number of people with our communication. We now have access to individuals all over the world. Not only that, but the amount of information we are creating and sharing is increasing dramatically. In just one minute on the internet, 6.3 million searches are done on Google. In that same minute, 3.5 billion Snaps, 231 million emails, and 16.2 million texts are sent. In that same minute, 625 million TikToks and 3.47 million YouTube videos are watched along with 452 thousand hours of Netflix. (Marino, 2023). With all of that information available, we need better strategies and better tools to help us find the good stuff.

It's not surprising that tools like ChatGPT and other AI platforms are booming, with ChatGPT alone now seeing 1.8 billion visitors per month - about 42 thousand per minute (Mortensen, 2024). AI tools and large language models can be great tools for helping manage information more effectively. But no matter how much data it consumes, AI still cannot do anything we don't ask it to do. It cannot decide to write a novel or draw a picture – it can only follow the instructions we give it, and it can only draw from data that is made available to it. Dr. Jeff Hancock, a Stanford University professor researching AI, puts it this way - "The more we think of [AI] as an assistant or a tool that is incredibly powerful, the more we can envision how it will be useful. But it's important to note that these systems are not ready to plug and play right off the shelf. They're not there yet, and neither are we humans"

(Stanford Report, 2023). We still need to take our role in creating and navigating this vast amount of information and our ability to distribute information seriously.

In the age of social media and digital communication, the likelihood of your presentations and conversations being recorded and posted on third-party electronic websites or apps is a reality. Therefore, holding to high ethical standards in speaking and conducting research is critically important.

As you can identify in the qualities described by the National Communication Associations' credo, the following are important as they relate specifically to ethics and online communication:

- Plagiarism
- Respecting the Message
- Being inclusive
- Respecting Your Audience
- Respecting Yourself

These topics are helpful in our understanding the nature of ethics and online communication and showing you how you can *practice* the ethics of communication in the digital sphere. This process or practice of ethics in online communication is made easier by our ethical standards. Ethical standards, or moral principles, are the set of rules we abide by that make us "good" people and help us choose right from wrong. Consider the following practices of ethics (Millner and Price, 2016).

Throughout this chapter, we will use the foundational criteria established here to provide concrete tactics for incorporating ethics into the process and delivery of messages in the online environment, which will not only make you a better communicator in the digital space but will also shield you from the possible embarrassment of the consequences related to unethical public communication practices. These consequences could include being shamed and smeared via social media, failing a college course or being expelled from school, losing your friends or even losing your job. In the next section, we will consider the key practices of ethics in online communication.

As a public speaker, you should take seriously the responsibility you have as a public communicator and the consequences of your communication. Below are five core ethical public speaking ideas and behaviors that you should consider.

Plagiarism

Plagiarism is using someone else's work or ideas without giving the source credit or acknowledgment. When it comes to online communication, we often become inspired by the content others post or others' ideas that we want to incorporate into our messages, which should be encouraged; however, even in the online environment, you must always cite or give credit to the source whenever you use someone's idea or work.

Today, the internet is full of all kinds of information. We can find anything; enter the right words in the search box. On at least one occasion or another, most people reading this have copied and pasted social media posts or even sentences into assignments or documents without sourcing the content creator. It is exceedingly easy to copy and paste information, making the likelihood of plagiarism more prevalent. The advent of AI tools like ChatGPT has made it easier to develop materials, but also increased the risk of including misinformation and disinformation in the outputs and of plagiarizing sources. As mentioned earlier, AI tools can only access public materials or data that it is trained on. Many scholarly journals and research materials are behind paywalls and not publicly available. This leads to AI hallucinating information, sources and citations – put bluntly, it just makes them up (Weise, 2023). As creators of content in the online environment, and as students creating and delivering presentations of all kinds, we are responsible for all of the content of our communication.

Types of Plagiarism
Global Plagiarism

There are three distinct types of plagiarism – global, patchwork, and incremental plagiarism (Lucas, 2011). **Global plagiarism**, the most obvious form of plagiarism, transpires when a speaker presents a speech that is not his or her own work (Millner and Price, 2016). This would include using a speech obtained from a friend or an online site, even if some changes are made to the original speech, or asking an AI tool to write a speech for you. Plagiarism is particularly easy to catch in the online environment when people can record your speech and upload the text to applications and websites that can easily detect plagiarism.

Patchwork Plagiarism

According to Millner and Price, 2016), **patchwork plagiarism** occurs when one "patches" together bits and pieces from one or more sources and represents the result as his or her own. Michael O'Neill (1980) also coined the term "paraplaging" to explain how an author uses the partial text of sources with partial original writing. Again, this is made easier by copying and pasting text or images from online articles into our own assignments. This form of plagiarism is increasing rapidly with the enormous amount of information available on the internet, and the use of AI tools that cannot give correct citations (Marcus, 2022).

Incremental Plagiarism

The third type of plagiarism is **incremental plagiarism**, which occurs when most of the speech is the speaker's original work. Still, quotes or other information have been used without being cited. Incremental plagiarism can occur if, for example, you provide a statistic to support your claim but do not provide the source for that statistic (Millner and Price, 2016). Again, this is prevalent in the online environment, as people copy and paste quotes from others across social media platforms without always citing the source. However, just because there is no way to penalize each person engaging in plagiarism does not mean it is ethical, good or right to engage in this practice. These considerations lead us to discuss *why* social media increases the prevalence of plagiarism and how you can decrease the likelihood that you will be engaging in plagiarism in the online environment.

Intended Plagiarism

Marketing and promotion are exceedingly popular online. Brands both big and small want to "go viral;" therefore, they want you to share their content. For example, when self-published authors or companies issue a press release online, their goal is to get the media and individuals to reshare it to spread the news about what they are selling or marketing. In essence, brands want you to plagiarize so that their content or product(s) reaches as many people as possible., This practice creates an ethical dilemma as *intended plagiarism* essentially allows us to get used to or comfortable with reposting or resharing content without necessarily citing the source. However, as an effective and ethical communicator, you need to be especially mindful and intentional not to cite the source (or brand) from which your messaging comes.

Convenience and access

No prior period in human history has allowed us to access the volumes of information and data that we have today. This access to information is not showing any signs of slowing down. As discussed, social media and online communication have made it exceedingly easy to access large amounts of information, including published papers, others assignments, and day-to-day messages that might aid us in writing speeches or completing academic assignments. We can now input a prompt or two into an AI tool and ask it to generate entire speeches and assignments. Just this year the College Board issued new guidelines on the use of AI and other tools such as Grammarly, a popular editing application, warning students that work written or reviewed with these tools could be flagged for plagiarism (College Board, 2024).

As a student who wants to adhere to the utmost forms of integrity and credibility (and is required to by the academic honesty policies of your school), it is incumbent upon you to put ethics before convenience and access. Therefore, we need to increase our adherence to ethical behaviors that protect the principles of ethical communication and creator content. Make it a habit of practicing ethical communication in the online environment by citing and sourcing the ideas of others. Doing this will become second nature, and you will avoid using the content of others without giving them credit.

Ethos, Logos and Pathos

Ethos, Logos and Pathos, which you will learn about throughout this text and as you learn to construct and deliver speeches, are integral to ethical public speaking practices. **Ethos,** appeal to ethics or character, will be diminished if you do not follow ethical practices in public speaking. **Credibility** is a speaker's trustworthiness or the audience's confidence in the information that the speaker is delivering. You can develop credibility throughout your speech, and often your reputation affords you a certain amount of credibility before you even deliver your speech. **Logos** appeals to logic, which means that you need to incorporate up-to-date, factual evidence into your speech. Using flawed information, actual misinformation or faulty data can destroy a speaker's character and, ultimately, the entire speech. Check and recheck your sources and data points. Make sure your data is factual, cross-referenced and sourced. **Pathos,** an appeal to emotions, requires that speakers use relatable evidence and examples to elicit emotion, helping persuade and inform their audience. Speakers who use fear-mongering or appeal solely to play on the audience's emotions can incite and provoke distress and disproportionate responses in listeners. Therefore, speakers need to be aware of their words' power and the significance of the psychology of public speaking, even in the online environment. That is, do not rely so heavily on pathos that you cloud the audience's critical thinking—doing so is unethical.

Respect the Message

You should not mistake inclusivity with disagreement. If your position is different from someone else's, that does not mean you are not inclusive. You can share an oppositional point of view without being divisive or offensive. One way to do this is to use accurate and factual information that credible supporting materials can verify. Verify your supporting materials by checking the claims you intend to use in your speech, with at least two reputable sources.

Reputable sources include peer-reviewed academic journal articles and vetted news outlines with a history of fair and accurate reporting backed by scientific data. Additionally, when using images, music, songs or the like, it is especially important to follow copyright law for media used in your presentation. In the academic setting, fair use likely applies to how you will use media in your digital presentation as your content is not for commercial use or sale. While this chapter is not about copyright law specifically, it is prudent to take a quick look at a specific section of the United States Copyright Act: Section 107 of the Copyright Act defines fair use as follows: {T}he fair use of a copyrighted work, including such use by reproduction in copies or phonorecords or by any other means specified by that section, for purposes such as criticism, comment, news reporting, teaching (including multiple copies for classroom use), scholarship, or research, is not an infringement of copyright. In determining whether the use made of a work in any particular case is a fair use the factors to be considered shall include —

1. the purpose and character of the use, including whether such use is of a commercial nature or is for nonprofit educational purposes;
2. the nature of the copyrighted work;
3. the amount and substantiality of the portion used in relation to the copyrighted work as a whole;
4. and the effect of the use upon the potential market for or value of the copyrighted work.

Copyright law can be extensive and often confusing. Still, as we discussed in the section covering plagiarism, the best way to avoid issues is to source and cite, do not give presentations for commercial use that include the work of others unless you have written permission, and if your presentation is for commercial use or sale, consult a lawyer. For this chapter, you want to understand the basics of "fair use" as detailed above. The Digital Media Law Project cited in the reference section of this book is a great place to learn more (Digital Media Law Project, 2021).

Be Inclusive: Speaker, Message, Audience Cycle

Being inclusive can mean a lot of different things to various people. We could talk about using inclusive language or delivering a more accessible presentation or simply getting people involved in the presentation. Therefore, in the spirit of practicing effective communication, we want to define what we mean by *inclusive* in the context of this chapter.

Inclusive here represents what Dr. Sheena C. Howard terms the **Speaker, Message, Audience Cycle (or SMAC). SMAC** is best represented using the following as foundational guidelines:

- Reject content that normalizes racism, sexism, classism, homophobia, and other forms of bigotry.
- Avoid gender-specific and gender-binary language.
- Use material that can be seen, heard, and experienced by all listeners.

You can best incorporate this foundational approach in your presentation by viewing inclusivity as something that involves both attention to accessibility and inclusion around identity. The Speaker, Message, Audience Cycle (or SMAC) means that public speaking is about the relationship between a speaker, the message, and the audience, with ethics being at the center of all communication. Therefore, if you have audience members who cannot participate in this relationship, you open yourself up to excluding listeners. As the speaker, you are generally in a position of power in that you have a platform to deliver your message and can potentially influence the behavior and perspective of others. . Remember to respect all three of these elements and center ethics. These four elements are interdependent and need to work in tandem as you construct and deliver your speech.

As the speaker, you should aim to research, create, and deliver a presentation that does not exclude audience members who may not look, think, or act like you. In this active process, you must continually remind yourself of the interdependency of the four outlined elements. If you simply focus on the speaker, message, and audience without centering on ethics, then you open yourself up to engaging in exclusionary practices.

As previously mentioned, you can deliver controversial content or content with which your audience disagrees. Still, it does mean that the content should not elicit fear, harm, or judgment of others based on their identities. You can best stay clear of excluding audience members by delivering a fact-based and well-sourced speech, using references that are verifiable, credible, and relevant to your thesis and main points. In short, construct your speech and deliver your content using SMAC as your foundational approach.

Respect Your Audience

Respecting your audience requires two things: accountability and responsibility. One way to engage in ethical public speaking practices is to set responsible speech goals to maintain accountability for the consequences of your public communication. To be accountable means that you have considered your audience and how your presentation will affect others when preparing your speech and the delivery stage of the public speaking process. Considerations such as inclusive language, avoiding hate speech, assuming responsibility for raising social awareness, and employing respectful free speech are all responsible speech goals that you should consider (Millner and Price, 2016). In addition, you should consider how you appeal to the emotional fears and concerns of your audience (to the detriment of logical appeals), as well as how you use false or unsound arguments—**fallacies**—to support claims throughout your speech.

Appeals to Fear and Fallacies

Typically, in courses on persuasion or more advanced public speaking classes, you will learn about fallacies. However, it is important to briefly mention them here as they have implications for ethics in public speaking. Fallacies are misleading arguments or attacks on someone's character or personal traits without addressing disagreement with an argument. For example, a fallacy would look like this:

After Rob presents a compelling case for immigration reform, Jim asks the audience whether we should believe anything from a man who works for the border patrol, has several outstanding parking tickets, and is unattractive.

Fallacies, although unethical, can be very effective in persuading audiences and winning arguments. Hopefully, you will continue to study communication and take advanced speech courses to further develop your knowledge around the different types of fallacies employed that often result in unethical public speaking practices. For now, be mindful of your approach to counter-arguments and persuasive speaking when writing and delivering your speeches.

According to Kaylene Williams (2012), in her article *"Improving fear appeal ethics" in the Journal of Academic and Business Ethics,* fear appeals are commonly used in many types of marketing communications (for example, the marketing of products, services, social causes, and ideas). Also, they are frequently used to get people to help themselves and generally effectively increase ad interest, involvement, recall, and persuasiveness. The literature conventionally agrees that more effective fear appeals result from higher fear-arousal followed by consequences and recommendations to reduce the negativity. Fear appeals have been criticized as unethical, manipulative, exploitative, eliciting negative and unhealthy responses from viewers, and exposing viewers to offensive images against their will (Williams, 2012), all unethical tactics people do use in public speaking. Thus, the ethical use of fear appeals can be improved, but public communicators should consider the often-blurry line between ethical and unethical fear appeals.

Kim Witte (1992, 1993, 1994), a prominent author in this area, defines fear appeals as "persuasive messages that arouse fear by depicting a personally relevant and significant threat, followed by a description of feasible recommendations for deterring the threat." Fear appeals work when you make the listeners very afraid and then show them how to reduce the fear by doing what you recommend (Williams, 2012).

As you move through this text, use the guidelines in this chapter to inform your research and delivery decisions. Starting with good habits, such as ethical listening, ethical research, productive public speaking qualities, and understanding the history of diverse approaches to communication, you develop "best practices" early on in your learning process. As we have noted in this chapter, employing these traits will benefit your personal, professional, and public life. Consider the following guidelines in incorporating accountability and responsibility into respecting your audience.

Topic selection

Understand that presentations are about your audience, not about you. Focus on framing your topic in terms of what you can provide the audience based on their needs and interests. One of the best ways to do this is to find out as much information as possible about who will be attending your speech, which might include age, title, positions, backgrounds and other variables that will help you position your speech and select the most appropriate topic based on who will be listening.

Identify with audience members

Establishing common ground is what Kenneth Burke termed the "new rhetoric." The process of identifying with your audience is powerful in engaging with listeners—whether you are there to persuade or inform. This process involves finding methods to connect with them in various ways, including but not limited to identity, issues, and perspective. For example, you may establish common ground by acknowledging that you and the listeners are in the same class, or go to the same school or work at the same place. In addition, you might acknowledge that you are all facing similar challenges overcoming the fear of public speaking. As a speaker, it is your job to engage in writing and delivering a speech that can establish common ground with the listeners.

Be honest

Never be dishonest about your intentions for speaking. Your speech should give a primer or preview statement up front, letting the audience know where your speech is headed and what you will cover in your presentation. Letting the audience know where you are going in your speech helps them feel engaged and follow along. After all, one of your goals as a speaker is to hold your audience's attention.

Respect Yourself

As previously discussed in this chapter, credibility, integrity, accountability, and responsibility are important, both inside and outside the digital space. However, these characteristics that you need to embody can only be practiced if you have respect for yourself. When you respect yourself, you can then respect the identity of the audience without delivering disingenuous content. At times, you might find that you have a highly critical or oppositional audience. The best way to deliver a presentation to such an audience is to first begin with being credible, having integrity, and being accountable and responsible.

Critics can only be persuaded when you have incorporated logos into the construction and delivery of your speech, which entails incorporating ethics in terms of being a "good person speaking well" and pathos in believing and being passionate about your content. Even critics can respect an oppositional viewpoint if they know the presenters have done their homework in terms of research (credibility) and display honesty (ethics) in their delivery. Thus, you respect yourself and your audience by maintaining your character and credibility when faced with an oppositional audience.

As you practice these guiding principles of avoiding plagiarism, respecting the message, inclusivity, and respecting your audience and yourself, it is important that you also include these in the process of listening. Listening as a speaker or presenter is just as important as listening to an audience member. As we conclude this chapter, we will focus on listening in the online environment and exploring how our foundational principles co-exist with listening.

Ethical Listening

In *Listening to Diversity,* Sally Lehrman (2016) outlines four ways news reporters can listen ethically in relation to understanding the values of marginalized communities. Her outline, though directed at understanding the values of a specific type of community, provides an excellent general approach to ethical listening. **She cites the following ways to better your listening by employing an ethical approach.**

- Quiet your mind. Don't assume your definitions are the same as your source's.
- Ask why? Look for the story behind the story. Listen for the reason behind the statement.
- Meet your source where she/he is, both literally and figuratively. You'll be able to hear better if you are in your source's comfort zone, not your own. And they will be more forthcoming.
- Ask what your source actually does, not just what he or she thinks and knows.

Lehrman's ethical approach to listening shows us that audiences have a responsibility, which involves a process of listening beyond simply hearing or receiving sound bites. It is the responsibility of the listener to acknowledge fairness and accuracy in the way they interpret and disseminate information. From a news reporting perspective this cannot be done without practicing ethical listening as outlined above. Think about the ways in which you can improve your communication skills, by simply incorporating these ethical listening guidelines into both your public speaking and interpersonal relationships. All of the guidelines laid out here can be improved upon by being polite and attentive, avoiding prejudging the speaker, and maintaining the free and open expression of ideas.

References:

Abbott, J., T., McDorman, D., Timmerman, & Lamberton. (2015). Public Speaking and Democratic Participation: Speech, Deliberation, and Analysis in the Civic Realm. Oxford University Press.

College Board. (2024). 2023-24 Guidance for Artificial Intelligence Tools and Other Services . Retrieved from College Board: https://apcentral.collegeboard.org/exam-administration-ordering-scores/administering-exams/preparing-for-exam-day/exam-security/artificial-intelligence-tools

Copyleaks Technologies LTD. (2020, October 20). The Impact of Social Media on Plagiarism. Plagiarism Checker: AI Based Anti-Plagiarism Online. https://copyleaks. com/blog/the-impact-of-social-media-on-plagiarism/.

Devito, J. (2017). The Interpersonal Communication Book. Boston: Pearson Education.

Digital Law Project (2021). Fair use. Retrieved from http://www.dmlp.org/legal-guide/fair- use

Gudykunst, W.B. & Y.Y. Kim, 1992). Communicating with Strangers: An Approach to Intercultural Communication, (2nd ed.) New York: McGraw Hill.

History of Public Speaking. (2016, May 26). Retrieved June 6, 2016, from Boundless website: https://www.boundless.com/communications

Lehrman, S. (2016). Listening for Diversity. Quill, 104(2), 38.

Lucas, S. E. (2001). The Art of Public Speaking, 7th ed. New York: McGraw-Hill.

Marcus, G. (2022, December 1). AI Platforms like ChatGPT Are Easy to Use but Also Potentially Dangerous. Retrieved from Scientific American: https://www.scientificamerican.com/article/ai-platforms-like-chatgpt-are-easy-to-use-but-also-potentially-dangerous/

Marino, S. (2023, December 4). What Happens in an Internet Minute. Retrieved from localiq.cm: https://localiq.com/blog/what-happens-in-an-internet-minute/

McCabe, D. (n.d.). Statistics. Retrieved April 26, 2021, from https://www.academicintegrity. org/statistics/

McKay, B., & K. McKay(2011, January 26). Classical Rhetoric 101: The Five Canons of Rhetoric â€" Invention. Retrieved June 5, 2016, from the art of manliness website: http://www.artofmanliness.com/2011/01/26/ classical-rhetoric-101-the-five-canons-of- rhetoric-invention/

Millner, A., & R. Price, (2016, March). Ethics in Public Speaking. Retrieved June 7, 2016, from Public Speaking Project website: http://www.publicspeakingproject.org

National Communication Association. (1963). Credo for Free and Responsbile Communication in a Democratic Society. Retrieved from Natcom.org: https://www.natcom.org/sites/default/files/Public_Statement_Credo_for_Free_and_Responsible_Communication_in_a_Democratic_Society_2017.pdf

Mortensen, O. (2024, April 24). How Many Users Does ChatGPT Have? Facts and Statistics 2024 . Retrieved from SEO.AI: https://seo.ai/blog/how-many-users-does-chatgpt-have

O'Neill, M. T. (1980). Plagiarism: Writing Responsibly. Business Communication Quarterly 43, 34-36.

Power, Mary R. and Camille Galvin, (1997) "The culture of speeches: Public speakin across cultures," Culture Mandala: The Bulletin of the Centre for East-West Cultural and Economic Studies: Vol. 2: Iss. 2, Article 2.

Schulz, P., & P Cobley,. (2013). Theories and Models of Communication. Berlin: De Gruyter Mouton.

Stanford Report. (2023, February 13). How will ChatGPT change the way we think and work? Retrieved from Stanford Report: https://news.stanford.edu/stories/2023/02/will-chatgpt-change-way-think-work

Weise, K. a. (2023, May 1). When A.I. Chatbots Hallucinate. Retrieved from New York Times: https://www.nytimes.com/2023/05/01/business/ai-chatbots-hallucination.html

Williams, K. (2012). Improving fear appeal ethics. Journal of Academic and BusinesEthics, 1-24. Retrieved June 05, 2016, from http://www.aabri.com/manuscripts/11906.pdf Witte, K. (1992). Putting the Fear Back into Fear Appeals: The Extended Parallel Process Model. Communication Monographs, 59(4), 329-349.

Witte, K. (1993). Message and Conceptual Confounds in Fear Appeals: The Role of Threat, Fear, and Efficacy. The Southern Communication Journal, 58(2), 147-156.

Witte, K. (1994). Fear Control and Danger Control: A Test of the Extended Parallel Process Model (EPPM). Communication Monographs, 61(2), 113-134.

Lupita Nyong'o
2014 – ESSENCE Awards

Best Breakthrough Performance Award: 12 Years a Slave

http://www.essence.com/2014/02/27/lupita-nyongo-delivers-moving-black-women-hollywood-acceptance-speech

I want to take this opportunity to talk about beauty. Black beauty. Dark beauty. I received a letter from a girl and I'd like to share just a small part of it with you: "Dear Lupita," it reads, "I think you're really lucky to be this Black but yet this successful in Hollywood overnight. I was just about to buy Dencia's Whitenicious cream to lighten my skin when you appeared on the world map and saved me."

The lizard brain is sending out hormones...

What's Happening

Anxiety is caused by several energy producing reactions in the various parts of the brain. In simple terms, the brain stem and cerebellum (the "lizard brain") which handle automatic, reflexive behavior, send out hormones that stimulate the limbic system. The limbic system creates an emotional response at the gut level causing an intense feeling and a heightened state of awareness. The hormonal activity related to these brain events leads to the symptoms we know as anxiety such as fast heartbeat, flushed skin, cold hands and feet, and constricting throat.

Coping with the Stress

Simple practices such as diaphragmatic breathing or getting a little exercise before your speech can really help to alleviate stress. We've mentioned the two parts of the brain that stimulate the reactions we call stress. Fortunately, human beings are also equipped with a third area of the brain, the neocortex and cerebrum. This part of the brain, otherwise known as the "thinking brain," is in charge of memory, problem solving, and thinking in general. You can use this part of the brain to manage both the physical and mental effects of stress. This is done through "relabeling" the feelings of anxiety as feelings of heightened energy. By using your thinking brain's understanding of the biology behind your anxiety, you will be able to analyze the situation for what it truly is: a physiological response. You can thereby transform your perception of such symptoms as rapid heartbeat and flushed skin into the physical signs of being excited to speak in public.

Speech Anxiety: Problems and Solutions

Dr. Tracey Quigley Holden
University of Delaware

One of the most common feelings associated with public speaking is anxiety - sometimes called stage fright, nerves, or just plain fear of public speaking. Comedian Jerry Seinfeld has joked that people in the United States are more afraid of public speaking than death – so much so that at a funeral they would rather be the deceased than give the eulogy! Yet there are some people who are quite comfortable speaking to a large group, but who feel anxious at a party, in meetings, or in one-on-one situations like interviews. Scholars in communication are well aware of the phenomenon and in research have found that people experience anxiety in many communicative situations, not just public speaking. More than forty years ago, Dr. James McCroskey (1970) labeled this common feeling "communication apprehension" and began developing measurements and scales for assessing the anxiety felt in many communication situations. But even a hundred years ago, teachers and practitioners of public speaking had been discussing how to manage stage fright and feelings of anxiety associated with communication. In this chapter you will learn about what "communication apprehension" is and how to manage it in ways that help you communicate more effectively, no matter how you are feeling in the moment. *Feel the Fear and Do It Anyway* was the title of a popular book in 1987 that quickly showed up on bumper stickers and posters and was used as a motivational quote for many people. More practically, it can be a personal mantra and a little extra push for facing and managing communication apprehension.

Glossophobia, Social Phobia, and Social Anxiety

In 2013, Google marketed a tablet as a research and education tool for K-12 students. In its advertising, it showed a middle school boy searching for "glossophobia", which Google defined as the fear of public speaking. Indeed, many if not most people experience feelings of anxiety and stress when asked to give a public speech. In fact it is estimated that 75% of all people have some degree of anxiety/nervousness when public speaking (Hamilton, 2013). Those feelings are uncomfortable, but not to the point of causing people to avoid giving speeches entirely.

Glossophobia and social phobia, however, are types of social anxiety disorder, a recognized mental health condition. The Mayo Clinic (2014) defines social anxiety disorder to include "fear, anxiety and avoidance that interferes with your daily routine, work, school, or other activities." These conditions can contribute to, but are distinguishable from the communication apprehension described earlier. Social anxiety disorder is characterized by intense and persistent feelings of fear of humiliation, judgment, failure, and anxiety that seem uncontrollable. They can cause people suffering from them to avoid a wide range of social situations, even when such avoidance is personally or professionally costly. It is estimated that about 7% of the U.S. population suffers from a social anxiety disorder (National Institutes of Health, 2017). Glossophobia is a performance-related anxiety. People with performance anxiety may not have difficulty in social situations, but instead feel anxious when called on to give public speeches or other forms of performance, such as dancing or playing music, sports competitions, or taking a test. There are very effective therapeutic and medical treatments for social anxiety disorder and for performance anxiety.

We know that about 7% of people have to deal with social anxiety; let's consider that in the context of a typical public speaking class of 20-30 students. That's about two people who are affected. For most students, the anxiety and stress they feel before giving a speech is normal, manageable communication apprehension. That's what made the Google ad so effective; it showed that good information and preparation could reduce anxiety. There is a predictable, physical response to the need for your body and brain to take action. Knowing what that is and how it works is what the next section is all about.

The Betrayal and Benefit of Biology

In order to understand and manage your communication apprehension, it helps to know something about human biology and the production of fear. It is well known that the human brain and body are wired to respond to stress of any kind with a "fight or flight" response. In the early twentieth century, Walter Cannon (1932) identified the response and began research on the physiological causes and effects in humans. There are two parts to the response, each produced by different areas of your brain.

When we experience stress of any kind, our brains and bodies produce a response geared to help us either fight or flee from the situation. One concept that helps us understand brain function is the "triune brain" (MacLean, 1990) or three general brain parts each with a specific function. While this is widely acknowledged to be a gross oversimplification of brain structures, it does give us a way to conceptualize brain activity. So the brain stem and cerebellum handle automatic, reflexive behavior – basically the things you should not spend time thinking about, like breathing and keeping your heart beating. This is sometimes called the reptilian or "lizard brain", since it is arguably the oldest part of our brains, is essential to life, but lacks the ability to reason. The limbic system, including the amygdala, handles emotional responses but at the gut level – it feels, but does not think. The cerebrum and neocortex form the larger part of your brain, and they handle memories, planning, and thinking in general. So in the **first** response to stress or strong emotions, your "lizard brain" signals the body to produce extra quantities of several hormones, including adrenaline and cortisol. Your limbic system contributes intense feeling and heightened awareness. Adrenaline heightens the muscular response and glucose available for immediate action, while cortisol suppresses the immune system and converts fatty acids to energy.

The lizard brain and limbic system are boosting all your available systems to give you maximum energy. Unfortunately, this hormonal and emotional activity tends to have some unpleasant side effects, such as increased heart rate, a feeling of flushed skin, cold hands and feet, the feeling of your throat constricting, butterflies in the stomach, shaking or trembling of your muscles, and others. The side effects and what is noticed in a stress response vary from person to person, but the physiology is almost identical.

Your brain perceives a need for energy, and enthusiastically dumps hormones into your system to provide it. But your lizard brain, the part of your brain that manages these responses, doesn't have rational thought capabilities - it doesn't care if you are seeing a saber toothed tiger or giving a two minute speech. Instead, it works on a stimulus-response basis. Got stress? Get energy! Your lizard brain and limbic system together can act a like a toddler with a box of cookies and no adult supervision, grabbing as much as she can as fast as she can from the box. More, more, more! Why have one when you can have them all? The result is a system overload and overreaction driven by physical and emotional reactions. This is the betrayal of our biology - our lizard brains and limbic systems have no ability to think. When your thinking brain, the neo-cortex, finally kicks in, it can help to assess and manage the thoughtless responses of your lizard and limbic systems. A key part of the thinking brain's job is to identify and label – give words to – our physical and emotional responses. This is the **second** response, and it can lag well behind the first response. Your thinking brain starts analyzing the situation, using language to describe and label the key pieces. Your thinking brain can tell the toddler to have one cookie, notices that there is no saber toothed tiger in the area, and recognizes that the audience of your peers is actually pretty harmless. That's the benefit of biology! If you were actually in danger, your lizard brain would have given you a quick response to save your skin. If there is no imminent danger, your thinking brain can usually take over, label the situation, and use the energy to produce an appropriate response.

So from the beginning, it is important to understand that the physical and emotional feelings you may have are driven by your brain and body trying to give you energy to cope with perceived stress. **The physiology is the same no matter what kind of stress you are experiencing.** This is where our thinking brain and our use of language can be a huge benefit. In our **second** response, when we think, we can assess the situation accurately and manage our physical and emotional response effectively. A key part of this process is to recognize the feelings for what they are – a response to stress, the creation of extra energy - and label them in ways that help us act effectively. Thinking is done with language. We cannot think about something until we name it, so we can use naming to help us manage the response.

Imagine for a moment that you are getting ready to go to a party. You're within minutes of departing, and everything is going well. You're rushing just a bit to be ready on time. You know that good friends will be there, the party is well planned with fun things to do, and even the weather is cooperating. As you grab your keys and head for the door, how do you feel?

Here's another scenario - you are getting ready to go take an exam. You've studied hard, but you're just not sure you really understand all the material. A big part of your grade depends on this test, and a lot of your classmates have been texting about how they're studying – some have been up all night. You got some sleep, you've had a good breakfast and an extra cup of coffee, and you think you're ready. As you grab your keys and head for the door, how do you feel?

Most likely for the first scenario, you imagined feeling excited, happy, and eager to get to the party. In the second situation, you probably imagined feeling anxious, stressed, and reluctant to go take the test.

Guess what? Your brain and body are responding to each of these stress situations with extra adrenaline and emotional intensity. The difference is that in the first scenario, your mind is labeling those responses and feelings with words like "happy" "excited" and "anticipation". In the second, your mind is grabbing different labels like "anxious" "stressed" and "worried". You are interpreting the same physical and emotional responses in your brain and body differently. In both situations, your brain and body are responding to stress with the same physiological actions, while your mind is applying different words.

If you understand that the physiological response is just energy, and that you can choose how to label it, you are well on your way to being able to manage your communication apprehension. The next section will discuss effective techniques for relabeling, reducing, managing, and even benefitting from the communication apprehension you experience.

Managing Communication Apprehension

Once you understand the biology of apprehension, you are in a much better position to get your thinking brain in gear and able to mitigate the intense response of the lizard brain and limbic system. In addition to managing your involuntary brain and body responses, there are a variety of exercises and techniques that will help you boost your confidence and focus. There are several things you can do to manage communication apprehension, starting well before your actual presentation.

3 | SPEECH ANXIETY: PROBLEMS AND SOLUTIONS

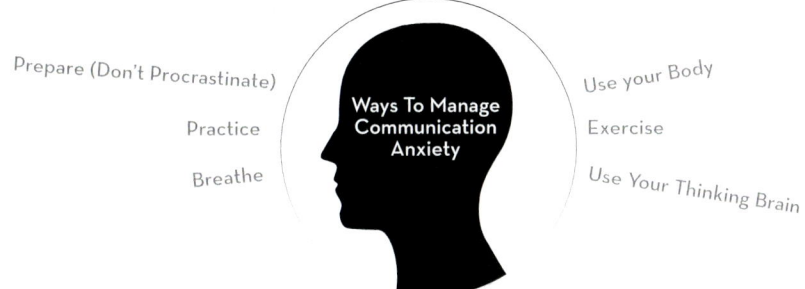

Prepare (Don't Procrastinate)

Normally, you have some time to prepare before you have to give your presentations. The single most effective thing you can do to reduce your communication apprehension is to prepare your presentation thoroughly, and well ahead of the due date. Taking the time to really know and understand the topic you will be speaking about, finding and organizing high quality information, and planning your presentation carefully for both the audience and the time available are all essential to giving an excellent presentation, and as a bonus, every aspect of preparation also reduces communication apprehension. The more familiar and comfortable you are with your material and your plan for presentation, the more confident and less apprehensive you will feel. Ideally, you would know the content of your speech so well that delivering your message is almost effortless – instead, you can focus on the response from the audience and adapting your message in the moment. When it comes to public speaking, procrastination is one of your worst enemies. Procrastination leads to stress, which can amplify your feelings of apprehension. Even if you feel that some spontaneity or inspiration is lost in the process, the advantages of thorough preparation of your materials far outweigh the disadvantages of leaving preparations until too late.

A second significant and helpful aspect of thorough preparation is that it allows you to focus on crafting the most effective message for your audience. It may surprise you that the message your audience needs to hear may not be the same as the one you'd like to deliver. Thinking through the likely composition of your audience members and some key elements of their current knowledge of your topic is essential to building and delivering a truly effective speech. Ask yourself, "What does my audience know, feel, or understand about this topic? What do I want them to know, feel, or understand after my presentation?" By focusing on the needs of your audience, you accomplish three things. You create a speech that contains the information most likely to add to what your audience already knows in a positive way. You shift the focus of the speech from yourself and your message to the audience and their communicative needs, which will reduce your concerns about being judged on your performance. Finally, focusing on audience needs always improves a presentation, because people enjoy feeling that you are giving them something "just for them". When you do just that, their opinion of you as a speaker goes up too.

Practice

Once you have the content and organizational plan for your presentation, practice is crucial. Moving from the written pages or notecards you have prepared to effective delivery to an audience takes practice, if only because what is written down does not always sound right when spoken aloud. Multiple rehearsals of your presentation will help you recognize the places where your speech flows smoothly, where you are comfortable with the material, and identify the spots that need polishing or where you need a note or reminder. As a management practice for communication apprehension, an additional benefit of multiple rehearsals is **desensitization.** Systematic desensitization is a psychological technique used for many fears and phobias. Exposure to a smaller level of the stimulus that provokes fear or anxiety in a controlled situation helps you to reduce your stress response. Over time your brain learns that stimulus X does not pose a significant threat, and your stress response decreases. When you practice giving your presentation, especially if you either imagine your audience there or actually have someone watch you, you are simulating the stress of the actual presentation but at a reduced level. By engaging in the behavior that your brain perceives as stressful in an environment that is more comfortable for you, you become 'desensitized' to the situation. The more often you practice, the more your brain recognizes the situational cues correctly and gives you just the energy you need, instead of going to full alert.

Breathe

An important technique you can use to de-stress is so simple and quiet, it can be done anywhere – just breathe. Oxygen is a great antidote to anxiety. Your body is ready to respond to any perceived threat with fight or flight, and part of that reaction is an increased heart rate and faster breathing. Those shallow, quick breaths cut down on the oxygen available in your system and heighten your feeling of tension. Taking a deliberately slow, deep breath, holding it for a second or two, and releasing it slowly, helps your body reset itself, and to know that it is not immediately threatened. That deep breath actually uses some of the energy being used to speed up your systems, and using the energy acts as a counter to the adrenaline boost in the system. Adding oxygen to the mix also tells your brain and body that you are not at immediate risk.

Taking a deep breath also gives your thinking brain time to take a little more control of the situation. It's a little like pushing a reset button. Once you've taken a good deep breath (or two) you can reassess your situation and take action to help your performance.

Use Your Body (Release, Redirect, Reframe)

When we experience stress, it's not unlikely that someone will tell us to "Keep Calm and Carry On" – borrowed from the famous British World War II poster. It's worth knowing that those posters were never distributed to the British people. They were kept in storage, to be used only in the worst-case scenario of a German invasion. The phrase was intended to help Britons endure hardship and extreme circumstances that might go on for a long time. "Keep Calm and Carry On" may sound like an effective way to manage unavoidable stress or anxiety, but it is very difficult to do in the moment. When your brain and body are in "fight or flight" stress response mode, calming down is an impractical goal. Instead, realizing that the physical response to stress creates an abundance of energy in the human body, you can find ways to release or redirect that energy. You can also use your body to create a physiological response that will help you perform better.

Exercise

Exercise is another simple technique to help you burn off some of the extra energy you have. If you have a choice between taking a few flights of stairs or taking the elevator, take the stairs. If you can walk around a bit, do so. If you have to stay in one place, squeeze your hands into fists and open them a few times, or tap your feet on the floor. Shrug your shoulders up and down. Any way you feel comfortable moving in a controlled way, move. As you burn off the energy, your sense of intensity and anxiety will diminish as well.

Use Your Thinking Brain (Relabel and Rename).

Even with thorough preparation and practice, you are likely to still feel some communication apprehension. As discussed earlier, this is a normal physiological and emotional response of your brain and body to any form of stress. You can still use your "thinking brain" to help you manage both your physical responses and the emotional feelings of stress. First, new research from Harvard Business School shows that recognizing the emotional feelings of stress and **relabeling** them more positively can "flip the switch" of your experience (Brooks, 2014). Excitement is the emotional twin of apprehension. Both involve some uncertainty in anticipation of action, but our labels are different. The technique used at Harvard is simple - as you notice the feeling of apprehension, you say out loud, "I am excited!" or "Get excited!" Instead of perceiving the situation as a threat, you relabel your perception to see it as an opportunity. That perceptual switch helps you relabel your feelings, switching from apprehension to excitement. The bonus of relabeling is that it also improved performance. Participants in the research who relabeled with "I am excited!" or "Get excited!" were scored higher by observers. When study participants were tasked with giving a speech, the participants who said "I'm excited!" out loud scored higher on persuasiveness, persistence, competence, and confidence. Those are pretty positive qualities for any speaker!

If switching from apprehension to excitement seems a bit of a stretch, or if you want an added boost for your performance overall, you can **rename** your physical responses. The technique is similar to relabeling, but focuses on identifying and directing the physical responses of your body as energy for your performance. The first act of our thinking brain is to find words for the feelings produced by the reptilian and limbic systems. Our words, especially those used for responses associated with emotions, have both denotative and connotative meanings. The denotative meanings are the dictionary definitions, the core meaning of the words. The connotative meanings are the additional interpretations imposed on the word by our experiences. For example, we all agree that "cat" has a denotative meaning of four-legged mammal of the feline species. For someone who loves cats, "cat" carries many other positive connotations – love, warmth, pleasure, purring. For a person who is not so fond of cats, "cat" might carry connotations of scratching, hissing, witches and bad luck. Neither connotation is wrong, but they are definitely different. Thus the words we use to name something bring their own connotations along with the core meanings. Recall our discussion of the lizard brain's contribution of adrenaline and cortisol. Both hormones act to maximize the **energy** available to you and the speed of your responses. By naming the physiological response as energy, your thinking brain helps to diminish the emotional aspect of the response and the connotations that are associated with whatever words you might have named those emotions. Energy is what we all need to accomplish the tasks on our to-do lists. Identifying and **renaming** your physical response as **energy** helps you direct that positivity toward your presentation.

These techniques can be used separately or together. Relabeling and renaming the physical and emotional response to stress does take some thinking effort, and a certain level of awareness of your own responses to stress. For some people, it is easier to relabel the emotional response; for others, renaming the physical response as energy is easier. There is no right or wrong way to use these techniques – try both and see what works for you!

Releasing your extra energy should still leave you with more than you need to give your presentation. This is where the **redirection** of your energy can help you. Elite athletes, musicians, and other creative people spend hours practicing their skills, but many of them also use visualization for specific elements of their performance. An active **visualization** helps redirect your energy into creating the actions you need to perform. Tennis players will visualize every motion of a perfect serve, golfers a perfect swing, musicians see themselves perfectly producing every note. Redirecting your energy through visualization teaches you what you need to do to perform successfully – it's a form of mental rehearsal of the physical performance. A short **visualization** of you successfully giving your presentation channels your energy into reproducing that success. As you visualize your movements, gestures, and "see" yourself giving a great

speech, you are simultaneously teaching your body and brain how to recreate it in real performance. Another visualization technique is called the Bubble. For the Bubble, you imagine yourself inside a lovely bubble, which smells and feels like your favorite place in the world. While in your bubble, you start your presentation and the bubble expands to include all of your audience members. Giving your speech is effortless! After you conclude, your bubble shrinks down to just enclose your body, and you can float happily along through your day. The Bubble also redirects your energy into your audience connection and your message, and away from your reactive state of apprehension.

The final technique for managing communication apprehension actually does quite a bit more than just help with a presentation. Dr. Amy Cuddy at Harvard Business School conducted research on the effect of particular physical positions of the body for people giving short presentations. The study showed that people who adopted "high power poses" for periods of two and five minutes prior to their presentation were evaluated more positively and their presentations were given better ratings than people who adopted "low power poses" for the same periods of time (Cuddy, Wilmuth & Carney, 2012). Cuddy's research and her TED talk explain that our senses of confidence and competence are affected by the way we hold our bodies. High power poses are expansive and take up more space; they increase feelings of dominance, action, risk-taking and increase pain tolerance. High power poses also reduce stress and anxiety – and of course we know that reducing stress and anxiety is the key to managing communication apprehension! One way to use this research is to simply hold a power pose for a few minutes, shortly before your give your presentations.

But more than just boosting confidence and reducing stress for a presentation, Cuddy suggests that power posing can alter how we behave across many situations, which fundamentally **reframes** how we act. As Cuddy (2013) says in her TED talk, "Our bodies change our minds, and our minds change our behavior, and our behavior changes our outcomes." Power posing increases our action orientation, so we are more likely to do or try something new. At the same time, power posing seems to foster positive evaluations from others. The combination of the two can act to **reframe** how we see ourselves in the world, as more competent and powerful. Competent, powerful, action oriented people might still feel anxiety and apprehension, but they are not going to let that get in their way. There is too much to do on the way to their goals!

Conclusion

In this chapter, we have discussed the challenge of communication apprehension, how the brain and body produce it and how our brains and bodies can help us manage and reduce it. We also distinguished communication apprehension from glossophobia and social phobia. It's important to remember that nearly every speaker experiences some form of communication apprehension. Recognizing the effects of communication apprehension from both psychological and physiological perspectives is the key to effective management. Preparation and practice can reduce anxiety before your presentation. Relabeling and renaming techniques can be used in the moment of your presentation. Releasing, redirecting, and reframing before, during, and after your presentation help to shape your experience and your response.

References

For additional information on references in this book, please visit rowanpublicspeaking.com

Brooks, A.W. (2014). "Get excited: reappraising pre-performance anxiety as excitement." *Journal of Experimental Psychology*, 143(3). pp 1144 – 1158.

Cannon, W. (1932). *Wisdom of the body*. United States: W.W. Norton & Company.

Cuddy, A.J.C. (2013) Your body language shapes who you are.
https://www.ted.com/talks/amy_cuddy_your_body_language_shapes_who_you are?language=en

Cuddy, A.J.C., Caroline A. Wilmuth, and Dana R. Carney. (September 2012) "The benefit of power posing before a high-stakes social evaluation." *Harvard Business School Working Paper*, No. 13-027.

MacLean, P.D. (1990). *The triune brain in evolution: role in paleocerebral functions*. New York: Plenum Press.

McCroskey, J. C. (1970). "Measures of communication-bound anxiety." *Speech Monographs*, 37(4), 269.

Mayo Clinic. (2017, March). *Social anxiety disorder*. Retrieved from: http://www.mayoclinic.org/diseases-conditions/social-anxiety-disorder/basics/symptoms/con-20032524

National Institute of Health. (2017). *Social Anxiety Disorder NIH Publication No. QF 16–4678*. Retrieved from: http://www.nimh.nih.gov/health/publications social-anxiety-disorder-more-than-just-shyness/index.shtml

---

AMY CUDDY
TED Talks— Your body language shapes who you are

https://www.ted.com/talks/amy_cuddy_your_body_language_shapes_who_you_are/up-next

3 | SPEECH ANXIETY: PROBLEMS AND SOLUTIONS

Audience analysis is one of the most important parts of your speech.

An audience can transform your speech positively or negatively. The speaker can transform an audience through powerful stories, proper use of verbal communication, and the appropriate nonverbal communication cues.

The successful speaker should dedicate a large portion of time to audience analysis and topic selection. Speakers have a responsibility to consider the powerful relationship of speaker and audience. The audience sees, hears, and follows the command of the speaker. As a speaker, you guide the audience, and have a unique role in creating a specific message and assisting the audience in their comprehension and retention of the message. To focus properly on one's audience requires demographic research, self-reflection, and adaptation.

Audience Analysis

DAVID PALLANT
County College of Morris

What Does It Mean To Be Audience Centered?

Being audience centered means knowing how to craft and deliver your message so that the audience reacts the way that you want them to. While you want to be aware of your audience's attitudes, beliefs, and values, you want to remain authentic to your own. Herein lies the art of good audience analysis. How can you best deliver your message given the audience and situation, while remaining true to yourself?

WHEN PRESENTED WITH A SPEECH OPPORTUNITY, ONE MUST FIRST ASK A FEW IMPORTANT QUESTIONS:

Why am I speaking to this audience?

Who specifically is in my audience?

What are the motivations or expectations of the audience?

In what context is this speech being made?

In what environment or location will I be speaking?

How is the topic I choose audience centered?

Why am I speaking to this audience?

It is likely that the answer to this question is, 'I am taking this Public Speaking course as part of my major requirement.' Different types of speeches require different approaches toward the audience. For example an **informative speech** seeks to provide clear and concise information in a logical order. The general purpose of an informative speech is to educate the audience. A **persuasive speech** employs certain communication strategies to motivate the audience toward a particular point of view. An **entertainment speech** uses both techniques to educate and motivate an audience. However, all successful speeches incorporate the speaker's story-telling ability.

Who specifically is in my audience?

The audience can consist of many different types of people, and it is important to gain knowledge from these people in formal or informal methods. The **demographics** of the audience are the unique characteristics and identities of the individuals. We have all taken surveys for employment or marketing purposes, and these types of surveys are formal primary research methods for demographic and product research. If you do have the time and opportunity to ask formal survey questions on expectations and overall knowledge of your speech subject, it is highly suggested that you use this method to collect some information from the audience before speech day. A simple survey including questions on your speech topic and audience demographics would assist the speaker in tailoring the speech to the audience's needs and wants. However, speakers do not always get an opportunity to deploy a formal survey to an audience before delivering a speech. In that case, it would still be important to do some secondary research on who the audience is, what previous knowledge they have of the speech subject, and come up with the best approaches to successful audience-centered speaking. For example, before presenting to the audience, why not consider the social background of the audience. Remember the individual audience members listening to a speech bring certain expectations and can assist the speaker by active listening and appropriate feedback.

Here are some examples of how demographics of an audience should be considered by the speaker:

- When speaking or presenting to a predominately Jewish or Muslim audience it might be wise to consider the religious restrictions on diet as pertaining to the consumption of pork products.
- A younger audience in comparison to an older audience may have different expectations when it comes to the speaker's use of audio/visuals or language usage.

What are the motivations and expectations of the audience?

Each member of an audience always brings pre-existing notions and experiences to each speech. The three types of audience motivations that are important to keep in mind when preparing and delivering a speech are **Attitudes, Beliefs, and Values**. The *audience attitude* is simply a liking or disliking of something or someone. The *audience belief* is an idea about what is true or false. *Audience values* are deeply held personal judgments about what is right or wrong. Keep in mind that audience attitudes can change daily or even hourly. Audience attitudes are the easiest elements to change during a speech, followed by the beliefs of the audience. Lastly, audience values are rarely changed during a single speech since individuals develop their commitments to what is right and wrong over extended periods of time.

ATTITUDES
Beliefs
Values

In what context is this speech being made?

The speech context refers to the occasion or historical time. Context matters to audiences because it can change how they receive the speech. Context includes how the speaker uses verbal and non-verbal communication. Context also includes the events that surround the speech. For example, a speech that is presented on terrorism before September 11th versus a speech given after September 11th has a very different context. Audiences would expect a speaker to adapt the speech to the new context, and here is where context matters in developing a successful speech. Another example of a speech given in a particular context is a wedding speech. The context implies that you will be considerate of the audience and not share too much information to embarrass or denigrate a dear friend or family member. The context is important to consider because you will need to provide personal stories and tribute to a close family member or friend, all while adapting your delivery to a diverse and often unknown audience.

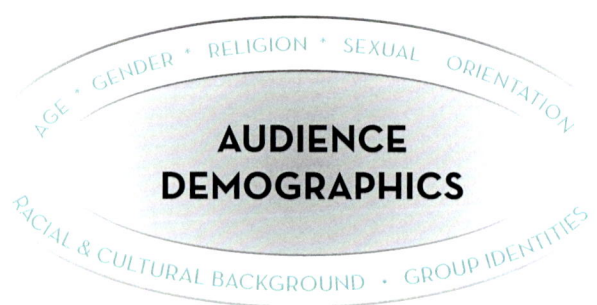

In what environment or location will I be speaking?

Where a speaker presents the speech is **environment or location** of the speech. This could include such settings as a classroom, auditorium, outside street, or a conference room. Certain environments for speeches require careful considerations. For example, if the audience is sufficiently large and your speech is scheduled for outdoors, you may want to consider amplification through a microphone or video screens to assist the audience in hearing and seeing the presentation. If the speech is being delivered in a large lecture hall that holds one hundred students, but your class only has twenty students, you may ask the audience on the day of the speech to sit in the first three rows to improve the distance between the speaker and audience. This type of request not only improves speaker credibility with the audience, but it also creates a better environment for audience comprehension.

How is the topic I choose audience-centered?

The initial brainstorm, research of the topic, and finally the selection of the topic are all-important steps to a well-crafted speech. However, there are many different types of audiences and topics; therefore, topics should be chosen to fit with your audience's expectations.

Different Types of Audiences

Here are some of the types of audiences that a speaker should consider when selecting a topic and delivering the speech.

- **Active Audiences**: An active audience is one that is engaged, enthusiastic, and works to listen effectively to the speaker and speech. For example, an active audience will provide more verbal and nonverbal feedback; you may be informing an audience on a select topic and witness active note taking and questions being posed at the end of the speech.
- **Passive Audiences:** A passive audience is one that is physically present but not fully engaged in the speech. A passive audience can easily be distracted and tune out during the speech. For example, you may notice that the audience is not providing proper eye contact, checking their cell phones, or are overall not attentive.

- **Captive Audiences:** Members of audiences can consider themselves as captive or forced to attend a speech or presentation. For example, a state required workshop or training for employees could be a context where the audience feels captive due to organizational or legal obligations. The speaker must not view them as captive and find a way to show the value of the speech to the individuals in the room.
- **Supportive Audiences:** A supportive audience is one that might have previously built a relationship with the speaker or topic. Essentially the speaker is preaching to the choir. For example, an audience at the Democratic or Republican convention would be considered supportive.

- **Voluntary Audiences:** The voluntary audience is attending the speech or presentation because of personal interest or value. For example, the audience that attends a stump or campaign rally speech during a presidential campaign is usually voluntary.
- **Involuntary Audiences:** The involuntary audience could be similar to the captive audience, but they have been chosen by someone else to attend a speech and may not be as difficult as a captive audience to deal with. For example, the audience present during a Public Speaking course is usually required to attend.
- **Hostile Audiences:** A hostile audience arises for many different reasons. One reason for a hostile audience could be due to previous failed attempts of the speaker to connect with an audience. A second reason audience members or a speaker can become hostile is if they believe their opinions have been ignored, or the speaker or audience has lost credibility. Lastly, audiences may have different goals than the

speaker's intended message and this might create conflict. An example of a hostile audience would be a press secretary for the president speaking to reporters during a press conference.

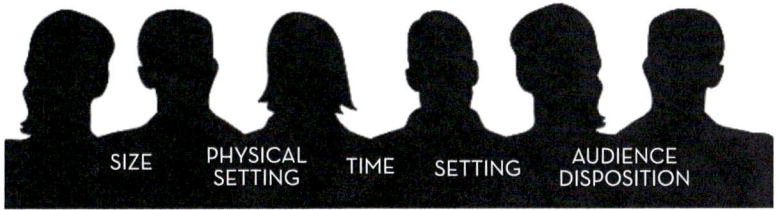

Situational Audience Analysis

When addressing audiences it is imperative that we consider the situation of the speech. Speakers should adapt to the *time, size, location,* and *occasion* of the speech. If you can take on the role of an audience member and be an empathetic speaker, it will be easier to successfully adapt your speaking style and delivery.

First, let us discuss the use of **time** in the speech making process. The actual day, specific time, and length of time that we will speak with our audience matters. The study of the use of time in nonverbal communication is called **Chronemics.** The speaker's or audience's Chronemic preferences can change depending on their cultural identity, power or control relationship, and time orientations.

For example, when scheduling an interview you may be provided a few options to meet, some in the morning and some in the afternoon. A competent speaker must consider when is the best time to speak. Ask yourself are you a morning person or afternoon person? Decide which specific time you will be most effective with audience engagement and persuasion.

When delivering your speech for a public speaking course, a professor usually sets a minimum and maximum time requirement for each assignment. This time requirement is usually calculated into your grade and also ensures that each student is given ample time to speak. Practice your speech to make sure it meets the time requirement. Be sure to incorporate appropriate pacing, pause, and potential audience feedback (such as time for laughter) into your practice.

The second key aspect of situational audience analysis is the total **size** of your audience. Audiences vary not only in individual demographics, but also in size. Larger audiences are more difficult to engage. Speaker communication apprehension can increase when more individuals are watching, listening, and judging the speaker. Larger audiences can lead to misunderstanding and inaccurate message dissemination. Each of the individual audience members has a unique listening and speaker style which can influence other members of the audience in the interpretation of the speech. A smaller audience also presents unique challenges. A speech delivered to a small audience can potentially become too personal and be considered an informal conversation that does not accomplish the intended speech goals. Informal conversation has very different verbal and non-verbal communication from a public speech. A smaller audience may be intimidated by an informal nature and have different expectations which in turn can create an awkward silence. It's your responsibility, whenever possible, to find out the size of your audience and adapt your speech as needed.

The third part of situational audience analysis is the **location** of the speech. It is important to remember that all speeches are a form of public communication or public address. A speech should be delivered with the notion that an audience somewhere will watch, listen, and react to it. Where a speech is delivered is not always the choice of the speaker, but speakers can work to improve the location or listening environment. You should always try to find out ahead of time where it is you're going to be speaking and, if possible, go and inspect the location. See how the room is set up. Will there be a podium, or will there simply be a stool and a microphone? What type of technology does the room have? Is there a lot of external noise? If there is a podium, do you plan on using it? These are all things that you can be prepared for if you pre-inspect the location of the speech and plan accordingly. If necessary, on the day of their speeches, speakers may be able to move furniture around. They also can ask the audience to move closer or close doors or windows to attempt to reduce external noise.

Lastly, the **occasion** or event speech can combine general purposes to inform, persuade, or be ceremonial. Ceremonial speeches include introduction, acceptance, presentation, dedication, toast, roast, eulogy, and farewell. This type of speech can utilize and sometimes combine general-purposes. Ceremonial speeches often have certain audience expectations for speakers. A speaker should consider the occasion of the speech and adopt the traditional expectations. For example, a eulogy speech is an important occasion that provides a tribute to a loved one and can assist an audience in the process of mourning by incorporating powerful empathetic storytelling. A speech like this, though often somber, can also employ some humor to heal and motivate an audience to overcome sadness; if it is delivered correctly it can actually transform a solemn audience into one of hope.

Speaker Adaptation with Specific Audiences.

In this section we need to consider the power of a word or combination of words to inform, entertain, and persuade an audience. In informative speaking, a speaker needs to use descriptive language and statistics that educate the audience, but it also considers the audience's level of knowledge on the topic. In narrative and entertaining speeches, a speaker needs to use language that elicits powerful images, stories that the audience can realistically relate too. In persuasive speaking, a speaker needs to craft strategic messages that take into consideration the audience's experiences, needs, wants, and fears. Persuasive speaking attempts to change the attitudes and opinions of the audience through the Aristotelian persuasive appeals of ethos, logos, and pathos.

In certain settings a question and answer period may occur after a speech. Treat audience members that are asking questions in the way that you would want to be treated. Listening to the questions carefully so that you can understand and formulate an appropriate answer is important. You should keep in mind how much time will be allotted for questions, so you can manage your time accordingly. In some cases the amount of time will be up to you and in others it will be predetermined. If someone asks a question that is not relevant, be polite but don't take too much time to answer it.

Predicting audience reaction to your speech can be difficult, but it is important to continue to adapt to the reaction of your audience. As we have discussed previously, different audiences present different challenges because of their different sizes, types and demographics. It is important to remember that audiences can help or harm your speech presentation. Speakers need to, in real-time, interpret verbal or nonverbal audience reaction into a positive aspect of the speech delivery.

Adapting to Your Audience During Your Speech.

"[I]t is not enough to know what we ought to say; we must also say it as we ought.... It is, essentially, a matter of the right management of the voice to express the various emotions—of speaking loudly, softly, or between the two; of high, low, or intermediate pitch; of the various rhythms that suit various subjects. These are the three things—volume of sound, modulation of pitch, and rhythm—that a speaker bears in mind."

— Aristotle

Let us now look at **paralanguage** or **vocalics** which is an aspect of nonverbal communication. Paralanguage studies the speaker's use of tone, rate of speech, volume, and pitch during a speech. As Aristotle states, management of these aspects of a speaker's voice are as important as what we are saying. The nonverbal communication that audiences provide during a speech is just as important as its verbal communication. The feedback of the audience should be considered and monitored throughout the speech delivery. Most formal speeches do not allow for feedback in the form of questions or clarifications during the speech; however, they may allow for questions at the end of the speech.

An audience provides numerous signals to the speaker that they are paying attention, agreeing or disagreeing, or are confused with the content of the speech or the delivery style. Great speakers have a unique skill for discerning audience approval or rejection, and can adapt to difficult audience situations. The obvious areas a speaker can pay attention are audience members' eyes, head, posture, and overall attentiveness. If the speaker notices that the audience members are taking notes, showing approving head nods, maintaining eye contact, smiling, and providing positive gestures, then the speaker can infer that the speech is connecting with this audience.

If the speaker notices that the audience is showing disapproving head nods, making eye contact to others in the room, frowning, and providing negative gestures, then the speaker will need to adjust or adapt the speech delivery to re-engage the audience.

So the next question would be, how does a speaker re-engage an inattentive audience?

Here are a few recommendations:

- Tell a story. Choose to tell a story that somehow connects the content of the speech to the audience's experiences, wants, or needs.
- Self-disclose to the audience so they can trust you, and find ways to re-build your credibility with the audience.
- Use humor or satire.
- Use an audio or video clip.
- Increase rate of speech or volume.
- Change the distance that you are speaking to the audience.
- Ask a rhetorical question or direct question to the audience to show that you are an audience-centered speaker.

Audience Relationships with the Speaker

A speaker should always consider if they have an existing relationship with the audience. Audiences that do not have an existing relationship with the speaker can be more difficult to speak to and may require additional outreach in order to succeed as a speaker. Why does it matter if you have a previous relationship with audience members? As you may recall there are different types of audiences; each audience has different characteristics, and speakers need to adapt to these specific characteristics. Naturally if you have a previous relationship with audience members, you will surely have established credibility or a trust with your audience. Once a speaker has established credibility, the audience is more prone to actively listen, and, in turn, your message will be effectively received.

It is also important to consider the power dynamics of speaker and audience. Speakers should think about the powerful position and opportunities a public speech provides, and try to balance out speaking to an audience versus speaking with an audience. Audiences can recognize the comfort of a speaker's verbal and nonverbal communication and will act accordingly. For example, if a president of a college is speaking to faculty during an end of the semester meeting, we can infer that he/she has formal power through title and position within the college. As chief executive, he or she realizes that when he or she speaks, employees will naturally listen due to the power to hire or fire employees. However, certain speakers may also have informal power over audiences. For example, if a faculty member who has worked at the college for 45 years delivers a last lecture to all employees of the college, we may find audience dynamics similar to those with the president of the college. Before delivering any speech, consider your existing relationship with the audience and how you can improve the relationship throughout your speech.

Challenges Faced In the Speaker/Audience Relationship

- **Credibility:** There are three types of credibility; initial, derived, and terminal. Initial credibility is the credibility a speaker possesses going into making a speech. Derived credibility is credibility that a speaker obtains from an audience during the speech. Terminal credibility is the credibility that a speaker has at the end of a speech. Some speakers already have credibility or trust with an audience. Others must gain it during the course of their speech. Generally speaking, audiences will not listen to a speaker who lacks credibility.

- **Self-Disclosure:** Each speech has a credibility statement; this is where the speaker shares something about himself or herself. When speakers self-disclose with an audience it can help connect the central idea of the speech with the audience. However, too much information or over disclosing can negatively impact an audience.

- **Polarization:** A speaker can push an audience toward a perspective by using extreme examples or language that may polarize the audience. An audience that is polarized can tune out the speaker or react negatively toward the speaker.

- **Misreading Expectations:** Audiences may have certain expectations based on previous encounters with a speaker, and a speaker may wrongly make a judgment about the dynamics of the audience, which creates a hostile audience.

- **Speaking Down to the Audience:** A speaker can incorrectly use his or her position of power as speaker and speak down to the audience. This can manifest itself in condescending statements, awkward silence, audience inattentiveness, and improper use of language. Audiences can feel inferior when a speaker speaks down to them.

- **Ignoring Nonverbal and Verbal Communication Feedback:** Speakers often make mistakes in interpreting, or completely ignore, the verbal or nonverbal feedback of an audience.

- **Allowing the Audience to Take Control of the Speech or Speaker's Intended Message.** A speaker who allows an audience to take control of the content of a speech or creates avenues of audience disruption can have difficulty getting back on topic. Speakers should develop a way to handle audience hecklers or disruptions in the speech.

- **Distracted Audiences:** The environment, location, or personal media devices can distract audiences. If it is possible, attempt to reduce the potential distractions before the speech takes place.

Strategies to Improve Speaker Dialogue

- Always attempt to put yourself in the audience's listening role.

- Understand that cultural communication competency is essential to successful speaker/audience dialogue. Cultural communication competency is the awareness of how to deliver a message to audiences in a way that is respectful and mindful of cultural differences and characteristics.

- Accurate nonverbal communication can many times be much more powerful than the verbal communication.

- If you are provided the appropriate time or opportunity, make sure to research who will be present in the audience.

- Speakers who appropriately decode the audience reaction during the speech can improve audience message reception and improve understanding.

- Certain audiences can have a transformative aspect with speaker and speech, taking control and redirecting the presentation. It is important that the speaker maintains the intended speech message and not allow the audience to negatively change the message.

Conclusion

As you may have noticed, a perfectly outlined speech, which has been well researched and practiced, can only be successful if the speaker seriously considers who will be in the audience. Public speech audiences and their feedback are crucial to a speaker's success on speech day.

There are many aspects of audience analysis to consider: individual demographics, attitudes, beliefs, and values. Without an audience the speaker has no real communication challenge. The speaker must inform, influence, and entertain audiences through a well-crafted blend of verbal and nonverbal communication. Let us especially realize the enormous responsibility the speaker has to look, listen, and adapt to an audience in a way that is collaborative and respectful.

Stephen Ritz
A teacher growing green in the South Bronx.

http://www.ted.com/talks/stephen_ritz_a_teacher_growing_green_in_the_ south_bronx

The first step in developing your speech is to choose your topic.

For most speeches, this will be determined by the occasion and the audience. However, in the classroom, students typically can choose their own topics, provided they meet the criteria for the speech. While this may initially sound appealing to you, this is the one part of speech writing that usually has students most concerned. There are a few things you can ask yourself when you start thinking of your topic choice. What do I already know that I can share with my audience? What do I want to know more about that the audience would also?

Selecting a Topic and Purpose

With contributions from
PAM MARSHALL
Rowan University

What Do I Already Know That I Can Share With My Audience?

When thinking about a potential topic, first think about your own knowledge and experience. What is something that you know a lot about that your audience may not? Have you had a lot of experience with something that your audience may not have? Is there a significant event in your life that people would be interested in hearing about? Do you currently volunteer somewhere and would like others to as well?

Here are just a few examples of speech topics based largely on students' personal knowledge or experience:

- *How to dress for a job interview*

- *Why it's important to understand your credit score and what you can do about it*

- *The basics of curling*

- *How you can all support the local animal shelter*

Exercise: Finding an Authentic Topic

Use the table below to identify unique and important experiences you've had with your interests and talents. Once you've done this, start to consider how these experiences, interests, and talents might be applied to a particular subject or topic. The stronger the relationship that exists between these four items, the more likely you have found your authentic topic.

Experiences	Interests	Talents	Applications

What Do I Want to Know More About That The Audience Would Also?

If you decide there isn't anything you currently know about that you'd like to share with your audience, then perhaps you want to choose a subject that you have some knowledge of but have always wanted to know more about. You may even want to choose a topic that you've never researched before and are going to do so for the very first time. For example, you've heard about Tesla cars but never really knew much about them. This would be a great opportunity to research something interesting and turn it into a speech your audience would also find enjoyable.

Is there something that you feel strongly about? Perhaps something on the national or international level, or maybe even something right here, such as the safety on campus. Maybe you want to propose a new parking garage on campus. These would all be possible topics for a speech as well.

Or perhaps there is something from one of your other classes that you found very intriguing and wanted to know more about it. *Is it something your audience would also find intriguing?* If so, that would be a perfect opportunity to research the topic more and create a great speech your audience would enjoy.

OVERALL QUESTIONS TO CONSIDER WHEN SELECTING A TOPIC

Who is the audience? (What are their demographics)?

What are the needs of the audience? (Do they need information? Do they want to be entertained? Should they be persuaded to do something that might help them in some way?)

What are the audience's expectations? (What rules are dictated by the context?)

Why should the audience care about this topic?

What are my goals in speaking to this audience?

Will the audience be receptive or skeptical? Friendly or hostile?

Will the audience be voluntary? Are they being incentivized in some way?

What questions might come from the audience at the conclusion of my speech?

IN ADDITION, THE TOPIC YOU CHOOSE SHOULD BE

- Timely and relevant to the audience
- Based on research instead of "common sense"
- Well-established with credible sources
- Interesting and engaging to the audience
- Commensurate with the audience's level of knowledge on the subject
- Authentic: based on your own experiences, interests, and talents

Your General and Specific Purpose

General Purpose

The **general purpose** refers to the overarching goal of the speech and may be to **(1) inform, (2) persuade, or (3) entertain (special occasion speech).**

- The purpose of an informative speech is to provide an audience with knowledge and understanding of a topic. An informative speech can also serve as a lesson, instructing the audience on a given subject.
- The purpose of a persuasive speech is to convince or reinforce a proposition in the mind of the audience.
- The purpose of a speech on a special occasion is to commemorate or celebrate special events in a person's life.
- All speeches should be able to be defined by a general purpose. This purpose informs strategy for both development and critique.
- The general purpose of a speech is defined by its central idea. If the central idea refers to a "lesson," the speech is informative, whereas if it refers to a "proposition," the speech is persuasive. Speeches on special occasions often lack a specifically stated central idea, but are defined by the purpose of telling an engaging (or perhaps entertaining) story or commemorating a person, place, or event.

Specific Purpose

Once you have your topic and know your general purpose, you now must narrow down your information to determine what the specific purpose is of your speech. The **specific purpose** refers to the goal of the speech itself and is dependent upon the topic you have chosen. Ultimately, to determine your "specific purpose" you have to ask yourself what you want the audience to do with the information you give them. Should they come away with a different attitude about something? Should they change their beliefs or values? Should they behave differently? What is the ultimate goal of your speech?

Determining your specific purpose will always start with reflection upon the general purpose of your speech. It will include consideration of the nature of your audience and then finally the goal of your speech.

General Purpose: *To persuade*
Specific Purpose: *To persuade* my class to use clean energy rather than fossil fuel energy.

General Purpose: *To persuade*
Specific Purpose: *To persuade* my class that adopting from an animal shelter is much better than buying from a breeder.

General Purpose: *To inform*
Specific Purpose: *To inform* my class about how credit scores work and what can be done to improve them.

Here are some things to keep in mind about your specific purpose:

- Make sure it is never written as a question
- Make sure it is limited to one specific topic
- Make sure it doesn't cover too much (too general)
- Make sure it isn't covering too little (too vague)
- Make sure you can accomplish it in the time you have
- Make sure it is relevant to your audience
- Make sure it isn't too technical for your audience

Central Idea

While the specific purpose of your speech is the ultimate goal of the speech, the **central idea** is a single sentence that is a declarative statement of what your speech will inform, persuade, or entertain your audience about. It tells your audience what it is you are going to be talking about. You will see this referred to as a thesis statement as well.

Think about your speech and how you would describe it in one sentence. It is more detailed than your specific purpose statement, but sums up your entire speech in one sentence. If your audience forgets your entire speech, but only remembers your central idea, what is it you want them to remember? Usually this will have something to do with your main points. The following would be an example for a speech on clean energy versus fossil fuel energy.

General Purpose: *To persuade*
Specific Purpose: *To persuade* my class to use clean energy rather than fossil fuel energy

Central Idea: *Clean energy* is more beneficial for human health, environmental health, and economic health, than fossil fuel energy, and we all should be using it.

You can see that the central idea is much more detailed and in fact, is what the three main points of the speech are. You know that this speaker is going to be talking about the human health, environmental health, and economic health of clean energy. Let's look at the informative speech on credit.

General Purpose: *To inform*

Specific Purpose: *To inform my class about how credit scores work and what can be done to improve them.*

Central Idea: *I'm going to explain to you what a credit score is, how having bad credit can harm you and how to build good credit.*

Again, from this central idea we can assume that the speech will have three main points. The first will explain what a credit score is, the second will explain how bad credit affects you and the last will explain how to build good credit.

Here are some things to keep in mind about your central idea:
- It should not be a question
- It should be a complete, full sentence
- It should be very detailed
- It should sum up your whole speech

Conclusion

Selecting a topic and purpose shouldn't be intimidating. Remember to remain authentic. Research your topic and use credible sources. Also, whenever possible, try to speak about something that is of interest to the audience. As you see and hear more examples of speeches, and as you learn more about public speaking, continue to be on the lookout for topics that might be of interest to you and your listeners.

Phillip Agnew
2013 – Dream Defenders

http://feministing.com/2013/08/12/end-your-day-right-with-this-amazing-speech-from-dream-defender-phillip-agnew/

I grew up poor. I never had what everybody else could have. But I remember a teacher telling me, "Phillip, some people are so poor that all they have is money." And so, I remember growing up and my father teaching me about faith. That faith is the substance of things hoped for, the evidence of things not seen. And I remember my father telling me stories of when one or two is gathered together, there is power. And I remember the stories of old, so today I've come to tell you all a bit of a story.

It's the story of a country called America.

Research can be defined as "The strategic acquisition of information."

Public speakers, especially politicians, are often accused of offering their audiences nothing but hot air—lots of words and energy, but little content. To be an effective speaker, you must have more than enough information about your chosen topic to share with your audience. The way to find that information is to do research. Research might sound difficult or intimidating, but it is something you do every day. You gather information about topics you're interested in so you can make better choices. If you were considering taking a job, buying a car, or getting a roommate, you would spend time gathering and assessing information about your options. That is research! Research for a presentation should be more thorough and more selective than deciding on a restaurant to eat at this weekend, but both tasks involve the strategic acquisition of information.

Research for Effective Communication

Dr. Tracey Quigley Holden
University of Delaware

In many train stations, metro stations, and even airports around the world, you will see signs and hear announcements telling you to "Mind the Gap." The gap in a train station is the space between the train and the platform, something you need to be aware of so you can cross it safely to get where you're going. One way to think about the information you need for your speech is to recognize existing "information gaps" you need to cross to reach your audience effectively. As you begin researching your topic, there is an information gap between what you know and what you need to know for your speech. There is also an information gap between you and your audience when you begin to present your speech. The gap between what you know, think, and believe about your topic and what your audience knows, thinks, and believes is what you want to bridge with the information you choose to include in your presentation. Recognizing these information gaps helps you think through the research process and begin to identify the information you need. You need to "Mind the Gap"! If you want to bridge an information gap, you will need to:

Gather the information you need about your topic;

Assess the information you find to determine its accuracy, quality, and appropriateness for your presentation;

Place the information in your presentation strategically so your audience has the best opportunity to understand your ideas.

Gathering Information

If you have ever felt like there was just too much information to take in, let alone to sort through, you are not alone. As far back as the 1660s, people noticed and complained about how much information was available. The term "information society" has become a common way of describing our current culture, and the burden of "information overload" is one we all carry. The concept of the information society emerged early in the 20th century, as the expansion of human knowledge moved toward an exponential pace. In the 1970s, the term "information society" was first applied as the economic impact of human knowledge and its distribution began to overtake the production of goods. (Crawford, 1983). In the years since the term was coined, the rate of information production and dissemination has only increased.

Research is done using **primary** and **secondary** sources. Primary sources are the original documents from history, accounts, or materials produced by people with first-hand experience.

Secondary sources are interpretations or analyses produced by people who did not have the experience themselves. Most of your research will be with secondary sources. Of course, you can do your **original** research as well. Speakers can sometimes **survey** their audiences to gain relevant information before a speech, such as an audience's knowledge about and attitudes toward a given subject. **The speaker could conduct interviews** to obtain first-hand accounts and comments from people with relevant experience or expertise with a topic area. However, in most cases, speakers must rely on secondary source research rather than original or primary source research as they look for information on their chosen topic.

The enormous increase in the amount of information available and all of the different sources of information noted above may seem daunting. But in the past fifty years, more and more information has been made available online. Project Gutenberg started digitizing books and cultural material in 1971 to offer free, global access to books (Project Gutenberg History and Philosophy, 2021). Material from books, journals, magazines, and other sources printed decades ago has been digitized and made accessible online, and nearly all new information is produced for online access. Although some publications are still behind paywalls, more and more researchers are posting their work publicly, and some research databases are opening their catalogs. Sites like z-library, libgen.li, and sci-hub allow users to download files of many books and journals, but they carry the risk of copyright or even ISP violations. Even so, a colossal amount of information is available at your fingertips, for free, if you have access to a computer and the internet.

Having so much information makes an effective strategy for gathering information one of the most important aspects of research. Thinking ahead and doing a little planning will significantly reduce the time you spend gathering information and improving the quality of the information you get. The saying, "Five minutes of planning is worth fifteen minutes of just looking," is even more true today than when E. L. Konigsburg wrote it in 1967 (Konigsburg, 1967). There are three steps to effective, strategic information gathering, and each one is described below.

1. Choose your search terms carefully.
2. Use the best available search tools.
3. Use your results to refine your search further.

Choose your search terms carefully. Our society now uses "Google" as a verb; most likely, you have "Googled" something recently. Google now processes over 40,000 search queries every second on average, translating to over 3.5 billion searches per day and 1.2 trillion searches per year worldwide, with each search producing hundreds of thousands of results. To make any search work for you, it should be focused and tailored to produce high-quality results. Starting with good search terms—the words and parameters you search for—is a critical step to finding good information. Knowing the topic you want to search for is a good starting point, but knowing a couple of related terms or possible subtopics is even better. Too broad a topic or search term will return too many results. Take five minutes to write down your topic's keyword or central phrase, and then add another three-to-five terms that are either directly related to your topic or indicate another area you are considering. For example, if your topic is "student activities," you might add "sports," "recreation," and "Greek life." Or you could start with "student activities" and add "funding," "diversity," and "campus culture." Using a combination of keywords and phrases will help you focus on your topic and will generate a stronger set of results from any search.

Usually, a search, especially in a public access search engine, such as Google, will produce more results than you can use. But if you don't get enough results, or if the initial results don't seem related to your topic, you need another approach. Changing your terms can produce very different results. It is important to keep in mind that the same topic can have several different names, and a simple change of terms could connect you to better resources. In the example above, "student activities" was the prime keyword. Another closely related term would be "student organizations" or "college clubs," which is when the concept of related terms can help you. If your initial keyword doesn't produce results, look for a synonym or a related term. Boolean *operators* are your friends. Boolean operators are the short words that connect your search terms into a searchable string. AND, OR, and NOT, with AND NOT used occasionally. Here is how they work when you have two related terms:

AND - tells the search engine to look for BOTH terms (Dogs AND Cats)

OR - tells the search engine to look for EITHER term (Dogs OR Cats)

NOT – tells the search engine to look for the first term but exclude items containing both the first and second term. (Dogs NOT Cats)

A search done using "prison reading programs," and one done using "prison AND reading programs" produce very different results within the same search engine. Substitute "correctional institution" for "prison" produces another set of results; trying "literacy" OR "reading" still another. As you work through your terms and combinations, you will likely see the same articles show up in multiple searches. Look at those articles first to see if you are getting the results you need.

Use the best available search tools. In the discussion of search terms, Google was an example of an effective and readily available search tool, which can get you **good** enough information. But in many cases, Google or other public access search engines will not produce the best possible results. Other information sites, such as about.com, ehow.com, and ask.com, have limitations that can lower the quality of the information you get. Online dictionaries and encyclopedias may offer a broad overview of a topic or a quick definition of a term for your personal use. Generally, they should not be used for more in-depth information.

For the most part, Wikipedia falls into this category as well. Wikipedia can be useful as a starting point to gain additional insights into your topic, to identify possible alternative search terms. It occasionally might have useful links to another more reliable source. These search mechanisms can provide you with a lot of information and sources to check. Still, they will also turn up a lot of junk and information from unknown, unverifiable, or poor-quality sources.

Artificial Intelligence (AI) tools like ChatGPT or Bard can seem like a great option for quickly gathering information, but they have limitations. First, AI tools are only as good as the data they are trained on and the prompts they are given. AI tools combine AI technology with large language models, allowing the tools to produce text that reads like natural human language. The text will sound grammatically and semantically correct. However, tools like ChatGPT can only duplicate what it has gathered from open resources, so it can't get any information that is behind a paywall. ChatGPT and other AI tools cannot assess the accuracy, value, or significance of anything it has read. Consider that one of the major sources of training data for ChatGPT is Reddit, the online forum where anybody can ask a question and anybody can respond. (Isaac, 2023) When you give it a prompt, it gives you a collection of statistically likely words in correct grammatical form related to that prompt, but it does not assess the truth of the statements it draws from or of the text generates. As a result, AI tools can produce wildly inaccurate statements called hallucinations. "Hallucinations can vary from flat-out fabrications to irrelevant and nonsensical responses. Hallucinations can be particularly dangerous, because AI is so good at sounding right, even when it's wrong." (Davis, 2024)

A **better** option is to use a search engine, which curates and reviews the indexed information. Google offers "Google Scholar" as public access but a limited-content search engine, which focuses on scholarly articles in recognized journals across a wide range of topic areas and scholarly disciplines.

Elsevier, Oxford University Press, Science Direct, and Wiley are all publishers of open access journals. Depending on your topic, searching in a scholarly and open access database could be very helpful. The articles and journals in these databases are usually peer-reviewed, which means experts in the field have read and approved the content, which can offer you a much higher caliber of information, especially for technical topics. Along the same lines, most industries have professional associations and publications within their field that offer well-edited, relevant information. These organizations and publications are geared toward people already working in that area who need to stay aware of important trends and innovations. If you are working on a related topic or have a strong interest in a particular industry, you should find out where professionals in the field look for their news.

If you have access to a good library, especially a college or university library, you may be able to use a database to do your search, which is almost always your **best** option for high- quality information. Some databases such as Nexus-Uni or General OneFile are wide-ranging, covering a huge variety of topics across tens of thousands of sources in popular media or publicly accessible records. Other databases, such as ProQuest and Academic OneFile, cover a wide range of topics and areas of knowledge but prioritize scholarly journals in their indexing.

Many databases are more specialized, covering a limited number of scholarly sources in a particular discipline. JSTOR, for example, indexes the contents of scholarly journals in the social sciences; including history, sociology, and political science. There are databases that only index newspapers, databases that index business and company information, and databases for science and medical information. *The New York Times* has digitized access to almost all of its issues going back to 1851, including advertisements.

Databases such as these offer access to high-quality information, often within a particular area of knowledge, and can include the most cutting-edge and recent research. Working in these databases can require patience and persistence. Unlike Google, where you can type in anything you want and start searching, or an AI tool that will generate a response to almost any prompt, scholarly databases often require you to set careful search parameters before starting to look. There can be layers of menu options to select from and multiple search terms to enter. Often you can set a specific date range, request only full text or peer-reviewed articles, even search for court cases or government proceedings. The process takes some getting used to, and what works in one database will not always work in another, but the overall quality of information is well worth the time.

Use your results to refine your search further. Once you have begun searching, you can do several things to help narrow and focus your results and sift out the best quality information. As you look at a results list, remember that most people never get beyond page 2. See how your results are reported. Many search engines and databases default to a ranking by "relevance," but how that affects your results can vary. It can mean only that the items at the top of the results had the most occurrences of your search terms. Viewing your results with different sorting criteria, perhaps in chronological order from newest to oldest, can help you identify the most current information.

Keep track of items that you have found that you want to review in more depth. If you are searching using a public search engine, it helps to open a file for notes and a folder for saving documents on your computer as you are searching. If you can open a file, keep a running list of the titles, authors, and, if possible, links to the most promising items. If you identify a document or an article that you want to review more carefully, download it and save it where you can find it later.

Most databases have a way to tag or mark items for later review; take advantage of that option if it is available. In some cases, you can have items emailed directly to you. With whatever approach you take, make sure your notes about your sources are complete enough that you can locate the item again. As search parameters change and as the search engines 'learn' what you're looking for, you can lose earlier items. Losing track of a good article is frustrating, and too often, it is impossible to recreate the search.

As you identify and review items, you can dig into them for additional pieces. There are links and lists of references to earlier research or related articles in scholarly articles and some Wikipedia entries. Especially in scholarly articles, those reference lists can lead you to the most important, earliest, or most reputable research in the area. They can also lead you to controversial issues and differences within a field. Either way, you have gained information and insight into your topic.

These strategies can and should be repeated until you have a reasonably large number of items to review. It is up to you to decide what is *enough* material to work with before you search again or move on to the next step. Putting time and effort into the information-gathering part of preparation is essential. As the saying goes, Garbage In, Garbage Out! Without good information to choose from, your presentation will not reflect positively on you as a speaker, nor will it help you bridge the gap to your audience. It's also helpful to review a few articles at a time rather than trying to plow through a giant stack. Knowing what you have and what you still need can help you search more effectively.

Assesing Information

When you have gathered several articles or sources, you are ready to review. Take a minute to consider your goals for your presentation. What do you want your audience to know, believe, or do after you speak? Having a clear sense of your goals as a speaker will help you look for the specific information you will use in your presentation.

The articles and other items you have gathered are raw information. What you want to pull out of that material is evidence. *Evidence* is the information you use to support the major claims and ideas in your presentation. Good evidence can stand up to close inspection, and all evidence should meet basic criteria before any of it is included in your presentation. You can use multiple types of evidence, and each type adds something a little different to your presentation.

Evidence also requires attribution; you have to let your audience know where you got it and who wrote or created it. Failing to provide correct and appropriate citations for your evidence is *plagiarism,* a form of theft with serious consequences. These three practices will help you identify the best information to include in your presentation.

- Evaluate the evidence carefully using multiple criteria.
- Choose a variety of types of evidence from your available information.
- Make sure you know the source of your evidence and cite it correctly.

Evaluate your evidence carefully, using multiple criteria. This evaluation step is the most important one you take in managing the information you have. You can't include all of the information available on your topic, nor would your audience want to listen for that long! Every presentation involves a selection process to decide what gets included and what gets left out.

Speakers have ethical responsibilities to their audiences to be accurate and honest. It is fine to present a particular perspective or to have an opinion about a given topic. However, ethically you must still ensure what you share with your audience is true, reasonably timely, and avoids obvious bias.

Evaluating your evidence for **accuracy** is the first criteria you need to apply, which can present some challenges, especially on controversial topics or with a topic about which not much is known. A good place to start is with the source itself. Where did your information come from? Is your source a reputable scholarly journal with peer-reviewed articles or a well-known source of current news? Within the article, can you determine how the information was created? Did the authors conduct their research, or are they reporting what someone else did? As you evaluate the information you have, it can help you look for facts or ideas in more than one source. That is not a guarantee, but it can indicate a higher likelihood that the information is accurate. This technique is called "lateral reading" and it is especially important if you used an AI tool to generate a draft or preliminary notes. Because AI tools cannot access materials behind paywalls, they cannot provide accurate citations for many sources. Instead, they hallucinate sources based on the likelihood of topic, title, or author's name occurring. AI tools are also used to produce mis- and dis-information which is then disseminated across the internet. These sources are designed to look real and sound accurate, but the information in them is not represented accurately or is actually deceptive. (Virginia Tech News, 2024) You need to double check every source an AI tool gives you to make sure it actually exists and contains the information AI says it does.

Assuming that the evidence you have is accurate, you will want to consider its **currency**. Generally, more recent information is most relevant to your audience and will add the most value to your presentation. With the fast pace of information creation and technological innovation, information from even two or three years ago is often obsolete or no longer applicable. If you are talking about a particular time in history or presenting a chronological perspective on your topic, then older information can still be relevant. But even if you were discussing the plays written by Shakespeare or the building of the Egyptian pyramids, it is a good idea to look for the most recent information available. New evidence and information still comes up on older topics and staying current matters more than ever before.

As you are assessing the **accuracy** and **currency** of your evidence, you should also consider the **relevance**. You could find a terrific piece of evidence, absolutely accurate and just out this week, but if it isn't relevant to your topic and what you want your audience to know, understand, or do, it isn't good for you. It is easy to get distracted by a compelling piece of evidence or an intriguing perspective you had not encountered before. Perhaps a great piece of evidence will make you rethink your approach to your topic or what you want to emphasize in your presentation! Be open to these possibilities. But as you are reviewing the information and looking for high-quality evidence, you should stay focused on your topic and presentation goals.

Depending on the time you have to speak, it is likely that you will be unable to include much of the evidence you find. Ask yourself, what will my audience get from hearing or seeing this? How does this support my ideas? Is it clear how this connects to my overall perspective on this topic? If you can answer these questions easily, you're on your way to a solidly supported speech.

Choose a variety of types of evidence from your available information. Once you have a collection of pieces of evidence, you will want to think about the types of evidence you want to include in your presentation. There are three major types of evidence, and each offers something useful and unique to your presentation. The three types are **statistics**, **examples**, and **testimony**. In your presentation, it is a good idea to include all three types to create a SET of excellent pieces of evidence within your speech.

Statistics are a powerful type of evidence using numbers to express information. Most statistics express a relationship, although often, the relationship is implied rather than explicit. According to the American Veterinary Medical Association, 36.5 percent of U.S. households own dogs and 30.4 percent own cats (AVMA, 2012). The statistic quantifies the relationship of pet-owning households to the total number of households. To put those percentages in more concrete terms, according to the AVMA, approximately one out of every three households in the United States owns at least one pet. Statistics are powerful because they tend to be accepted rather than questioned, and the use of numbers carries a tone of authority and competence.

Stephen Colbert coined the term "truthiness" to describe information that feels true, whether it is actually true or not. For many audience members, statistics feel true. As a speaker, you also gain credibility and authority when you use statistics effectively. Statistics can make you sound more knowledgeable on your subject. For that reason, it is important to evaluate the statistics you use in your speeches carefully and to explain them clearly to your audience.

Statistics are generated from many sources for many reasons, and not all statistics are created equally. As with any piece of potential evidence, you want to make sure the statistics you use are accurate, current, and relevant. More specifically, make sure the statistic you use supports the claim you are making with it. For example, suppose your speech is about pet ownership. In that case, the statistic about dogs and cats could be useful to help your audience get a sense of how prevalent pet ownership is in the United States. Still, it does not say if those pet owners are responsible and care for their pets properly, nor does it account for households with multiple pets. It is up to you to determine if the statistical evidence supports your claim and explain the numbers to your audience in a way that makes sense but does not overstate or misrepresent the statistical evidence.

Election polls are a good example of statistics that are often misrepresented or not fully explained. A poll will offer statistics such as Candidate A has support from 47 percent of the voters and Candidate B has support from 51 percent, and so Candidate B is the leader. But in small print, the same poll will indicate a "margin of error" of plus or minus 4 points. If the gap between the candidates is just four points, and the margin of error is four points, then the poll results are meaningless. Such examples of statistics with serious limitations and shortcomings are all too common. Again, it is up to you to find statistics that support your claims and explain what those numbers mean to your audience. The credibility and power of statistics can work to your advantage if you handle them well!

Examples are another form of evidence and probably the most commonly used form. Examples come in three forms: the **specific instance**, the **brief example**, and the **extended** or **narrative** example. The power of examples is in the way they help your audience to imagine and connect to your topic. Examples can create vivid images and evoke strong emotions for your audience members. They can act as the human-interest stories in the news, providing a connection to the personal experiences of your audience.

Specific instances are items on a list, usually given in sets of three. In your pet ownership speech, you might say, "The most common pets in the United States are dogs, cats, and birds." Those are specific instances. A list gives your audience the

chance to identify with some aspect of your speech. While they might not own a dog, they might own a cat or a bird, and the list brings them into the speech and encourages them to continue to listen.

Brief examples are short stories, approximately three to five sentences long. Brief examples connect to our human affinity for stories. Stories build understanding, and a brief example can act as a small window into a new idea or concept. The audience can identify with the story in your brief example, even if the example is of something they have never experienced. The key to effective brief examples is to keep them short, vivid, and related to your topic. For example, for the speech on pet ownership, a brief example could describe a pet wedding. "Rocco and Brie spent $5,000 on food, fancy clothes, and themed decorations for their wedding last month. More than fifty of their close friends and family members gathered at Rocco and Brie's house to celebrate. When the groom walked around the room and sniffed all the guests, no one was worried – because Rocco and Brie are dogs." Such a short example paints a vivid verbal picture for your audience, helps them connect to your topic, and yet does not take up a lot of time. Brief examples are points of connection and understanding between you and your audience members.

The last type of example is the **extended** or **narrative** example. Just as it sounds, extended or narrative examples are longer and more detailed stories. The benefit of an extended example is the amount of detail you can include within the longer story framework. If a topic is particularly complex or difficult to understand, an extended example can be very helpful for your audience. However, extended examples also take much more time to deliver properly. If the example does not go over well with your audience, it can become a long and painful experience. It is also easy to get caught up in the details of a narrative example and miss the point of the story, especially if the example is a personal experience. No matter what type of example you choose, it should be vivid, help your audience connect to your topic, and clearly relate to the ideas and claims you want to make.

Testimony is another form of evidence that offers a unique contribution to your presentation. Testimony is evidence from someone with specific expertise or first-hand experience and is usually presented as a direct quotation. Carefully chosen testimony can be a powerful form of evidence, as it has both **authenticity** and **authority**. A good piece of testimony conveys the authority of the person you are quoting and the authenticity of someone's actual words. Testimony is commonly categorized into two major types – **expert** testimony and **peer** or **lay** testimony. Expert testimony most often comes from a person with recognized professional credentials in their area. The Surgeon-General of the United States or the Director of the Center for Disease Control would both have advanced medical degrees, perhaps additional credentials in public policy, and extensive experience with the policies and practices related to national health issues. They would be considered experts in public health.

Prestige testimony is a special type of expert testimony, often from an organization or person well-respected by other experts. The Mayo Clinic is a well-respected health organization, and statements from Mayo carry high credibility. Peer or lay testimony comes from a person with significant experience in a particular area, but not necessarily professional credentials or degrees. Basketball player Stephen Curry would likely be considered an expert on his sport, but he does not have a degree in basketball. His authority comes from his personal experience, and he could offer highly authentic peer testimony. Two key aspects for assessing testimony are the person's qualifications on your topic and the quality of their words. First, it is important to clearly and briefly explain the qualifications of the person to your audience.

You get credit from your audience for the quality of the testimony you use. You are borrowing the credibility of the person you are quoting. Additionally, you have the option to use a direct quotation or to paraphrase the person's words. If you quote the person, be sure that you are absolutely accurate in the quotation. Use the exact words, and make every effort to keep the quotation in the correct context. It is just as acceptable to paraphrase the person. Unless the quotation is so good or so striking that you cannot even come close to matching it, often you can convey the same information in your own words.

The famous quotation from John F. Kennedy's 1960 inaugural address, "My fellow Americans, ask not what your country can do for you; ask what you can do for your country," is so iconic and so powerful, there is no good way to restate it. Kennedy also spoke about the importance of physical fitness and was a strong proponent of the President's Council on Physical Fitness. During his presidency, Kennedy expanded and promoted the program. His support was a significant factor in the program's success and recognition of the importance of fitness, especially for school children. In a 1961 speech supporting the program, Kennedy said, "Physical fitness is not only one of the most important keys to a healthy body, but it is also the basis of dynamic and creative intellectual activity." This is a strong quote, but it could be reasonably and effectively paraphrased to "Kennedy viewed physical fitness as an important part of creative and intellectual work as well." Use quotations when they are so great or so eloquent, you can't possibly say it any better; use paraphrases when the quotation is good, not great, and can be effectively restated.

Make sure you know the source of your evidence and can cite it correctly. While doing your research, keep track of the sources of the information. You will need to know the author, the publication name or site, and the date your source was published. If you are using information from a website, you need the URL and the date and time you accessed the site. Given the likelihood of a link being taken down or revised, that combination allows reasonably precise identification of your source.

Oral citations are often different than the written references given at the end of a paper or in the closing visual aid of a formal presentation. You should ALWAYS give attribution for any information that you did not create yourself, including images in your visual aids. If you used any AI tools like ChatGPT, Bard, DALL-E, or Grammarly, remember that they cannot generate accurate sources, and they will hallucinate fake ones. They can help format citations for sources you have found on your own. You should also check with your instructor about how to cite AI generated material and see if your school has a policy. Citation requirements can range from none at all, to a statement of use, to a detailed cite including your prompts and how you used the tool (Guidry, 2024). Bear in mind that the abundance of material available on the internet or through social media does not mean you can use whatever you find. Many images, website materials, and other accessible forms of information are protected by copyright. Even if no copyright is present or asserted, never use anything you find without crediting the source. YouTube videos, Vines, tweets, Instagram photos, blogs and Facebook posts are examples of public sources that still require citations for anything you use.

In digital presentations, it can be difficult for the audience to see the citations on your visual aids. If that's the case, you may choose to provide a reference slide at the end of your presentation and orally cite the sources for your visual content in your speech. For oral citations, you want to provide your audience with enough information to find the source if they wanted to get more information. Sometimes this will mean giving the entire formal reference orally; more often, you can give the most relevant and necessary information about the source without formal reference. This abbreviated form of citation allows you to speak more naturally and stay in the flow of your presentation. For example, if you are citing an article written by Nicholas Kristof in the *New York Times*, you might not include the author in your oral citation, but instead say, "In a *New York Times* article from May 21, 2016…." If your topic is relevant and your audience is familiar with Kristof's work as a journalist and advocate, you might want to cite him more directly, "In May 2016, Nicholas Kristof's column in the *New York Times* covered….." Both oral citations will let your audience know that the material came from a credible source and where they could find more information; neither is a complete and formal reference. As noted above, failing to cite your sources properly is plagiarism.

Placing Information

When you have gathered and assessed a substantial collection of possible pieces of evidence, it's time to work through the process of deciding what to use and how to place it in your presentation. You already know that the different types of evidence offer different benefits within a presentation. It's also important to consider your audience's abilities to understand and process information. We know that the average rate of speed for a speaker is about 100-175 words per minute, and we know that the average listener can take in about 300 words per minute. But those rates do not factor in the time it takes to understand and evaluate information that is unfamiliar, of high interest, or verbally complex. So here is another gap for you to bridge—the gap between your speech rate and your audience's ability to understand.

One good way to think about how much evidence to include is a concept known as the Magical Number 7, Plus or Minus 2 (Miller, 1956). Miller's concept suggests that most humans can manage about seven pieces of information at one time. Here, "manage" means to understand, hold in short-term memory, and put in context. In more (or less) challenging situations, or with audiences who are more (or less) capable or interested, the number rises to about nine or drops to about five. As a speaker, you can be thoughtful about how much information you give your audience at any one time and how you can place it within your speech to maximize comprehensibility, which is accomplished in three ways: by limiting how much evidence you include; by "chunking" your information to maximize audience comprehension; and by positioning your strongest evidence for maximum effect.

First, select the best possible evidence, limiting the total amount of evidence you present. Knowing that each type of evidence offers different benefits, you will want to try and choose what to include based on the quality of the content and the effect of a given type of evidence. Too much of any one type of evidence can seem unbalanced and sound awkward. For most speeches, choosing various types of evidence to create a **SET** is an effective approach. Creating a **SET** for your speech means you have included at least one or two pieces of each type of evidence: **S**tatistics, **E**xamples, and **T**estimony in your speech. A more technical speech would likely have more statistics, a speech to share an experience, more examples or testimony, but creating a **SET** gets you off to a good start.

Second, "chunk" your information into fewer pieces and give your audience clear cues about the "chunks" you have created for them. Using an outline can be very helpful in this process. As you think through your main points, subpoints, and the supporting evidence you want to include, you are already chunking your information. The structure of a typical speech or essay—introduction, three main points, conclusion—effectively chunks information into just five pieces. Within each of the major sections, information can be added in a similar pattern. For example, one of your main points could include two subpoints, each with two pieces of supporting evidence.

Even adding an opening and closing statement within that main point still gives you only eight pieces of information to convey to your audience. With good signposts and verbal cues from you, your audience will process those eight pieces and associate them with your main point, which turns the eight pieces into one chunk, freeing up processing capability. Now your audience is ready and able to take in more of your great information!

Finally, think about the overall goal of your speech and what evidence you have that most powerfully supports that goal. Listeners tend to recall the first and last things they hear, a result known as the "primacy–recency effect." Additionally, listeners tend to recall more details about recently heard information (Crano, 1977). Depending on your topic and content, placing the strongest basic concepts at the beginning of your speech and more specific details at the end might be an effective strategy. It also helps to repeat and restate the important concepts you want your audience to remember long after you've concluded your presentation.

Conclusion

In this chapter, we discussed the basic principles and strategies for effective research and information gathering. Understanding the "information gaps" that must be bridged for your presentation to be effective is a basic building block of effective communication. Three key concepts have been presented to help you "Mind the GAP."

Gather the information you need about your topic;

Assess the information you find to determine its accuracy, quality, and appropriateness for your presentation;

Place the information in your presentation strategically so your audience has the best opportunity to understand your ideas.

With these concepts and the accompanying strategies, you have the tools you need to do effective research for your presentations. In our information society, the ability to gather, assess, and place high-quality information is a critical skill. This chapter has provided the directions you need to navigate through your information gathering effectively and efficiently.

References

Crano, William A. (1977). "Primacy versus Recency in Retention of Information and Opinion Change." The Journal of Social Psychology. 101(1) pp.87-96. DOI: 10.1080/00224545.1977.9923987

Crawford, Susan. (1983) "The Origin and Development of a Concept: The Information Society." *Bulletin of the Medical Library Association,* 71 (4) pp. 380-385.

Dictionary.com. (n.d.). *Audience definition & meaning.* Dictionary.com. Retrieved August 3, 2022, from https://www.dictionary.com/browse/audience

Isaac, M. (2023, April 18). Reddit Wants to Get Paid for Helping to Teach Big A.I. Systems. Retrieved from New York Times: https://www.nytimes.com/2023/04/18/technology/reddit-ai-openai-google.html

Konigsburg, E.L. (1967) From the Mixed-Up Files of Mrs. Basil E. Frankweiler. New York, NY: Dell.

Miller, George A. (1956) "The Magical Number Seven, Plus or Minus Two: Some Limits on Our Capacity for Processing Information." *The Psychological Review,* 63, pp. 81-97.

Project Gutenberg History and Philosophy. (2021, January). Retrieved from Project Gutenberg: www.gutenberg.org/about/background

U.S. pet ownership statistics. American Veterinary Medical Association. (2012). Retrieved August 3, 2022, from https://www.avma.org/resources-tools/reports-statistics/us-pet-ownership-statistics

Virginia Tech News. (2024, February 22). AI and the spread of fake news sites: Experts explain how to counteract them. Retrieved from Virginia Tech News: https://news.vt.edu/articles/2024/02/AI-generated-fake-news-experts.html

Outlining— An effective outline will help gather and organize your thoughts...

Outlining – An effective outline will help you gather and organize your thoughts so that you can clearly present your topic to an audience. This chapter will also instruct you how to turn your preparation outline into a speaking outline and provide you with examples of both types of outlines.

Key Terms:

I. Preparation Outline: This outline is written in complete sentences and fully encapsulates the topic you plan to present. The crafting of a preparation outline is like the piecing together of a puzzle; you must figure out where all the pieces of information fit and how they fit together in the bigger scheme of things. Also see Speech Structure.

II. Speaking Outline: Once the preparation outline is complete you can convert it into a speaking outline. Shorten those complete sentences you wrote for the preparation outline into brief phrases and keywords to guide you through the delivery of your speech.

Outlining

Dr. Sandra French
Radford University

Think of your outline as a structure that will support your speech. We are living in an era with access to more information than at any other time in history and unless we properly understand and implement outlining, our message risks being lost in a deluge of that information. Information found on the Internet can be read over and over to increase comprehension, but a speech unfolds moment-by-moment for an audience. A well-placed car horn, a missed lunch, a conflict with a co-worker, or a momentary daydream can prevent an audience from following the message a speaker is trying to convey. Because we are so prone to distraction, both from within and without, effective outlining is crucial to effective public communication. An effective speech is organized in such a way as to repeatedly emphasize the main points for listeners: even if attention wavers, they can easily rejoin the speaker's message and fill in the gaps. Think of outlining as a gift you give to your audience to give them the best possible chance of really hearing what you have to say.

After thoroughly researching a topic, a speaker must be clear on what he or she wants to share with the audience. Outlining helps a speaker to see connections between research materials and to pick out quotations or examples that are likely to have the biggest impact on the audience. Most importantly, outlining provides clarity and helps a speaker stay on topic and make the information more understandable. The preparation outline is written in complete sentences and fully encapsulates the topic you plan to present. The crafting of a preparation outline is like the piecing together of a puzzle: the key is figuring out where all the pieces of information fit and how they fit together in the bigger scheme of things.

The Preparation Outline

The preparation outline, true to its name, helps you to prepare your presentation. This is the stage at which you will try out several different organizational patterns to find the best approach to sharing your information. At this stage, you will also finalize your thesis statement and experiment with different main points based on your research and the speaking situation. You should be prepared to do a lot of reorganizing and rearranging of information.

Visual Framework: Labels, Symbols, and Indentations
A good preparation outline begins with a clear and well-organized visual framework consisting of labels, symbols, and indentations. Variations to this framework exist but the most common is detailed below.

- *Labels*
  The outline should consist of three main sections labeled Introduction, Body and Conclusion. These labels themselves don't get assigned Roman numerals. They are typically positioned closest to the left margin.

- *Symbols*
  An numeric alpha system is employed to mark the main points, sub-points and sub sub-points of the outline. Main points are denoted by Roman numerals. Capital letters are used to identify sub-points. Sub sub-points are identified by numbers.

- *Indentations*
  By indenting the smaller ideas you create a hierarchy of importance and precedence within the visual framework of the outline. In addition, consistent and correct use of indentations will provide a logical continuity to the flow of information and how that information is expressed.

  For an example of this visual framework see the preparation outline example later in this chapter.

Criteria for Content of an Effective Preparation Outline

Full Sentences

The preparation outline is written in full sentences. There should be one sentence per symbol except in the case of multi-sentence quotes and grouped statistics. Your preparation outline should also include transitions: well-thought out sentences that move an audience from one main point to the next or one part of the speech to the next. Transitions help to make a speech flow better and turn disjointed ideas into a unified whole. (see chapter 8)

The last component of a preparation outline is a complete references list, created according to the assignment specifics and including all relevant information so that your sources can easily be found by others. Most instructors will suggest a standard style for citations, such as APA, MLA, or Chicago. Be sure to check the assignment specifics and provide the reference list in the appropriate format. Your library or writing center are good places to obtain assistance for compiling adequate citations.

Keys to Creating an Effective Preparation Outline

1. *Start with your General and Specific Purpose*

2. *Identify and Label the Introduction, Speech Body and Conclusion*

3. *Use Labels and Symbols to create a Visual Framework that will help you to structure your speech*

4. *Create a Main Point/Subpoint, Sub-subpoint Structure (see the outline example later in this chapter).*

5. *Use full sentences to fully encapsulate the topic that you are planning to present.*

6. *Include formal citations in your outline. By using signal phrases, also known as introductory phrases, within the text of the outline as opposed to citing all of your source information parenthetically, your oral citations will be easier to include on the speaking outline.*

Symmetry in Rhetoric
Symmetry in rhetoric is not about language. It is about creating balance within the visual framework of your outline. There must be at least two of each symbol to maintain this balance.

To begin your preparation outline, start with your general purpose – is this a speech to inform, persuade, or entertain? Next, craft the main idea (sometimes called the specific purpose statement) of the speech.

- **General Purpose:** To Inform
- **Specific Purpose:** To inform my audience about strokes and the actions needed when someone presents the warning signs.
- **Central Idea:** By understanding strokes and the actions to take when someone presents the warning signs, lives can be saved.

Now that you have articulated your general and specific purpose, it is time to begin writing the preparation outline. Remember to follow outline form but to write in full sentences. If any individual component takes more than one sentence, subpoints should be used. Your preparation outline is a visual framework of your talking points and their relationship to one another, so be sure and use not only the symbols associated with outlining format (I, A, 1, a, etc), but also labels in parenthesis to clearly indicate the element of the speech. When outlining, be sure to follow proper indentation. Indenting provides consistency and helps clarify the relationship between your points. Be sure that text is under text (not under an outlining symbol) and that you follow the subject of your previous sentence. See the Sample Preparation Outline with labels on later in this chapter for further assistance.

Once, the preparation outline is written, use it to gauge whether your speech successfully meets the criteria of the assignment. Read through your preparation outline as if you were delivering your speech. Is it too long? Too short? Take note of how long it takes you to read through each main point. Are the main points out of balance? Remember that you want to keep each main point within a similar time frame so that your points are not out of balance.

Read through your preparation outline several times, using the following questions to guide you as you assess its effectiveness:

- **Are my main points clear?**
  - If you read through your preparation outline for a friend and they cannot easily pick out your main points and repeat them back to you, see how you can better emphasize them. Repetition of main ideas is key to helping them stand out to an audience.
  - Do I use complete sentences?
  - Do I restrict myself to one sentence per symbol (exception: multi-sentence quotes and grouped statistics)
- **Are my supporting materials clear and supported?**
  - Are you orally citing your sources?
  - Do I have at least one source to support each main point?

Your library or writing center are good places to obtain assistance for compiling adequate citations.

While your individual speaking assignments will vary, most preparation outlines should include these components. At the end of the chapter you can find a full-length example of a Preparation Outline, complete with full sentences.

For more on Compiling Citations, see Purdue University's Owl Website: https://owl.english.purdue.edu/owl/

Converting the Preparation Outline into the Speaking Outline

Once you've practiced your preparation outline in front of a live human audience (pets do not count!) several times, and received their feedback on the clarity and power of your message, then you are ready to transfer from your preparation outline to your speaking outline. Many speakers try to skip this step, opting to use their full-sentence outline to deliver a speech. Trust me friends, this is a mistake! A full-sentence outline leads to a memorized, or partially memorized speech. Delivering a speech from a full-sentence manuscript offers the speaker no wiggle room. The pressure is on to deliver the speech exactly as it is written on the outline – word for word! This often leads to an audience perception of "wooden" delivery on the part of the speaker, and added stress for speakers who lose their exact place in the outline trying to deliver it exactly as written.

Instead, opt for the *speaking outline, an outline using key words and brief phrases to prompt you through your materials.* This forces you as a speaker to really know your material, rather than relying upon a manuscript or full-sentence outline. One key benefit of speaking from a speaking outline, rather than a full-sentence preparation outline, is the freedom it affords a speaker. Speaker's using a preparation outline are free to actually respond to audience feedback and adjust their message accordingly, rather than blindly delivering a fully pre-scripted performance. A second benefit is that a speaking outline is much briefer and can easily be put on index cards or printed on paper, as determined by the speaking situation and/or assignment requirements. If you prefer to use index cards, 5 x 8 note cards are a much more acceptable alternative. You should still write out any quotations in full to ensure that you deliver them accurately, and often speakers will still include the introduction and conclusion in full-sentences to help ensure the presentation starts and ends smoothly. If you choose to use index cards, be sure to number them! Speakers who fail to heed this advice often find out the hard way that they should have listened. While teaching public speaking at a large East Coast land-grant, I encouraged all my students to follow this rule. One speaker, a Big 10 football player with a serious case of nerves, failed to heed my advice. While speaking, his hands began shaking violently, resulting in his index cards falling to the floor in a scattered heap. Failure to number his cards caused him to lose his place and only regain it after what seemed an eternity, both to him and to his audience. Remember that even numbered index cards can get disorganized if you shuffle them in your hands. When using a speaking outline on index cards, either place your cards on the podium (if you have one), or practice holding them in one hand only so your other hand can freely gesture as appropriate. Whether you use a full 8 ½ x 11 sheet of paper or index cards, you should practice with your speaking outline so that you feel comfortable with a quick look at your cards to prompt your next speech point.

A final benefit of using key words and brief phrases in the speaking outline is that it frees up space on the page for other directions you want to remember.

In a different font color, in the margins, provide yourself key reminders such as "pause here for a count of three" "look up" "smile!" It can be difficult, particularly for novice speakers, to keep these things in mind when presenting. These reminders serve an important role in seamlessly weaving together the components of speech structure, speech content, and speech delivery.

Benefits to Using a Speaking Outline

1. Allows for more freedom than the preparation outline

2. Briefer and easier to put on index cards

3. Frees up space on the page or cards for other prompts
   (i.e. smile, pause here, look up etc)

Sample Outline Structure
Title

Introduction
- I. Attain the attention of the audience
- II. Establish Credibility
- III. Relate to the audience
- IV. Reveal the Topic
- V. Preview the Body of the Speech

Speech Body
- **I. Main Point One**
  - A. Support
  - B. Support
- **II. Main Point Two**
  - A. Support
  - B. Support
- **III. Main Point Three**
  - A. Support
  - B. Support

Conclusion
- I. Signal the ending, Reinforce the Central Idea, and Restatement of Main Points.
- II. Refer Back to the Introduction

Many word processing programs, such as Microsoft Word, and Google Docs, have built-in automatic outlining. It is strongly recommended to use your word processor's outlining feature rather than manually typing the numerals and letters; however be aware that not all programs create this particular format and some changes may need to be made, so be mindful of that.

SAMPLE PREPARATION OUTLINE

Title: *Time Loss is Brain Loss – The Dangers of Strokes*

Specific Purpose: To inform my audience about strokes and the actions needed when someone presents the warning signs

Central Idea: By understanding strokes and the actions to take when someone presents the warning signs, lives can be saved.

Introduction
I. The scariest day of my life was April 12, 2012, when my grandfather had a stroke and almost died.

II. Since my grandfather's stroke, I've been researching more about strokes.

III. According to the Centers for Disease Control and Prevention webpage "Stoke Facts," "Stoke kills about 140,000 Americans each year. That's 1 out of every 20 deaths."

IV. Today, I'm going to inform you about strokes.

V. I will share with you the different types of strokes, as well as how to recognize the warning signs.

Speech Body
I. There are two types of strokes: Hemorrhagic and Ischemic
  A. Hemorrhagic strokes occur due to the rupturing of weakened blood vessels.
    1. This causes bleeding around the brain.
    2. Blood accumulates and compresses surrounding brain tissue.
    3. This is the rarer of the two main types of stroke.
  B. According to the Stroke Awareness Foundation's webpage "Stoke Information," 87% of strokes are ischemic stokes, which makes them the most common.
    1. Ischemic strokes occur when blood vessels become blocked, often by a blood clot.
    2. Blood clots can form due to vessels being clogged with fat and cholesterol.

3. The blockage keeps blood from reaching the brain, depriving it of oxygen and key nutrients.

TRANSITION: *Now that you know about the two main types of strokes, let's discuss the four major warning signs.*

II. To remember the four warning signs of stroke, the Stroke Association encourages people to remember the acronym FAST ("Warning Signs").

A. The "F" stands for dace dropping, where one side of the dace droops or is numb.
  1. To check this symptom, simply ask the person to smile.
  2. Check his or her smile to see if it is uneven or lopsided.

B. The "A" stands for arm weakness because often a person having a stroke cannot lift both arms evenly.
  1. Ask the person to raise both arms.
  2. Check to see if one arm drifts downward or if he or she complains of numbness.

C. The "S" stands for difficult speech or blurred/slurred speech.
  1. Ask the person to repeat a simple sentence like, "Ocean water is blue."
  2. Can he or she repeat the words back correctly or is he or she speaking in ways that do not make sense?

D. The "T" stands for time.
  1. This is the most critical points of all as "time loss equals brain loss" according to the Nittany Valley Rehibition Hospital ("Time Loss").
  2. If any of these symptoms appear, it is recommended that your call 911 immediately, even if the symptoms subside.

Conclusion

I. In closing, I hope you are now better informed about strokes; remember there are two main types of strokes, hemorrhagic and ischemic, and four warning signs, easily remembered with the FAST acronym.

II. April 12, 2012 was the worst day of my life due to my grandfather's stroke, by Mom's quick thinking to recognize the symptoms and call 911 saved his life. Now you know the signs too!

SAMPLE SPEAKING OUTLINE

Introduction
 I.   April 12, 2012
 II. Today I'm going to inform you about stokes. *EYE CONTACT*
 III I will share with you the different types of strokes, as well as *PAUSE HERE* how to recognize the warning signs.

Speech Body
 I.   Two types: Hemorrhagic and Ischemic
   A. Hemorrhagic- Rupturing of weakened blood vessels.
     1. Bleeding around the brain.
     2. Compresses surrounding brain tissue.
     3. Rare
   B. Ischemic - more common, 87% of all strokes
     1. Blocked – blood clots.
     2. Clogged with fat and cholesterol.
     3. Deprives brain.

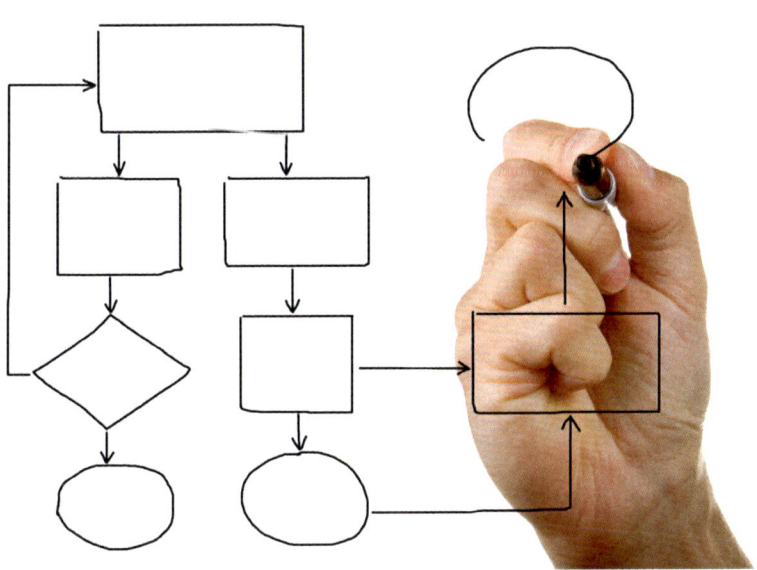

TRANSITION: *Now that you know about the two main types of strokes, let's discuss the four major warning signs.*

    II. The Stroke Association - the acronym FAST.
        A. Face Drooping
           1. Smile
           2. Lopsided?
        B. Arm weakness. *DEMONSTRATE*
           1. Raise Arms
           2. Numb? Drifting?
        C. Speech problems.
           1. Repeat "Ocean water is blue."
           2. Make sense?
        D. Time.
           1. According to the Nittany Valley Rehabilitation Hospital's website, "time loss equals brain loss.
           2. Call 911.

Conclusion
    I.   In closing, I hope you are now better informed about strokes.
    II. Remember that there are two main types of strokes – hemorrhagic and ischemic – and four warning signs, easily remembered with the FAST acronym.
    III. April 12, 2012, was the worst day of my life due to my grandfather's stroke, but Mom's quick thinking to recognize the symptoms and call 911 saved his life. *PAUSE FOR EFFECT*
        Now you know the signs too!

References

Preparation outlines need to show a full source page. Check with your teacher to see what type of format you are to use to cite works.

Conclusion

Invest the time in creating both the preparation and the speaking outline. Outlining helps speakers craft more organized, more concise, more memorable messages. By utilizing a preparation outline, speakers better learn their material, and develop a rhythm and flow in their speaking. As you move from the preparation outline to the speaking outline, you can be more confident in your presentation of the material. This will help you be a more compelling, more memorable speaker.

JK Rowling
The fringe benefits of failure

https://www.ted.com/talks/jk_rowling_the_fringe_benefits_of_failure

There's a reason why great music like Beethoven's Fifth Symphony sounds so grand, why a beautifully proportioned structure like the Golden Gate Bridge fills us with awe.

If we take away the structure of a song, a story, a film, or pretty much anything we create, we take away the foundation from which it stands and will more often than not be left with a chaotic cloud in which the initial message is lost. That is why art, music, literature, and rhetoric through the ages have all developed structures to provide their practitioners the most efficient and effective ways of reaching their intended audience.

In this chapter you will learn how to structure your speech. A speech is divided into three sections, the beginning or **introduction**, the middle or **speech body**, and the end or **conclusion**. In the introduction, the speaker should attain the attention of the audience, state the main idea of their speech, and preview the main points therein. The speech body consists of information, usually broken up into main points that support the speaker's thesis or convey the main content to the audience regarding the topic of the speech. Finally, the conclusion ties everything together. This is done by signaling that the speech is ending and summarizing the main points. It can also include challenging the audience to act, providing an appropriate quotation to sum up the points, or returning to a story or joke from the introduction. This chapter will also discuss connectives or transition statements that help move the speaker through the sections of his or her speech in a fluid way.

Speech Structure

Dr. Sandra L. French
Radford University

Crafting an effective message is key to getting an audience to understand your message. In order to do this, speakers must organize their message in ways that are relatable and understandable. When speeches are well organized, it increases the ability of speakers and listeners to create shared meaning and understanding.

A speech cannot be well organized if you are unsure what you are really talking about! After thoroughly researching a topic, a speaker must be clear on what he or she wants to share with the audience. Have you ever listened to a presentation and thought, "I don't get it?" Sometimes speakers have so many ideas to share with an audience that the listeners are really unclear about what to take away from the speech.

How does a speaker gain clarity about what it is he or she really wants to communicate to an audience? Try answering this simple question:

"When I'm finished with my speech, I want my audience to know that _____."

The second portion of the sentence is the main message of your speech, and the speech should be organized so that all the research and the information you provide helps the audience remember this main point. The general purpose of a speech is always either to inform, to persuade, or to entertain, but using this technique will help you figure out what main points you plan to develop in your speech. It's trickier than it sounds to create one sentence that captures the essence of a speaker's purpose. Too often speakers fail to realize that this simple step is the key to deciding how to organize a message. Given all the knowledge you have acquired on your topic through your research, how will you zero in on the essence of what is most important?

Once a speaker is clear on the main idea of the speech, it's time to figure out how to put all the pieces together into main points that can be easily followed and understood by the audience. At their most basic level, effective books, movies, and TV shows follow a simple structure; each has a beginning, a middle, and an end. Similarly, our speeches should have a *clear introduction, easy-to-follow middle, and satisfying conclusion.* To begin, start with the body of the speech, crafting the "meat" of the message. Once you know the points you wish to convey, you can then formulate your introduction and conclusion that will wrap around your speech body.

Speech Body: A Review of Organizational Models with Examples

When crafting his or her main points, a speaker must decide how to arrange them. Effective organization of supporting materials provides a logical and smooth flow to a speech. Speeches that are well organized are easier for the speaker to deliver and for the audience to understand. A speaker needs to ask one main question, *"What's the best way for me to show the relationships between my materials?"* In answering this question, a speaker will often clearly decide on one of several organizational patterns:

Organizational Patterns

Chronological

Spatial

Cause-Effect

Problem-Solution

Topical

Recency

Primacy

Monroe's Motivated Sequence

Compare and Contrast

It is important to note that the same topic, organized differently, will produce a drastically different speech. Later in this chapter, we will see how speeches about the same topic can look quite different and provide much different information, depending on which organizational pattern we choose. Pay particular attention to which organizational patterns are most appropriate for informative and persuasive speeches.

Chronological

A chronologically organized speech is one arranged according to time. This organizational pattern works well for speeches that take an audience through the history of a person, place, or idea. For example, a speech about the life of Walt Disney lends itself to a chronological organizational pattern, because its main points are easily divided into periods of time.

MAIN IDEA: *When I'm finished my speech, I want my audience to know that Walt Disney spent much of life failing before he succeeded.*

BODY:
I. Disney's early years were impacted by war: 1901 – 1918.
II. Disney's early cartoons were a string of failures: 1919-1928.
III. Disney's successes were unpredictable: 1929-1966.

This chronological organizational pattern divides Walt Disney's life into decades and takes the listener through his failures and successes from birth to death. Other organizational patterns might include some of the same research, but they will inevitably have a different focus.

Spatial

A spatial organizational pattern follows a direction. A spatially organized speech, in effect, makes you the tour guide for your audience. A speech about Walt Disney that focuses on The Walt Disney World, for example, could be arranged spatially as you take your audience through each separate park, or on a tour of one particular park, say the Magic Kingdom. This would mean including different information and additional main points.

MAIN IDEA: *When I'm finished my speech, I want my audience to know that there are five main sections of the Magic Kingdom.*

BODY:
I. Main Street, USA
II. Tomorrow Land
III. Fantasy Land
IV. Liberty Square
V. Frontier Land

The spatial organizational structure works well for describing some kind of landscape, such as a theme park, the D-day beaches of the Normandy Invasion, or an archaeological site.

The next two organizational patterns divide a speech into two main sections: *Cause and Effect and Problem – Solution.*

Cause-Effect

This pattern of organization is particularly useful when giving persuasive speeches, as it shows the relationship between various conditions and their impacts. While it is possible to use this organizational structure for informative speeches, one must take care when discussing effects not to cross into telling the audience what to do. For example, if the purpose of one's speech is to inform the audience about skin cancer, the cause-effect structure could work well:

BODY
I. **What causes skin cancer?**
II. **What happens to a person who has skin cancer?**

When using the Cause-Effect structure, a speaker might choose to discuss various causes (reasons) first, then explain their effects (consequences), but a speaker can also discuss the effects first, and explain the causes second. Suppose you were giving a speech about the lack of worldwide access to childhood vaccines. Your speech might start with the effects of non-vaccination and then discuss the reasons why vaccinations are not readily available worldwide.

Problem Solution

The problem-solution structure divides a speech into two main sections: a discussion of the problem (or problems) and its solution (or solutions). This organizational structure is used primarily in persuasive speaking, as the speaker's purpose is usually to convince the audience to support or engage in some type of action to alleviate a problem. The speaker first attempts to convince an audience that a problem exists, and then attempts to convince the audience to change either a pattern of thought, attitude, or behavior as part of the solution. In the first section, a speaker uses their research to demonstrate to the audience that a problem exists, and shows its different facets, its impact, seriousness, etc. In the second section, the speaker identifies a potential solution to the problem, and shows how the audience can participate in making the solution a reality. For example, in crafting a speech about the problem of obesity in America, the outline for the speech body might look like this:

BODY

I. Problem: Rising levels of obesity in America
   A. Increased medical problems in children
   B. Earlier death in obese adults
   C. Rising costs of health-care associated with obesity

II. Solution: Make eating healthy easier
   A. Decrease the prices of healthy food
   B. Take junk food out of schools

It is not mandatory to have the same number of sub-points in the problem and solution; just be sure to adequately address each of them. However, exceeding three sub-points may give the audience more supporting material than they can remember!

Topical

Topical organizational structure, where you divide a larger subject into logical sub-topics, is the most commonly used organizational method. There is no right or wrong way to divide a topic; just use ways that make sense given your overall main purpose for the speech.

MAIN IDEA: *When I'm finished with my speech, I want my audience to know that marriage rituals are different in China than in the United States.*

BODY:
I. Chinese wedding attire
II. Chinese wedding banquet
III. Post-wedding rituals

Notice the logical structure to the speech body and that each main point is an independent idea. The topical organizational structure can be used for almost any subject and is the most frequently used of all five organizational patterns.

There are four additional organizational patterns that generally relate to persuasive speeches.

1. **Recency:** The main points of the speech are organized so that the best arguments and evidence come last. This leaves the audience with the strongest possible impression of your persuasive message.

2. **Primacy:** The opposite of recency. Main points of the speech are organized so that the best arguments and evidence are presented up front. This is especially useful with skeptical or hostile audiences. Initially impressive arguments may capture their attention and give you a chance to make your case.

3. **Monroe's Motivated Sequence:** This strategy is a variation of problem/solution. The first step is to gain the 'attention' of your audience and to turn their focus to your topic. The audience is then offered a "need" (a problem that needs solving), a "satisfaction" (a solution to the problem), "visualization" scenarios where the problem is solved and/or not solved, and "action" where the audience is called upon to do something to enact the satisfaction/solution.

4. **Compare and Contrast**
   The Compare and Contrast structure is another common way to organize a speech. An example would be a persuasive speech that attempts to convince students that they should all live on campus. The compare/contrast organizational pattern could be used to compare living on campus with living off campus throughout the whole speech.

Introductions – The Beginning

Once the material has been researched and organized, it's time to start thinking about how you will introduce the topic to your listeners. The beginning of a speech is often the hardest to create. Have you ever heard the saying that it only takes 7 seconds to create a first impression (Goman, 2011)? Your introduction is your first impression. Use it to pique the interest of your listeners and establish common ground. Too often speakers give little time and attention to how they will begin a speech, opting instead for the strategy of simply stating, "Hi, I'm Sandy, and today I'm going to talk to you about ways to reduce pollution." This type of introduction generates little enthusiasm on the part of listeners and fails to convey a speaker's genuine interest in sharing information with listeners. Effective introductions help create a favorable first impression with listeners. It also boosts your confidence as a speaker and generates interest in the speech.

What is an audience looking for in an introduction? Effective introductions include the following elements:

1. **Get the attention of the audience**
2. **Establish credibility**
3. **Relate to the audience**
4. **Reveal the topic**
5. **Preview the body of the speech**

Step One: Getting the attention of your audience

When it comes to getting the attention of your audience, there are many options for speakers. While the options for introducing a speech are many, we will focus here on five key ways to make an impact:

- **Share a startling fact or statistic.**
- **Use a relevant quotation.**
- **Tell a humorous story or joke.**
- **Use a real or hypothetical illustration.**
- **Ask a question.**

Remember, there are many other ways to get an audience's attention! Be creative while remaining appropriate.

Share a startling fact or statistic. Providing a startling fact or statistic can attain the audience's attention by jolting them out of complacency. For example, one student began her speech on clean drinking water this way:

I see several of you brought water or something else to drink to class today. How long did it take you to get that drink? Probably not very long. We basically can get clean water whenever we want it, but in many areas of the world, this is not the case. In countries that lack access to clean water, women and girls spend up to six hours daily collecting water. That's more time than a student taking a normal load spends in class on a daily basis!

This method of attaining an audience's attention is most effective when not overplayed. Don't overdramatize the situation – present the facts in a clear and compelling manner. Often when we start with a startling fact or statistic, we need to pause and let what we have said "sink in" for our audience members. The idea is to cause your audience to reflect.

Use a relevant quotation. Starting a speech with a relevant quotation can provide a theme or frame to the rest of your speech. Often speakers will use a quotation from someone famous, but the most important point is that the quotation be relevant to your speech. Starting with John F. Kennedy's famous exhortation, "Ask not what your country can do for you, ask what you can do for your country," might make sense in a speech about volunteering, but it would be less relevant to a speech on spring break vacations. Where can we find useful quotations? Of course we can search the Internet for "famous quotations," but did you know there are actually books that compile this information for you? Check out *Barlett's Famous Quotations* or *The Oxford Dictionary of Quotations* in the reference section of your library. These books do the hard work for you and organize quotations by author, including ancient, modern, and pop culture sources.

Tell a humorous story or joke. The first rule of joke and humorous story telling is what I like to call "the grandma rule." If you wouldn't tell the story or joke to your grandmother, you probably shouldn't put it in your speech! As with quotations, your story should be short, simple, and relevant. Like quotations, jokes can be found in books, magazines, and online, but these too should be relevant to the speech. Also keep in mind that an attention-getter should utilize your strengths as a speaker. If you routinely forget the punch line when telling jokes to your friends, then this may not be the opener for you! For example, when my daughter ran for a position in student government at her school, her speech emphasized her skills as a problem-solver. She decided to open her speech with a relevant joke: "What did one math book say to the other? We've got problems!" Be sure your joke is clean, easy to deliver, and relevant to the topic.

Use a real or hypothetical illustration. An illustration could be a real story, or a story from literature, or even just a plausible tale. Like our other options for attaining the attention of an audience, the story must be relevant to the main point of your speech. Such stories can come from newspapers, magazines, sermons, and your own life experiences. For example, one student used just such a story when giving her informative speech:

I'm leaving a late night movie with my father when suddenly, as he's driving, we hear it and see it. Those dreaded lights and sirens! My father pulls over and the police officer politely asks him if he's been drinking. With slurred speech, and the smell of alcohol on his breath, my father responds, "No, officer." In that moment, if my father had been arrested for drunk driving, he could have died. You see, my father wasn't drunk, but slipping into diabetic shock. Nearly 29 million people in America are diabetics. Today I'm going to share with you some information about diabetes: its causes, symptoms, and treatments.

This student used a personal illustration to great effect. She attained the attention of the audience by drawing them in with a story that was true, personal, and cleverly told.

Ask a question. When a speaker begins with a question to the audience, the answer is usually an obvious one, but the question is asked in order to make a point to the audience. Let's say you are going to do an informative speech on cancer. A speaker might ask audience members to stand up if they know someone affected by cancer. This type of visual "answer" could help a speaker show the widespread impact of the disease and "set the stage" for the speech. However, a speaker must analyze the audience adequately so as to have confidence in the answer listeners will supply to the question.

An example would be the following: a student wanted to convince his fellow classmates to ride the university-provided bus transportation around campus, rather than driving their cars, in an effort to protect the environment. He conducted research about the percentage of students that drove to campus daily rather than using the bus system, and he felt well prepared to give his speech. However, he neglected to analyze the particular audience to whom he would be speaking, his classmates. As he began his speech with the following question, "How many of you drive to campus to get to your classes?" he anticipated a large number of students to nod in agreement or perhaps even raise their hands. Unfortunately, he was met with puzzled looks instead, because this particular class was made up mostly of freshmen who aren't allowed to have cars on campus and who all used the bus system already! It was a painful eight minutes listening to him try and convince the audience to do what they were already doing – ride the bus around campus.

Using a question to attain the attention of your listeners need not involve them standing, raising hands, or answering out loud. **Rhetorical questions** are asked without expectation of a response, usually to create a certain effect within the audience. Rhetorical questions can be effective in attaining an audience's attention IF you have confidence your listeners will answer (silently or otherwise) in the way that you expect.

Step Two: Establish credibility
It's important to establish for your audience why you are a credible speaker. Explaining to your audience why you are an expert on your topic may seem a bit uncomfortable at first. Often in the "real world" speakers are introduced by others who share and explain the speaker's credibility with the audience. However, we must become comfortable providing our credentials on our own behalf. This sets the audience expectation that you have solid, important information to share and that you are well-versed in your speech topic. However, we must remember that credibility is perceived by the listeners. Even being a Ph.D. (presumably an expert) on a topic does not guarantee that audience members will find a speaker credible. What exactly, then, does it take for an audience to grant a speaker credibility? To answer this question, let's return to the roots of the communication discipline: Aristotle. Aristotle divided the art of persuasion into three main components: pathos (emotion), logos (logic), and ethos (character/credibility). Establishing one's ethos is multi-faceted. Audiences need to know if they can respect you, if you are generally trustworthy, and if you can speak on your subject with authority. To help establish your credibility, inform the audience of your preparation and readiness to speak on the subject.

Step Three: Relate to the audience- What is in it for them?
This is a crucial question that effective speakers must clearly answer for their audience. After establishing your authority to speak on a subject, you can further enhance your credibility by explaining to the audience how listening to your speech will benefit them and how the information you share will be relevant to their lives.

Step Four: Reveal the topic.
In addition to establishing your authority and explaining how your speech will benefit your listeners, you want to clearly explain the topic you will be presenting. Leave no doubt in listeners' minds exactly what you will be speaking about: "Today I will share with you the benefits of learning a foreign language in college."

Step Five: Preview the body of the speech.
The final step is to preview the main points to be covered in the body of the speech. Once an audience member knows the speech is about benefits of learning a foreign language, it is important to them to know how the speaker plans to discuss those benefits, and how many benefits will be discussed. The preview statement helps listeners stay on track and follow the speaker: "I want to share with you three benefits of learning a foreign language while in college: enhanced cognitive function, improved multitasking, and increased employability upon graduation."

Be sure to include all five steps for an effective introduction: gaining the attention of your audience, establishing your credibility, relating your topic to the audience, clearly stating your topic, and previewing the body of the speech.

Conclusions – The End

Like introductions, conclusions are often neglected by the speaker. Students sometimes end speeches by thanking the audience for their time or asking for questions, but these are not truly effective endings. A solid conclusion reviews the main points of the speech and leaves the audience with a sense of closure. In order to prepare an effective conclusion, a speaker should do the following:

- **Provide an appropriate quotation**
- **Challenge your audience to do something**
- **Return to a story or joke from your introduction**

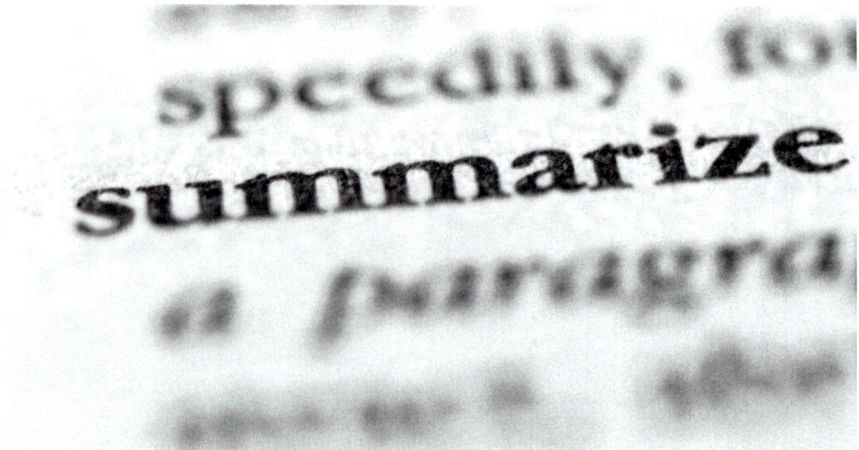

Step One: Signal the ending/Reinforce the central idea/Summarize the main points.

A transitional word or phrase such as "finally" or "to conclude my speech" usually precedes the ending of a speech. The next section on transitions will address this in greater detail. Once you signal to your audience that your speech will soon be ending, it's important to reinforce the central idea and summarize your main points. Remember the statement of the central idea is akin to a thesis statement in the paper. When you remind your audience what the central idea of your speech is, you are reminding them about the main purpose of your speech. In addition, repeating the basics of your main points helps cement them in the minds of your audience.

Step Two: Refer back to the introduction.

Consider the mood you wish to create in your audience in the final moments of your speech. What techniques are available to help a speaker create a memorable ending? This is often done by referring to your introduction in some way. Reminding the audience of the interesting information you provided to begin your speech "brings them around" full circle at the end. The following are some examples of how one might provide closure and a sense of finality in the conclusion:

Provide an appropriate quotation. Just as you can use a quotation to gain the attention of the audience in your introduction, you can use a quotation to bring a note of finality to your speech. For example, a speech about the benefits of active listening might end with the proverb, "We have two ears and one mouth, because listening is twice as important as speaking." A brief and relevant quotation at the end of a speech can stir an audience and help them reflect on the information you have just shared.

Challenge your audience. Particularly when doing a persuasive speech, a challenge to the audience to do something can make for an effective and emotional conclusion. For example, if a speaker is trying to persuade the audience to get involved in the worldwide lack of clean drinking water, a challenge to the audience to donate the money they typically spend on bottled water in a week could be an effective call to action.

Return to a story or joke from the introduction. Returning to a story or joke you mentioned in your introduction provides a greater degree of coherence to your speech. One student gave a speech on the problem of human trafficking and started her speech this way:

43,200. That's the number Karla Jacinto told the CNN reporter to remember. It's the number of times Karla was raped during her time in captivity due to human trafficking. That's 30 men per day, seven days a week, for almost four years.

After giving a stirring and disturbing informative speech on the current state of human trafficking, the student returned to Karla's story for the conclusion:

Karla is now 23 years old. She's told her story to the United States Congress, the Pope at the Vatican, and speaks out at conferences and events aimed at stopping human trafficking. But Karla is one of the lucky ones. She escaped. Won't you get involved to help others like Karla?

These three strategies for ending the speech with the appropriate mood can be used separately or together.

Your conclusion creates the final impression in the minds of your audience. Don't leave it to chance. Carefully plan out your conclusion and practice it so you are ready to leave a forceful and lasting impression on your audience.

Connectives

Even the most logically organized speech needs connections to help the speech flow from one point to the next. These connections are known as **connectives** or words and phrases that signal to the audience when a speaker is changing between main points or between main sections of a speech (from introduction to speech body to conclusion). Proper use of connectives helps a speech flow smoothly and assists the audience is following a speaker's logical progression of ideas.

Transitions help the audience to follow the organizational pattern of the speech through **signposting** or verbally cueing the audience about a move from one completed thought or idea to a new one. "The first symptom of skin cancer is…The second symptom is…" Questions can also be used effectively as signposts. Questions invite answers, and even signpost questions invite the audience to silently or subliminally follow along and receive the answers to your questions. For example, in a speech on identity theft a speaker could introduce a main point with the following question: "So just how prevalent are skimming devices?" This lets the audience know what will be covered in the next main point and prepares the audience for the answer to the question.

Internal previews and summaries can be used as connectives. An internal preview or summary previews (or reviews) multiple points and provides a link to the next point. "Now that I have told you about the prevalence of skin cancer and the importance of sunscreen, let's talk about what ingredients to look for in sunscreen products." Such a sentence assists the audience in remembering the points you have already covered and prepares them for how they connect to the material left to be shared.

Use **parallel structure** (also known as parallelism) in your connectives whenever possible. Parallel structure means using the same pattern of words or phrases. Parallel structure can be used to introduce main points or to emphasize subpoints in a speech. Here's an example of using parallel structure to introduce main points from Steve Jobs' Stanford Commencement Address:

It means to try to tell your kids everything you thought you'd have the next 10 years to tell them in just a few months. *It means to make* sure everything is buttoned up so that it will be as easy as possible for your family. *It means to say* your goodbyes. Here we see parallel structure effectively employed to keep the speech moving and to help the audience follow along.

An important corresponding principle is to keep your main points **in balance.** In other words, for a speech with three main points you should try and provide a similar amount of information in each main point; it shouldn't take three minutes to cover main point one, seven minutes to cover main point two, and four minutes to cover main point three. For some useful transition words and phrases check out Purdue's Owl Website:

Try not to get bogged down in what type of connective you are using. Just remember that it is important to include connectives, and they help make a speech more understandable to your audience.

Conclusion

In this chapter, the basic methods of organizational structure have been discussed. Understanding how to organize your information is crucial to effectively communicating your ideas to an audience. Effective speeches have a clear beginning, middle, and end. In your introduction, remember to attain an audience's attention, establish your credibility, relate the topic to your audience, state the main idea of the speech, and preview its structure. Additionally, organize your message using chronological, spatial, cause-effect, problem-solution, topical, compare and contrast, Monroe's Motivated sequence, recency, primacy, or topical structure. Use transitions to keep your speech flowing from point to point. Finally, conclude your speech by signaling to the audience that the speech is ending and summarizing the main points, referring back to the introduction, and reinforcing the central idea.

References

Goman, C. (2011). 7 seconds to make a first impression. *Forbes*. Retrieved from http://www.forbes.com/sites/carolkinseygoman/2011/02/13/se 0ven-seconds-to-make-a-firstimpression/#3c9a8724645a

Laverne Cox
2014 Creating Change Conference

https://www.youtube.com/watch?v=6cytc0p4Jwg

Some days I wake up and I'm that sixth grader who swallowed a bottle of pills because I did not want to be myself anymore. Because I did not know how to be anybody else and who I was, I was told was a sin, was a problem and I didn't want to exist.

For many speakers, preparing their speeches — topic selection, research, organization, creating visual aids — is the easiest part of their presentation.

When it comes to the actual physical delivery of their message, a new set of issues to coordinate and manage come into play. Unlike the earlier preparations, preparing to deliver your speech is all about you and your physical presence as you share the information you've so carefully put together. The good news is that you can prepare for and practice your physical delivery so that how you present your speech actually improves it, helps your audience understand your message, and increases your confidence as a speaker. But it takes thoughtful practice to get there. In this chapter, we will discuss multiple methods of delivery, how physical and vocal presence can be practiced to support and even enhance your presentation, and a step by step approach to rehearsing your speech.

Rehearsal and Delivery

Dr. Tracey Quigley Holden
University of Delaware

Modes of Delivery

There are many ways to deliver your message to an audience. Earlier in this text, we talked about the various channels of communication, including speech. Traditionally, there are four modes of delivery when giving your speech.

The four modes are memorization, manuscript, extemporaneous, and impromptu. Each has advantages and disadvantages related to the speaking situation in which your message needs to be delivered. **Memorization** involves the most pre-delivery preparation. For a memorized speech, the entire speech is written out word for word exactly as you wish to deliver it; then you memorize it until you have every word; then you practice your physical and vocal delivery of the memorized text. The advantages of memorization are limited. However, there are situations where you simply cannot have notecards or other speaking assistance, and yet it is critically important that your message be conveyed precisely and thoroughly. The disadvantage is the tremendous amount of preparation a memorized speech takes and the risk of going blank in the moment you need to deliver. You also cannot change a memorized speech, no matter how your audience responds. If you're familiar with TED talks, you may think that the speakers have all memorized their presentations. But Chris Anderson (2016), the current director of TED, says memorization is not the secret to a great talk – the real secret is being comfortable onstage and having a great story to tell. If you watched the Amy Cuddy speech on power posing, you may remember her story about her car accident. Cuddy (2017) said after the speech, she didn't decide to include that story until she was on stage, when the moment and the story called for it. Some of the

TED speakers do memorize, but most simply rehearse over and over until the speech is so much a part of them they can deliver it naturally. Many of the TED speakers do create a **manuscript** for their speech, but, unlike manuscript delivery, they don't read from it. That is what manuscript delivery is – practiced reading. Truly exceptional and highly practiced speakers can make a manuscript sound energetic and fluid, but it's a challenging task. Manuscripted speeches have the advantage of allowing you to decide every word in your speech ahead of time, which can be critical when you need to make a strong argument or be sure you don't leave anything out. The disadvantages include the challenge of reading in a way that connects with your audience and the lack of adaptability. Like memorization, you can't change anything in a manuscripted speech while you're delivering it.

That adaptability is the biggest advantage of the **extemporaneous** speech. Extemporaneous speeches are carefully prepared and organized and practiced many times. But the speech is not written out word for word, and it is not memorized. Instead, the speaker practices the speech many times until the content and organization are so familiar that the speech can be delivered as if the speaker were having a conversation with the audience. That **conversational tone** is what most speakers try to achieve and what audiences appreciate – the sense that the speaker is communicating *with* the audience, not talking AT them. Because extemporaneous speeches are so thoroughly prepared, the speaker is so familiar with the material and the organization that they can focus on the audience response. If audience members seem bored or look like they have questions, the speaker can add vivid examples or more detailed explanations. Extemporaneous speeches allow immediate, on-the-spot adaptation to the audience by the speaker; in general, they allow for a strong connection between speaker and audience. This is the type of speech most frequently given in public speaking classes and in most business presentations.

The last mode of delivery is one you probably use every day without thinking about it at all. **Impromptu** speaking is done in the moment with little or no preparation. Nearly all of our conversations are impromptu with the topic and content generated in that moment. Casual conversation is the most familiar form of impromptu speaking, but we use it at other times as well. When you respond to a question or make a comment in a meeting or in class, that's likely to be impromptu. While impromptu speaking is by definition unplanned and you often cannot prepare for a specific topic, you can still speak in an organized and effective way. Taking just a moment to think through a comment or before responding to a question allows you to organize your thoughts and edit unnecessary material. Your audience will appreciate it.

Delivering Your Speech

Now that you're familiar with the general modes of delivery, let's take a closer look at the details of delivering your presentation as effectively as possible. In this section, we will discuss the entire process of delivering a speech. The focus here is on physical delivery, so it is assumed that all of your content and organization is done – you have already done the preparation including presentation aids.

Your presentation begins well before you take your place in front of your audience. Take a minute to recall the material on communication apprehension, commonly called speech anxiety or stage fright. As you get ready to approach your audience, a few deep breaths will reduce any tension you feel. Check your presentation aids – visuals, sound if you're using it, notes – before you move to your primary speaking position. Once you are in front of your audience, hold yourself as tall as you can with your feet about shoulder width apart. Take a moment to look across all of your listeners, and take one more deep breath. You're ready!

Using Your Body Movement

One of the most frequently asked questions from speakers is "Can I move?" The easy answer is "Yes! You can and probably should!" But of course there is more to the story. First, movement is not required, and too much movement can be detrimental to your speech. We have all seen speakers who fidget constantly, or pace back and forth, or just can't seem to stop moving, ever! A lot of random movement is generated by the energy in your body needing somewhere to go, and if you don't direct it, it shows up in distracting movement. Human biology demands that we track any type of movement, a throwback to our days as predators or prey. So when you are moving, your audience has to pay attention to your movement – and that reduces their ability to pay attention to your message.

Avoiding unnecessary and random movement will improve your presentation significantly. Second, you might think, if moving is distracting, should I just stand still? That is certainly an option, but standing still reduces your connection with your audience. In many speaking situations it can be difficult to move in the most effective ways. If you are speaking from a lectern or podium, or if movement might block your presentation aid too much, you may have to stay in place. Standing still won't necessarily reduce your overall effectiveness as a speaker, but do your best to connect with your audience as directly as possible. Assuming you can move and do not have to remain in place, there are two fundamental principles for effective movement while speaking. They are as follows:

1. Move only 2 or 3 steps and STOP.
2. Move with intent.

Most of the time, the space you have in front of an audience is limited. Even on a relatively large stage, moving too far to one side or the other decreases your ability to connect with audience members on the other side. The other issue is keeping your audience engaged with your message. Knowing that movement is distracting and yet can add energy and dynamism to your speech, use it sparingly and in small doses. Taking two or three steps and then stopping strikes the right balance.

The timing of your move matters as well. Of course, you can take your two steps at any point during your speech, but there are ways to make the movement work for you. Ideally, your moves come at the same time the speech 'moves'- on transitions between your main points or ideas. Imagine you've spent a few minutes speaking about an important idea, provided several pieces of evidence, and drawn a conclusion about that material. Now you want to tell your audience how the information applies to a current issue. As you give your transition comments, take those two steps. Then **STOP** before you begin speaking about the next idea. That small movement signals your audience that something new is being introduced, gives them time to process the last bit of information you delivered, and adds dynamism to your overall delivery. When you **STOP**, you signal that they need to pay attention again, you reduce the level of distraction, and give yourself a moment to focus on your next words.

Whenever you give directions or instructions, ALWAYS stand still. If your audience needs to be able to follow a process step by step, you need to **STOP** *while you give them the steps!*

With that in mind, the key to truly polished and effective movement is moving with intent. Just taking a couple of steps in random directions, even if done on transitions, won't add the kind of positive energy you want to create. Additionally, the manner in which you move can contribute to how you feel during delivery and how your audiences perceive you. Moving with intent – firmly taking a step or two to address a new section of the audience, or to direct attention to a presentation aid, or to re-center yourself in the speaking space – contributes to your overall presence as a speaker. *Before you speak, think through your presentation and consider, when should I move?*

Last but not least, there are some types of movement that should be avoided. Pacing back and forth, especially if repeated several times, will only make your audience think of zoo animals. Stepping up and back or side to side, rocking back and forth, twisting on your feet, kicking your feet, tapping your heels or toes, bouncing up and down, leaning on a lectern, table, or chalk board, or the classic wrapping one foot around the other flamingo style won't help you or your audience with your message. *So - take your two steps, move with intent, and* **STOP**.

Gestures

It's possible that THE most frequently asked question from speakers is "What do I do with my hands?" As with the rest of your body, you can use your hands to support and enhance your presentation. Also as with your body, using your hands poorly can distract your audience from your message and even contradict what you're trying to say. Imagine you run into a friend who you know just went though a difficult experience. You say, "Hi, how are you? Everything okay" And he says, "Yeah, fine." But when he says that, his arms are wrapped tightly around his body, his head is down, and he barely looks at you. Is everything fine? No. His non-verbal communication, and especially the tightly wrapped arms, tells you that very little is fine for him at that moment. The gesture – or in this case, the lack thereof, contradicts his words. On the other hand, if he had waved to you as you approached and in response to your question said, "Yeah fine!" with a dismissive wave of the hand, a strong voice, and looking you in the eye, you would probably think he was doing fine. His gestures effectively reinforced the message of his words.

One of the amazing things about the human body is how well it is designed to do all the things we want it to do. Consider your arms and hands. Your arm hangs down from your shoulder and bends nicely at the elbow a little above your waist. Your hands can move, point, and rotate on your wrists. All of this happens just underneath your face and your mouth, where your main message is coming from. Although you can't literally talk with your hands in the sense of producing sound, your arms and hands do create a second, powerful line of communication between you and your audience. Using your hands to gesture can reinforce, enliven, and enhance your message. If you use your hands to hold notecards as a speaking aid, these also help you keep your speech organized and offer support during your speech. ***What a brilliant design!***

So back to the question – what do you do with your hands? First, keep them between your shoulders and your hips. Old speaking textbooks and speaking coaches used to say to "let your hands hang naturally at your sides." Unfortunately, that doesn't look or feel natural, and it certainly doesn't add to your speech. Nor should your hands be above your shoulders, unless you're doing a cheer or discussing the wonders of aviation or outer space. The idea is to keep your second line of communication in a supporting role and place. With your hands between your shoulders and hips, arms bent at approximately a 90° angle, you are able to use them most effectively. If you are using notecards, they should be in one hand at a time. If you need to change hands, make sure you complete the pass to your other hand.

Note cards should be kept relatively low so you can glance at them as needed. It's easy but ineffective to wind up with your note cards clasped in both hands creeping up towards your face like a tiny shield.

Whether you use notecards or not, you can use your hands to reinforce and support your message. It can be helpful to hold up a few fingers as you explain that there are 3 additional points or 2 compelling ideas. Moving your hands together, palms facing each other, indicates compressing or shortening something, while slicing your hand through the air horizontally can indicate emphasis. An open, upturned palm helps invite your audience into your message, and when you sweep your arms wide with upturned hands, you're inviting everyone into the communicative moment.

While all these techniques can prove useful, what is **most** important is to deliver your speech in a way that feels natural and comfortable. So be aware of your hands and gestures, but don't become overly consumed with adhering to a specific style or tradition. While fidgeting and fussing with your hair are not desired patterns of gesturing, a speaker should not feel confined by the recommendations provided in this chapter alone. Remember, it is your authentic self that will connect the most with an audience.

The setting and size of an audience could also have a great effect on how much gesturing and body language you choose to use. In small groups and with co-workers moving and gesturing more is to be expected. At a eulogy, the situation would likely call for the speaker to be more reserved in his or her approach. Being comforting and and being aware the mood of your audience is key to affecting authentic body language.

There are many powerful and useful gestures, so think about what you're trying to share with your audience and what is most significant about any given part of your speech. Sometimes cueing what is to come is most helpful. At other points conveying emotion or building a connection is more important. As you prepare and practice your speech, mentally note where it feels natural to gesture and what those gestures do for your message. Good gestures add to your speech, reinforce your message, and help your audience understand your words and your meaning.

An analysis of TED talks shows the most popular TED speakers use the most gestures. In some cases, that's over 600 gestures in just 18 minutes (Van Edwards, 2015). But like movement, too much gesturing without purpose, especially the same gesture, can distract your audience from your message. Most of us have preferred gestures that we use more frequently than others. President Barack Obama often used an open hand with slightly pointed or pinched together fingers to signify an important idea, sometimes followed with a thump on the lectern for emphasis. You can probably think of other public figures with distinctive gestures.

When a speaker repeats a gesture over and over, the audience can start to watch the gesture rather than listening to the speaker. These repeated hand movements are called **frozen gestures**, and they should be avoided. Gestures that are more fidgety than meaningful should be avoided as well, as they tend to convey tension and uncertainty. Don't slide charms on a necklace or bracelet, touch your face, twirl or flip your hair, or jingle change in your pocket. Your hands should not be in your pockets during your speech at all. Neither the fig leaf nor drill sergeant (sometimes called "handcuff") hand positions inspire audience confidence, so avoid both. Your gestures should invite your audience into your speech, not shut them out!

Remember that gestures can have different meanings in different cultures. Be careful not to accidentally insult someone with a gesture that is normal to you, but may have a different meaning and may be considered offensive in another country.

Using Your Voice

Now that you've got a clearer idea about how your body can help you deliver your speech, it's time to consider the instrument carrying your message – your voice. **There are six qualities to your speaking voice: *pitch, tone, rate, volume, fluency*, and *articulation*,** and five of them are within your control. Each contributes to how your audience hears your message.

The *pitch* of your voice is where you have the least control. The sound of your voice moves across a range of sound, and pitches are the points where a specific sound is heard. You can't control your range, but you can pitch your voice within that range, at least briefly. *Tone* is the quality of the sound as we hear it. Singers and speakers can have great pitch, but still have bad tone. We tend to associate lower, fuller tones with authority and confidence. *Rate* is how quickly we speak, while *volume* is how loudly or softly our voices sound. *Articulation* is our ability to form sounds clearly and cleanly. Articulation is distinguished from *pronunciation,* which is making the right sounds within a given word. "Nuclear" is pronounced "noo-klee-er," not "nu-cul-your". *Fluency* is our ability to speak without hesitation or *verbal fillers/vocalized pauses* - those sounds we make when we don't have the words, such as um, uh, and like. Fluency also relates to *pauses,* those moments when we stop talking.

Your voice is an incredibly nimble and powerful instrument, and we often fail to take full advantage of how it can enhance speeches. It is worth remembering that for you to speak, you have to breathe first. At the beginning of this chapter, we discussed taking a couple of deep breaths before you start your speech. While it is beyond the scope of this book to detail all the nuances of breath control, you can certainly practice breathing deeply and controlling your breath as you speak. Take a few minutes to breathe in completely, feeling your body fill with air. Then breathe out slowly. You're aiming to breathe out twice as slowly as you breathed in, controlling the exit of the air. Do five or ten practice breaths, and see how you feel. We tend to breathe rapidly and shallowly when we feel stress – so reminding yourself to breathe deeply (and then doing it) will both help you feel calm and focused and support high vocal quality.

When you are ready to give your speech, start by taking at least one or two of those deep, full, controlled breaths. With your vocal quality adequately supported, you will be able to use your optimum pitch and a rich vocal tone. You'll sound great, so you can focus on adding ***vocal variety*** to your speech to engage your audience. Vocal variety refers to choices you make throughout your speech with all of the vocal qualities. How quickly you speak, when you pause, where you add emphasis, whether you raise or lower your pitch – each aspect contributes to effective communication with your audience. You want your voice to enhance your speech and keep your audience listening. Speaking in a ***monotone*** – staying on the same pitch, with little variation in rate or emphasis - dulls your voice and bores your audience. It's about as far from an engaging conversational tone as you can get. Word of warning: a monotone sound is much more likely to happen if you try to read your speech word for word.

Looking back at the vocal qualities, what's optimal for most speaking situations? We have discussed avoiding a monotone already. The kind of vocal variety you're aiming for will vary depending on the speaking situation and topic. It would be appropriate to speak slowly, with a lower **pitch** and restrained **tone,** if you're speaking about a serious topic. For a topic that is more light-hearted, you can speak a bit more quickly with a higher pitch and lively tone. We tend to associate authority and competence with lower pitches and deeper tones, regardless of the gender of the speaker (Klofstad, 2012).

As a general rule, you do want to slow your **rate** when you speak, regardless of the topic. Speaking just a little more slowly than you usually do allows you time to breathe and maintain high vocal quality and gives your audience time they need to hear and comprehend your message. It also helps to make sure that you **enunciate** (pronounce clearly) and that your **pronunciation** is correct. There are regional differences in articulation, such as the dropping of 'r' in New England ("pahk" for park, "heah" for here) and dropping of the closing 'g' in some parts of the South ("fixin'" for fixing, "goin'" for going). Failing to correctly pronounce a key term is seriously damaging to a speaker's credibility. Make sure you know how to pronounce all the words in your speech, and look up any you are not sure of the correct pronunciation.

Your **volume** is guided first by the size of your audience and speaking space. Make sure everyone can hear you clearly throughout the room, then consider when you could increase or decrease your volume to add emphasis or intensity. **Fluency** is often influenced by the rate of your delivery. When you increase your rate, you also increase the likelihood of stumbling over a word, not **articulating** clearly, or mispronouncing a term. It may sound contradictory, but trying to speak too quickly can also increase verbal fillers/vocalized pauses, those "uhhs" "ummms" and "likes" that creep in when your brain lags behind your lips. **Pauses** are related to fluency – they're like antidotes to a rate that's too fast, and they should be silent.

Pauses can be used for many reasons in a speech – they add emphasis, give you time to think through your next words, and give your audience time to process what you've said. If you lose your place, taking a short, silent pause of up to 15 seconds to check your notes or mentally review what you've said and what you want to say next won't hurt your effectiveness with your audience. In fact, most of them won't even notice a short pause. Planned pauses are great markers of important points. Because our culture is so saturated with noise, a pause can direct attention to an idea in a way that additional speech can't. Consider a slightly extended pause after particularly important or challenging information to let your audience fully comprehend what you've said.

What's most important about your voice when you speak is that it conveys your sincere interest in your topic and your audience. If your voice sounds like you're bored or uninterested in what you're saying, your audience will hear that and tune you out. Why should they care if you don't? On the other hand, even if your topic isn't the most dynamic, if your voice expresses interest and energy, then your audience will listen to you and what you have to say. Remember you want to talk with them, not at them.

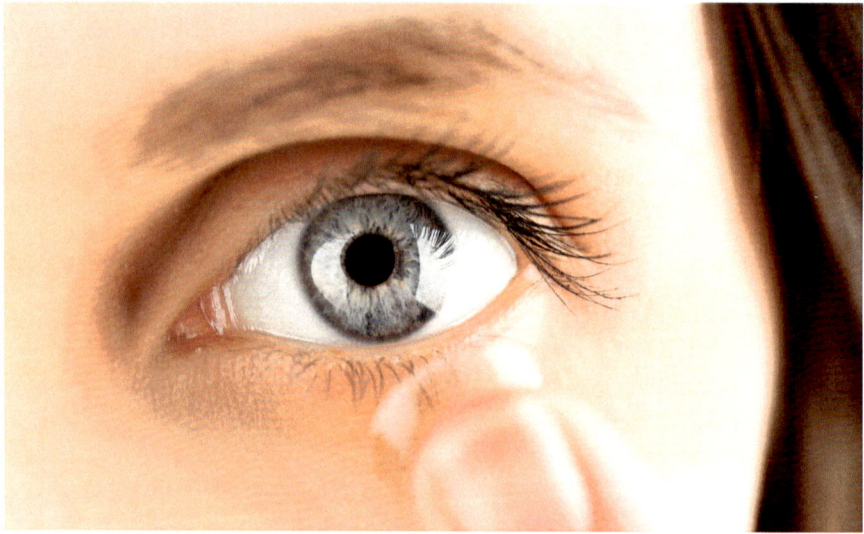

Eye Contact

Now that you know the basics of effective movement, gestures, and vocal quality, let's discuss eye contact. The eyes have been called the "windows of the soul" and for good reason; we pay a lot of attention to when, how, and what kind of looks people give us. It's important to remember that there are significant cultural differences in what constitutes appropriate and effective eye contact. Here we're primarily considering public speaking from a North American perspective. In that context, looking directly at your listeners, making an effort to include everyone in your audience, is considered the most effective and personable form of eye contact. Looking someone in the eye is associated with trustworthiness, truthfulness, and positivity; looking away, at the floor, or up in the air is associated with lying, uncertainty, and lack of knowledge. Good eye contact from a speaker means spreading eye contact across the entire audience, pausing to look directly at individuals for a second or two before moving on. Human beings are visually oriented; we want both to see and be seen by others. Making brief eye contact with members of your audience builds on that innate human orientation and our desire to be acknowledged. Your goal is to include everyone in your audience by letting them know you've seen them and appreciate their attention.

You may have been told to look just above your audience's heads but not directly in their eyes. Don't do it. That is an old theater technique called 'cheating the house,' and it only works with very large audiences who can't actually see exactly where you are looking. As a speaker, you want to connect with your audience, not avoid them. At the same time, you don't want to focus on one person or one section of your audience to the point that others feel excluded. We tend to have a dominant side, usually the same as your preferred hand for writing, and will naturally spend more time looking to that side. Just like crossing a street, look both ways and directly in front of you.

Looking at the floor, the ceiling, or at your speaking notes all disconnect you from your audience. Speakers who are trying to remember something – like their memorized speech - will often look up and away from the audience, or at the floor, searching for the missing words. Either one conveys a lack of knowledge and confidence. It's okay to glance at your notes for a second or two, but not much more than that. It's also acceptable to glance briefly at your screen or your presentation aid, but you should not look at them for long. Don't be one of those speakers who reads from their visual aids or explains them at length with their backs turned to the audience.

In the previous sections, we've discussed important aspects of the physical delivery of your presentation from your feet to your eyes. Bringing all of these pieces together into a smooth, strong, confident final presentation is what makes the difference between a competent speaker and an excellent one. In this last section, you will learn a five-step plan for practicing your speech so that you are able to bring together all of these aspects into a polished final presentation.

The Three "C's" of Language

With the content of your speech prepared, speaking notes and presentation aids in progress, and having thought about the place you're going to give your speech, you're ready to practice. Keep in mind that what you've written on the page is likely to sound different when you speak it. Practicing your speech aloud lets you hear the words, how they sound together, where you are comfortable with the material, and where you may need extra practice. An important part of practicing your speech is listening to yourself and adapting your content with strategic choices about the words you use. Because it is very likely that you will find that some of your written words sound awkward or don't flow well as you speak, this is a good time to consider the language you use and how it can work for you.

Barack Obama is a great example of a speaker who combines a rich vocabulary with word usage that reaches a wide audience. His command of words can inspire and motivate his listeners, weaving a rich tapestry where complex concepts and difficult decisions are made easy to understand.

Words often have meanings beyond their dictionary definitions. The most basic definition of a given word is its ***denotative*** meaning; the extra nuances and implications are the ***connotative*** meaning. In order to use language most effectively, you need to be aware of all the meanings of your words. As a speaker, you want to give your audience a speech with language that follows the ***Three Cs:*** it is clear, comprehensive, and compelling. Language that is ***clear*** uses words that are readily understandable by your audience, minimizes ***jargon,*** and most closely describes the ideas you're sharing. Jargon refers to terms that require additional information or knowledge for understanding. In most cases, jargon is related to a specific area of technical knowledge, but it can be a reference to an "inside joke," so you need to be part of a group to understand. Either way, overuse of jargon excludes members of your audience and should be avoided. Using clear language does not mean avoiding words with more than two syllables; it means using language that your audience readily grasps. Accuracy is the most important aspect of speaking clearly; you can explain unfamiliar terms in plain language. Putting technical terms into layman's terms is a necessity when the audience members are not experts in your topic.

Language that is ***comprehensive*** ensures that all of your audience members are included equally and respectfully. It can be easy to slip into colloquialisms that sound inclusive, but really are not. If you are speaking to a group of women or a mixed gender group, saying "You guys, let's talk about…" inherently excludes people. You can probably think of a time in your own life when this has happened. In addition, comprehensive language seeks to avoid disparaging or pejorative terms. The free exchange of ideas and information depends on civility, and it is possible to be accurate in your descriptions without being unnecessarily negative or judgmental. Using language that is comprehensive and unbiased maximizes your effectiveness as a speaker. Addressing all the members of your audience appropriately and avoiding pejorative comments builds your credibility as a knowledgeable and reasonable speaker.

Finally, language that is ***compelling*** adds a level of dynamism to your speech; it makes you more powerful as a speaker and your speech more interesting for your listener. Compelling language is vivid, distinctive, and can elicit an emotional as well as intellectual response from your audience. Interestingly, precise language is often more compelling than a more general term. Think about the difference between saying "The sky is covered with grey clouds" and "The sky is covered with steely thunderheads." When you have the opportunity to use vivid language, especially for key points in your speech, do so. Even a little drama will add energy and interest to your presentation. As a bonus, not only will your audience appreciate it during your speech, but it will also make your speech more memorable in the long term.

Paying attention to the language you use and the 'Three Cs' as you practice will pay off during your presentation. ***So how do you practice?***

Practicing Your Speech – Five Steps

The five steps all work together to prepare you to speak fluently, confidently, and with positive energy. Each step in the process builds in a key element of effective presentation, so that when you've completed the five steps, you are truly ready to deliver your speech. It's strongly encouraged that you do each of the steps at least once. As you follow the five steps, you may decide that repeating a step helps you feel more comfortable and confident.

Step 1. Sit in a comfortable place, preferably without distractions, with your speech outline or preliminary speaking notes. Go over the structure of the speech aloud. You are NOT giving your speech word for word in this step – you are checking and practicing the organization of the speech to see if it works and if you are comfortable with it. For example, while sitting with your outline, you would say aloud:

"I will start with the joke about the chicken. Then I will state how this topic is relevant to my audience. I will make my thesis statement and give my three preview points, X, Y, and Z. I will use another chicken story as a transition to my first main point, X. In my first point, my subpoints are P and Q. I have evidence from source M and source N to support P. More evidence from source M also supports Q, and I have an additional source L for that subpoint."

Go through your entire speech structure in this way. As you are doing so, make notes on your outline for where it flows well, or where you feel a bit hesitant or awkward. Note if you are missing any evidence, or if the evidence doesn't sufficiently support your points. When you are done, consider if any changes need to be made, new evidence included, points moved, or where you need to be more familiar with your material. When you have those changes in place, move on to Step 2.

Step 2. Stand with your revised notes, and again, go through the structure of your speech aloud. The purpose of step 1 was to identify the places where content was missing or changes needed to be made in your overall organization. In this step, you will review the changes in more of a delivery style. For step 2, try to go through the entire speech with minimal stops. If you notice a change that needs to be made, note it and keep going. You are using this step to check any changes from step 1, and also to build your familiarity with the 'feel' of the speech as it is delivered. By the time you are done with step 2, your speech should be very close to its final form, and you're ready to give it with very few full stops at all.

Step 3. For this step, you need a draft of your speaking notes and room to move. You should be very familiar with the structure and content of your speech by now. In Step 3, deliver the entire speech - not the structure – in plain language and with movement if you plan to use during your speech. Do your best to get through without stopping, but if you need to, stop and check the structure or your familiarity with the content. Step 3 is your rough rehearsal – you just want to get through the speech from beginning to end so you know you can. If you hesitate, if you stumble over words, if you have to stop and check your notes, that's fine. Just keep going from where you needed to check, and repeat Step 3 until you can get through the entire speech with no more than 5 stops. Then you're ready for Step 4.

Step 4. "Mirror, mirror, on the wall" - you will want to be able to see yourself for Step 4. In Step 3 you became familiar with the physical part of delivering your speech with minimal stops. In Step 4, you will deliver your entire speech from beginning to end with NO stops, watching and timing yourself. You need a mirror and whatever limited speaking notes you are allowed for your presentation. If you hesitate, stumble, have "Umms" and "uhhs", or forget what you meant to say, that's okay - but you have to keep going until you reach the end **WITHOUT** checking anything other than the notes you will use. The mirror helps you to see what your gestures look like, where you tend to make eye contact, when it seems appropriate to move, and gives you a little sense of an audience.

Step 4 is also where you check the language of your speech – are there places where you tend to say "Umm", or can you change a word to make it more vivid and compelling? Keep in mind you are your own worst critic, so be kind. Repeat Step 4 until you can deliver the entire speech with only your presentation notes within your allotted time.

Step 5. This is your dress rehearsal step. In Step 5, you will deliver your speech in as close to your final form as you can, to an actual audience, even if that is only one person. Before you start, tell the audience that you would like two kinds of feedback from them - one thing that you did well in the speech, and one thing you could change to make it better. Giving these directions will help them give you useful, constructive feedback. Then give your speech as if it were your presentation day, or as close as you can get. Make sure you time yourself if you have a time limit.

When you are done, ask the audience for their feedback and consider their response to the speech. Review the entire speech from beginning to end, including where you moved, what gestures you made, and your vocal delivery. By the time you get to step 5, you are polishing your presentation – you should be so familiar with the content and organization that it's nearly automatic. In step 5, you can work on details of your physical delivery and gauge your effectiveness for your audience.

Now you're ready to present – and hopefully your speech is at least a day or so away. As with any performance, taking care of your physical self is important to doing your best. So get a good night's sleep, drink plenty of water (in most cases, it's perfectly okay to bring a water bottle to your presentation), and take time to do your power pose and breathing before you present. If you have followed the five steps and the other guides for effective presentations in this text, you're thoroughly prepared. Bring your best self to the moment and share your ideas with confidence and pride.

Conclusion

In this chapter, we have discussed how to prepare for and practice delivery of your speech. By considering physical delivery, vocal quality, eye contact, and language, you now know exactly *how* your speech can support *what* you have to say. Practicing your delivery will improve both the how and the what of your speech. It will help your audience understand your message, and it will increase your confidence as a speaker. The Five Steps will guide you through the process of tying all of your preparation together and bringing your best speaking self to your presentation. You're ready to speak!

References

Anderson, C. (2016). TED Talks: The Official TED Guide to Public Speaking. New York: Houghton Mifflin.

Cuddy, A. (2017). Presence: bringing your boldest self to your biggest challenges. New York: Little Brown.

Klofstad, C. A. (2012). Sounds like a winner: voice pitch influences perception of leadership capacity in both men and women. Proceedings of the royal society of biological sciences, 2698-2704.

Van Edwards, V. (2015). Secrets of successful TED Talks. Retrieved from Science of People: http://www.scienceofpeople.com/2015/03/secrets-of-a-successful-ted-talk/

CHRIS ANDERSON
TED Talk—Secret to Public Speaking

https://www.ted.com/talks/chris_anderson_teds_secret_to_great_public_speaking

Wherever we go in this world, our eyes are met with signs and symbols

Wherever we go in this world, our eyes are met with signs and symbols, visual aids that we connect with on a day-to-day basis.

Street signs inform us as to where we are going. Billboards try and persuade us to buy an advertised product. Simple symbols let us know where the bathroom is and which receptacle is for trash or recycling. In the world of public speaking, visual aids can be an important part of a presentation, helping to convey your message in a way that can't be achieved through words alone.

Visual aids, when properly used, can be a wonderful addition to any speech. However, it is important to make sure your message is clear before employing them. Be selective about what information you decide to make visible to the audience. Make sure you have a variety of visual aids to illustrate various points in your presentation. Also, be sure you are able to explain and display each visual aid with maximum effect. Also, when making your presentation, focus your attention on the audience and not the visual aid.

We are all aware of technology's role in the modern world. In presentations and public speaking technology has its place. However, what is most important is that the speaker knows his or her subject well. While technology can help enhance a speech it can also be unreliable, potentially distracting and can even become a crutch, causing the speaker to connect less with the audience.

Visual Aids for Effective Communication

Dr. Tracey Quigley Holden
University of Delaware

There are two phases when you use visual aids with presentations – development and application. In this chapter, the Five-By-Five approach will help you through both phases. When you are developing visual aids, there are five rules that will guide you as you create effective visual aids. When you have developed your visual aids and are ready to use them, there are five application principles to guide you so that your message and aids work together to make your presentations as effective as possible. Before we discuss developing and applying visual aids, let's take a look at some common types.

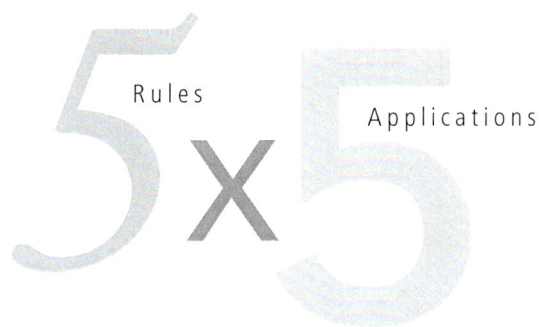

Graphs

Advantages: Graphs can render what are complicated figures into visual images that convey statistical information and numerical data in ways an audience can easily understand. The *line graph* has an x and y axis and a line correlating with statistical information. Such a graph can illustrate the change in sea levels or the decrease in land line telephone usage over time.

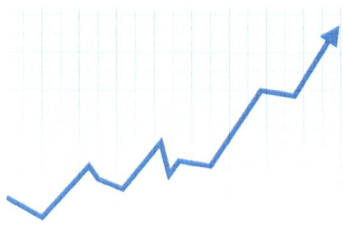

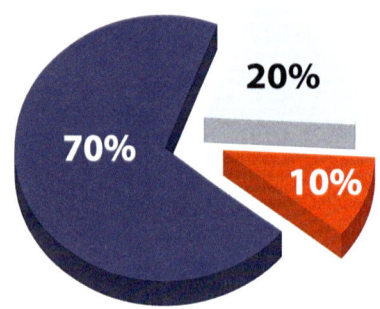

Pie graphs are good for representing different slices or segments of information related to a specific topic.

Bar graphs are well suited for comparing and contrasting two or more things.

Potential Challenges: Make sure the information conveyed on the graphs is easy to read and easy to explain. On pie graphs, make sure the number of segments is not too large, ideally between two and five per graph.

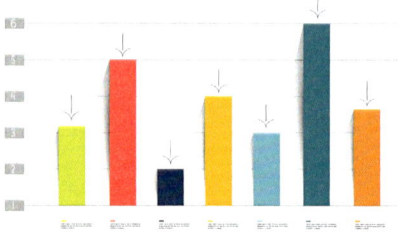

Charts

Advantages: Like a graph, you can fit a lot of data on a chart. A chart would be a great way to list the largest cities in the world by population or to list the league leaders in a statistical category of a professional sport.

Potential Challenges: Charts are not as visually stimulating as graphs or photographs and can leave less of an impression on the viewer. Also, in creating a chart a presenter can fall prey to including too much information and thus confuse the audience.

Drawings and Photographs

Advantages: What better way to add to a speech about the architect Frank Lloyd Wright then to include sample drawings of his work? Drawings could also come in handy when presenting on archaeological findings from a Mayan temple or Roman tomb. Likewise, a photograph can be useful in conveying the visual power of something like the Golden Gate Bridge when a model or the object itself is unavailable.

Potential Challenges: It is crucial that the drawings and photographs are large enough for the audience to see. PowerPoint is an excellent way to show these visual aids during your presentation. If there is text on these images make sure it is legible for the audience.

Presentation Technology (PowerPoint)

Advantages: A program such as PowerPoint can integrate a variety of visual aids into one clean and colorful mode of presentation.

Potential Challenges: Problems can occur when speakers rely too heavily on the program and not the presentation.

Video

Advantages: They say a picture is worth a thousand words. The same can be said of a video. Suppose you were making a speech about hurricanes. Video footage of such storms could really bring the point home about their power and effect on buildings and infrastructure, not to mention, the heavy human cost.

Potential Challenges: If the video is too long, poorly edited or set up improperly it can take away from the speech itself. Poor resolution and other technical issues can be detrimental. Also, be sure that your video is not too long. It certainly shouldn't be longer than a minute.

Objects

Advantages: Using objects related to your speech can be a great way to shed light on your message and make a powerful impression. A historical speech on mining might call for you to bring in an old pick axe. A speech on how kites are made might warrant bringing in a kite.

Potential Challenges: Sometimes the physical characteristics of an object can make it difficult to use in a presentation. If your object is in any way dangerous it shouldn't be part of your speech. For your presentation on mining it wouldn't be a good idea to bring in a case of dynamite. Similarly, the physical properties of certain objects make using them in a presentation prohibitive. Make sure the object is not too large to transport and not too small so the audience will have to strain to see it.

Developing S.M.A.R.T. Visual Aids – Five Rules

Before you begin to develop visual aids for your presentation, make sure your central message, main points, and supporting evidence have been thoroughly prepared. In our visually oriented society, too many speakers make the mistake of starting with the preparation of their visual aids, rather than their message. A good visual can inspire a good message, or even be the focus of your content, but the message must come first. In order for your presentation to be effective, your message must be at the center of your presentation. Imagine if your presentation was to introduce a new car. You could have dozens of pictures of the vehicle, engineering graphics of its mechanics, video of the car's performance, and even a model of the car itself – but without a clear and compelling message explaining how the car works and what is new and terrific about its performance and design, the presentation would fall flat. Your visual aids need to be tailored to the information you want your audience to understand. Visual aids can help your audience more readily comprehend complex ideas and increase their interest in your topic, but even the best visual aids cannot deliver your message as effectively as you can. The acronym **SMART** describes how to prepare visual aids to enhance your presentation. If you choose to use visual aids, you can use these ideas to develop **SMART** visuals that help your audience and you feel **SMART** about your topic and the effectiveness of your presentation.

Strong, supportive visual aids are built on five key qualities. Each quality is linked to how humans process information and how speakers are most effective in delivering information. The five rules for creating **SMART** visual aids are discussed below.

The first rule - *Simple visual aids are easy for your audience to understand. Any visual aid you use should be designed so that your audience can see and understand the key concept within **10 to 15 seconds**.* If you are using a chart or graph, the audience may need a little more time to read all the labels, but the concept being presented should not require more than a quick glance at the graph or chart title. Keep in mind you want your audience to be paying attention to you and your message, and not spending their time trying to understand a complicated visual aid. One basic design concept that helps keep visual aids simple is to think in terms of statement + image. Each visual aid should make (or have as a label) a single statement contributing to your message, and have an accompanying image to demonstrate that statement. Other information may be in the visual aid, but the central idea and image should be immediately apparent to your audience.

S
M
A
R
T

The second rule – *Memorable visual aids are striking to the eye;* they present information using strong visual cues and elements to draw the viewer in and highlight important aspects of the information being presented. An easy way to add memorability to your visual aids is to **limit the amount of text and add color.** Most likely you have been to a presentation where the speaker showed slides with lots of text, and perhaps even read from the slide. This all but defeats the purpose of a visual aid. Showing information you can give verbally is a waste of time and can create boredom and restlessness in your

audience. This is especially true of written text! Instead, use a eye-catching visual image with minimal or no text. Color should be used as an accent – too much and your audience gets distracted or overwhelmed. Think about how a good designer will use a neutral color as a base, then add contrasting colors in accessories. The smaller "pops" of color attract attention to those pieces, while at the same time adding depth to the base. Good design, color, and strong images should showcase the features of your visual aid that give your audience insight into your message.

S
M
A
R
T

The third rule – *Add information to your presentation.* Good visual aids do more than just present a pretty picture – they provide information to your audience in a way that words are not as efficient in doing. The old saying "a picture is worth a thousand words" is true in many situations, but not for all pictures. If you are trying to explain a complex process or object, a picture or model can convey that information efficiently and effectively. Never show an image or use a visual just for the sake of having a visual. For example, if you are giving a presentation about the harmful effects of poaching on African elephants, it is probably safe to assume your audience knows what an elephant looks like. Showing your audience a picture of an elephant adds no information to your presentation. Creating a graph using elephant icons to show the numbers killed by poachers each year would add information and do so in a visually memorable and effective way.

Along with making sure your images add to your presentation, make sure that you are using images appropriately. Pictures, images, graphs, charts, and other visuals are subject to the rules of plagiarism just as text or any other form of evidence. Many pictures and visuals available on the internet are copyrighted, and you cannot use them without permission and often paying a fee for their use. Sometimes images will have a watermark or copyright imprint on the image to indicate their restricted use. Unless you have created the image yourself, always provide a reference or URL directly on the visual aid to credit your source correctly. However, copying and pasting an entire URL is not desirable.

The fourth rule – *Readable text and clearly visible images are a must for any visual aid you use.* The classic elementary school poster with the words bunching up to one side or trailing around the edge should be a warning to you. Generally, your font size for any text should be at least 24 point; the person in the back row of your audience should not have to squint to read your text. Along with being large enough for easy reading, keep the amount of text to a minimum. Too much text on a screen is both distracting and boring to your audience, and tends to increase your likelihood of reading it! A good rule to follow is the *5 x 5 rule* - have no more than 5 lines of text on a slide, and no more than 5 words per line. That means you are limited to 25 words per slide. The 5 x 5 rule usually allows you to increase your font size as well, which increases your readability.

Just as your text should be easily readable, any images used should be clear and sharp. Keep in mind that when you project images on to a screen, they quickly become grainy and faded as they expand. Finally, limit the number of images you use. One image and a caption are far more powerful than a collage of small images and small text, or even a group of images. Five images on a screen should be your limit, and those should be carefully placed and sized. Too many images at once quickly become visual clutter, rather than contributing to your audience's understanding.

The fifth rule–*Be Technologically Independent.* While the use of technology for visual aids has become almost ubiquitous, your presentation should not depend on technology. In fact, many presentations don't need technology, so don't force the use of it. A video isn't always necessary to explain something that you should be explaining yourself, for example. Be careful not to use technology as a crutch. You must also be prepared for technology to fail, and need to give your presentation without any visual aids at all.

Technology fails. Projectors don't connect, links don't work, videos don't load, programs crash, and systems are incompatible or simply not available. No matter what happens, your message and content should be so well prepared that you can give your presentation effectively completely independent of technology. If you have it in mind that you can present with or without visual aids, you won't be flustered if something goes wrong. The most important aspect of any presentation is delivering the message!

Preparing your visual aids according to the **SMART** guidelines will help you be ready to present with great visuals. But as mentioned above, you need to use those great visual aids in the most effective way possible. The next section of this chapter will discuss five principles for using visual aids to enhance your presentation and support your message.

Things to Keep in Mind When Using Visual Aids

Once you have created your visual aid using the Five Rules, you can make sure you use it most effectively by following the Five Principles. Each principle stands alone, but also works with the other four principles and the Five Rules to help you prepare and deliver your final presentation with poised confidence and maximum effect.

Have a Clear Message

Make sure your message is clear before you consider adding visuals. That means your research, key points and evidence, organization, and overall presentation form are all complete. At that point, you are ready to consider what, if any, visual aids would be most useful to your audience. Visual aids are just that – aids to support and facilitate our messages, not replacements of our messages. If we are not clear about our content, about what we want to communicate, visual aids can only clutter the message. If our message is well prepared and clear, good visual aids can help our audiences more readily understand and grasp the meaning and significance of our messages.

Be Selective

Be selective about visual aids. For most presentations, a good guideline to follow is to have no more than one or two visual aids per main point. If you have three main points, that means no more than six visual aids total (screen shifts or views would be the Prezi equivalent). There is some flexibility with this principle. You may have a topic that is highly visually oriented, or need a couple more visual images to help your audience understand a particularly complex or technical concept.

But starting with just one or two visual aids, slides, or views per main point will still help you select only the best and most helpful visual support for your message and your audience.

Use Variety

There are almost unlimited possibilities for adding visual interest to your presentation. Although current trends are toward electronic visual aids, there are many other options. An actual example or model of an item you are discussing can be very effective. If you were talking about 3D printing, bringing in a 3D printer, samples of what can be printed, or even demonstrating how to use the printer would be a highly effective visual aid. If you want audience interaction within your presentation, using a blackboard, whiteboard, or even large flip charts on easels to illustrate ideas or record audience responses might be a great visual representation of your core message concepts. Simon Sinek, the ethnographer and leadership expert, gave a terrific TED talk in 2009 on "How great leaders inspire action" using a flip chart and a marker to illustrate a few essential ideas. That TED talk now has over 27 million views and is one of the top rated TED talks (Sinek, 2009). If you use the SMART design principles discussed earlier, even a basic poster can be an effective, low-cost and low tech visual aid. Just make sure to keep the appearance professional.

If you choose to use some form of technology, you still need to apply the principle of **variety.** Too many slides in the same format, even with a good basic design, quickly become repetitive and less effective. Slides with bullet points, heavy text, or too many images are also ineffective. Not only should you limit your use of text and number of images on any single slide, you should also make sure you mix up slides with text and slides with images, creating variety within your overall presentation. For example, you might show a slide with a strong image and a short caption, then another slide with an image, then a slide with a graph or bar chart and some detailed labeling or a single number with a caption. Varying the content of your slides helps keep your audience engaged and attentive. Using a short video can be a very effective visual aid and can add sound to your presentation. Video clips need to be carefully considered – they should be short, on point, and readily available. Downloading the video and embedding it in the presentation you plan to use, along with the link for the video (just in case) is your best option; depending on access to YouTube or some other site is always a risk.

Explain and Display

If at all possible, you should only show your visual aid when you are talking about it or explaining it to your audience. If you have a model or other physical aid, covering it or turning it around is one solution. If you are using an electronic presentation, it is a good practice to build in blank slides or neutral background views in between those with information or images. The blank slides allow your audience to return their full attention to you and your message. When you do show a visual, it is important to ***explain*** how the visual aid connects to your message and any detailed content you want your audience to understand. You should never show something to your audience without commentary, no matter how clear it may seem to you. If you are showing a video, be sure to set up what they are about to watch so your audience understands what they are looking for in the clip. When using graphs or charts, be sure to state the overall purpose of the chart, and then explain the specific details or concepts that are being illustrated. If you have a particularly complex or detailed image, you do not have to explain every label or facet of the visual. Your role as the presenter is to verbally highlight the information related to your message, not to explain every detail of the visual aid. If there is something particularly obvious and striking about a visual, but unrelated to your message, acknowledge that aspect and redirect your audience to the relevant parts of the visual aid.

Don't Talk to Your Visual Aid

You are there to present your message to your audience. Talking to your screen or your poster or your model defeats the purpose of your presentation, and actually disconnects you from your audience. A quick glance at your visual aid as you initially present it, or a guiding look as you actually point to something specific on the visual aid are acceptable, but you should make every effort to keep your eyes and your focus on your audience members. It should be obvious, but reading from your visual aid is an absolute taboo. If you need to read an extended quote or detailed statistic, put them on your notes rather than read from the screen or visual, and only if you believe the information is so powerful it has to be included. Reading to your audience implies that they are unable to do so for themselves – avoid it at all costs.

Conclusion

In this chapter, you have learned **Five Rules** for developing **S.M.A.R.T.** visual aids and some tips for using visual aids effectively. If you keep in mind that your message should always be the first priority of your presentation, the process of preparing and using visual aids will not only be easier, but your visual aids will contribute more to your presentation and your audience's understanding. Visual aids can support and enhance your message and your content, but they cannot replace either your message or you as the presenter.

References

Sinek, S. (2009) How great leaders inspire action.
Retrieved from www.ted.com/talks/simon_sinek_how_great_leaders_inspire_action

Simon Sinek
How Great Leaders Inspire Action

There is a big difference between hearing someone speak and listening to them.

The mere biological process of hearing but not taking in the full meaning of a speaker's statements is called **pseudo-listening**. The act of processing a sound, interpreting meaning and remembering what's said is known as **active listening**. Active listening is considered the most effective mode of listening.

The four stages of listening are **sensing, understanding, evaluating, and responding**. **Physiological barriers** such as brain lag, **psychological barriers** such as personal concerns in the listener or delivery of the speech for the speaker, and **environmental factors** such as external noise or uncomfortable seating can all play a role in affecting these stages in the listening process.

Different people listen differently. **People-oriented** listeners prioritize the speaker over the message. **Action-oriented** listeners focus on the tasks or jobs that need to get done. **Time-oriented** listeners are strict about how much time they can dedicate to a speech or presentation and often become impatient when the speaker goes over the time limit they allotted for a presentation. **Content-oriented** listeners focus on the message itself and enjoy diving in to the details of a given speech or presentation. Be aware that an audience may be filled with many types of listeners, some of which listen in more than one of the above styles.

How can you improve your listening skills? You can make an effort to **pay attention** and **resist distractions** such as external noise. You can incorporate verbal and nonverbal feedback into your listening. You can try to **empathize** with the speaker's message and if possible restate that message in your own words. You can also improve your **note-taking** skills by recording the speaker's message in a way that makes sense to you.

Listening and Evaluating

Dr. Sandra L. French
Radford University

Most people think of themselves as good listeners, but in this multi-tasking, technology-laden modern world, many of us are simply good actors. We engage in *pseudo-listening:* the fine art of maintaining eye contact, nodding with interest, all while taking a "mind vacation" and thinking about something or someone else!

Becoming a more adept listener can benefit us in the classroom, in the public speaking environment, in our personal relationships, and in our careers. Studies repeatedly list listening in the top skills employers are looking for. It's important to work on our listening skills because it is the communication activity we perform the most. According to research cited by the International Listening Association (n.d.), approximately half of all human activities involve listening and 45% of the time we spend communicating is spent listening. Listening is also important to you as a speaker. Most of your speech topic ideas will probably come from things you have heard – on the television, in the news, or from discussions with friends and family. As you can see, improving our listening skills has benefits in many facets of life.

So now that we know it's pretty important, what exactly is listening? Listening is not to be confused with *hearing,* which is biological process of receiving and interpreting sound. **Listening**, however, is a conscious choice that requires concentration and cognitive processing.

Types of Listening

There are four principle types of listening: appreciative, empathic, comprehensive and critical.

Appreciative Listening-This type of listening is done for fun. Examples would be listening to a favorite album or listening to an entertaining program on the radio.

Empathetic Listening-This type of listening occurs when the goal of the exchange is to provide emotional support to the speaker. An example would be when you listen to a friend that is going through a break-up and in need of a sympathetic ear.

Comprehensive Listening-This type of listening occurs when the purpose is to achieve an understanding of the speaker's message. An example would be listening to someone explain how to tie a bowtie or listening to a flight attendant describe how to use your oxygen mask.

Critical Listening-This type of listening occurs when the purpose is to evaluate a message in order to determine if it is valid or not. An example of this could be when a juror listens to a testimony in a courtroom and must determine of the person giving the testimony is telling the truth.

We have already discussed one popular type of listening: **pseudo-listening.** As we do more multi-tasking, we find ourselves utilizing this non-listening type of listening more often. The type of listening that yields the most effective communication is **active listening,** a cognitive process that involves processing sound waves, interpreting meaning, and storing interpretations in one's memory (Zarefsky, 2016). To better implement active listening, it is helpful to understand the process, or stages, in which listening occurs. Within each type of listening (appreciative, empathetic, comprehensive, and critical) we can be either pseudo-listeners or active listeners.

The Stages of Listening

Listening occurs in four stages: sensing, understanding, evaluating, and responding. ***Sensing,*** the first stage, happens when sound waves travel to the ear and are received by the brain. ***Understanding,*** the second stage, is when a listener interprets the sounds in order to determine their meaning. Crucial to successful understanding is the ability of the listener to determine the context as well as the meanings of the words they have heard. The third stage, *evaluation,* occurs when a listener assesses the information and figures out how to respond to the message. During this stage of assessing the message and figuring out how to respond, the listener forms an opinion of what they have heard. Additionally, the evaluation stage may best be considered the "judging" stage, or the point at which listeners consider how what they have heard might impact their own values and beliefs. Because each listener brings their own perspective and life experiences to each communication interaction, multiple listeners may evaluate the same message very differently. The fourth and final stage provides evidence that we are listening *(a response)* and confirms for others that a message has been received. It is important to note here that refusing, or failing to respond to a message is also a form of response. Unfortunately, at any one of these stages, we can, and often do, encounter barriers, which short circuit our successful navigation through the stages of listening. Let's take a look at some barriers to listening.

Barriers to Effective Listening

In order to accurately assess barriers to effective listening, we must first distinguish between *hearing* and *listening.* Hearing is a physiological process of transmitting sound waves to the brain, while listening is an active process of mental engagement and reflection. If poor listening is the result of poor hearing, then medical intervention (hearing aids, cochlear implants, etc.) may be necessary. In this chapter we will discuss three main barriers to effective listening: **physiological barriers, psychological barriers, and environmental barriers.**

Physiological barriers. Our biggest barrier to effective listening is our own brains! Studies show that people tend to forget what they hear at a rapid pace and have trouble recounting information as little as 15 minutes after hearing it. What accounts for this poor performance? **Brain Lag.**

The brain is amazing. Made up of over 13 billion cells, this highly complex organ is capable of processing around **600-700** words per minute, but the average rate of speech is only **125-175** words per minute. This means that by nature, our minds are predisposed to wander when people are speaking!

In addition to our brain power working against us, we also can encounter other physiological challenges. Other physiological challenges include not feeling well, being too tired, or too hungry to pay attention. Perhaps you have three classes back-to-back, or the dreaded three-hour night class. Your stomach is telling you it's time for a break, but you still have 90 minutes to go! Such challenges can be overcome by packing snacks, ensuring you eat before class or an important meeting, and trying to get enough sleep.

Psychological barriers. Psychological barriers, or mental obstacles to listening, always come from the listener. By training ourselves in the art of listening, we can reduce these barriers. There are two types of psychological barriers, *speaker-related*, and *listener-related*. These barriers are sometimes referred to as "internal noise" because they take place largely inside the listener's mind.

Speaker-related. Speaker-related psychological barriers are those aspects of a speaker or message that we find personally disruptive. In general, these barriers all stem from *focusing too hard on the speaker.* While we could list endless annoyances that people find disruptive we will focus here on four of the most common: ***delivery, triggers, message confusion, and lack of credibility.*** For example, it is impossible for a speaker's delivery to please everyone, but certain ***delivery*** characteristics can become a big stumbling block for listeners. If a speaker's voice is too loud or too low-volume, it can hinder the audience's ability to listen to the speaker's message. Additionally, listeners have preferences for the rate of speech – a speaker talking ***too fast, or too slow,*** can cause irritation and an excuse for a listener to "drift away" during a speech. Speakers can also unknowingly use a word or phrase that ***triggers*** a mind to wander. For example, let's say a speaker is talking about holiday traditions. The speaker shares a Christmas tradition of having hot chocolate as a family every Christmas morning. As a listener, you begin to think about your own family's holiday traditions. Now you are thinking about the family piling in the car to go see holiday decorations in your neighborhood, and the big blue house on the corner with the Snoopy inflatables in the front yard….and suddenly you pull yourself back to realize you have missed an entire main point in the speech! Third, when a speaker fails to properly organize their message, ***confusion,*** or an inability to follow what the speaker is saying, can cause listeners to stop listening. Finally, while listeners can be distracted by a speaker's delivery, or a portion of the message that causes the mind to wander, listeners may feel justified in "tuning out" if they do not find the speaker to be **credible.** This is another reason it is so important to carefully research and rehearse as a speaker. A listener's willingness to listen is often tied to whether or not he or she perceives a speaker to be using unreliable or biased sources. If the information, or the speaker themselves, is deemed "not credible" the listener has no compelling reason to listen.

Listener-related. Sometimes psychological barriers come from the listener and not the speaker. Again, the list of possible barriers is long, but we will focus on two of them: **personal concerns**, and **premature evaluation. Personal concerns** would include having a disagreement with your roommate or coworker right before class or an important meeting, which leaves you replaying the incident in your mind, rather than focusing on the speaker. Personal concerns can also be work or class-related. Are you the next speaker in class? Have a big test in your next class? These personal concerns can hinder your ability to focus on the message at hand.

The second main type of listener-related psychological barrier is **premature evaluation**. In our modern world, life moves at a very fast pace. Sometimes we get accustomed to making quick decisions and snap judgments. Listeners can fall into the trap of making a premature evaluation of a speaker's message as a result of habit. **Jumping to conclusions** about a speaker's message short-circuits the listening process. Judgments are not easily changed and it is important to listen to a message in its entirety before forming an opinion.

There is little a speaker can do to overcome these types of barriers. Rather, as listeners, we must be aware of the distractions we bring to a speaking environment and make every effort to be attentive listeners. We will discuss strategies for improving our listening later in the chapter.

Environmental barriers. These distractions, sometimes referred to as "external noise," cause us to focus on our surroundings, rather than the message. Environmental barriers include noise, unusual smells, uncomfortable seating, a room with bad ventilation that seems too hot or too cold. While experiencing these types of distractions, a listener must work diligently to keep attention focused on the speaker.

Upon review, it might seem that there are so many distractions it is impossible to give anyone your full attention. By becoming aware of the barriers and practicing effective listening techniques, we can better participate in the communication interaction. Remember that effective communication is the responsibility of both the speaker and listener.

Listening Styles

While recognizing that all listeners will encounter barriers, it is also helpful to recognize that we all have listening styles, or preferences. Listening research conducted by Barker (1971) and further developed by Watson and Barker (1995), suggests that listeners tend to fall into these four categories: people-oriented, action-oriented, time-oriented, and content-oriented. Listening preferences can change over time, and listeners can have dual or even triple listening preferences. It is helpful to identify not only your own listening preferences, but to remember that your audience members will have different listening preferences as well. This can help you as you craft a speech to include information in ways that appeal to a wide variety of listeners. Let's look at each of the listening preferences.

People-oriented. As the name suggests, people-oriented listeners prioritize the person, or speaker. These listeners demonstrate a high concern for the feelings of others. In terms of receiving information, they tend to focus on the speaker more than the message. One benefit of having people-oriented listeners in your audience is that they often provide clear verbal/nonverbal feedback to the speaker. One drawback to listeners with a people-oriented preference is that they can sometimes lose themselves in thinking about the speaker rather than focusing on the message. Further, a people-oriented listener who has strong positive feelings for a speaker may overlook inconsistencies in the speaker's message.

Action-oriented. Action-oriented listeners focus on the tasks, or actions, that need to be done. They tend to ask the "so what?" question of speakers, seeking what actions will be completed and by whom. Action-oriented listeners like messages with structure that stay focused and get quickly to the point. The action-oriented listener has the ability to quickly identify how to translate new information into action, but can also grow impatient with a speaker that starts with the "big picture."

Time-oriented. These listeners expect people to respect their time. As a speaker, if you have 10-12 minutes to give a presentation, don't try to stretch it to 15 with a time-oriented listener in the audience! According to Ripley and Watson (2014), only 7 percent of people identify time-orientation as their sole listening preference. These listeners are impatient with "wordy" speakers and often let speakers know with the verbal/nonverbal feedback if they feel their time is being wasted.

Content-oriented. The content-oriented listener focuses on the message itself. Is it accurate? Does it make sense? These types of listeners enjoy dissecting complex information and can look at an issue from many points of view. While their primary focus is usually on the message itself, content-oriented listeners also assess the credibility of the speaker. It is important for these listeners to hear the oral citations of sources and for the speaker to establish any unique expertise they may have on the topic at hand. One drawback of presenting to content-oriented listeners is that they can appear accusatory during a question and answer session if the message seemed unclear or if they judge sources to be unworthy. Keep in mind that your audience will be filled with these different types of listeners, many of whom will use more than one listening orientation.

Effective Listening – A Plan for Improvement

- *Often we are in the habit of listening passively – to music, television, or perhaps even to a parent, teacher, or other authority figure.* We listen, or pseudo-listen, rather than really engaging with the speaker. As we have already discussed, ***active listening*** is a learned skill requiring you to focus on the speaker, make sense of the information they share, and when possible, provide feedback to ensure understanding (Shwom & Synder, 2013). The following is a list of behaviors to practice in order to improve your active listening ability:
  - Making an effort to pay attention and resist distractions
  - Incorporating verbal/nonverbal feedback into your listening
  - Empathizing with what a speaker is saying
  - Restating what the speaker said in your own words to check for misunderstandings
  - Improving your note-taking skills

In a study conducted by Canpolat, Kuzu, Yıldırım, and Canpolat (2015), students who use these active listening techniques had higher academic success than students who did not. Many students reported using the techniques listed above including the following:

- **Paying attention**-My mind is disorganized sometimes, so I can't listen to my instructor effectively. However, when I'm paying attention to the class, I listen to the subject carefully (Student 2);
- **Incorporating verbal/nonverbal feedback**-I direct all of my attention to the person talking by looking into the instructor's eyes, by nodding, by using body language, and by supporting points with my eyes and facial expressions (Student 6); and
- **Note-taking**-I try to take notes of topics in ways that make sense to me, not everything that speakers talk about (Student 5).

There are many activities that can help improve your active listening. Let's try one!

Active Listening Activities

Activity 1: In order to assess your current active listening abilities, try this activity. Get with a partner and be sure you are seated facing one another. Move your desks if necessary. Each of you will take a turn being the speaker and the listener. Have someone time you; each person will spend two minutes talking about a favorite childhood memory. It does not matter particularly what the memory is, as long as it is appropriate to share in the classroom environment. While the speaker is speaking, the listener should practice these active listening techniques – focusing on the speaker, and giving nonverbal feedback. When the two minutes have passed, the listener should try and paraphrase back to the speaker what they heard. **Paraphrasing** is expressing what you think you heard in your own words to check for understanding. You can begin paraphrasing with a statement similar to this: *"So what I'm hearing you say is…."* The speaker should guide the listener and offer corrective feedback if necessary. Now reverse the roles. How did you do?

Because active listening often involves restating what a speaker has said in your own words, active listening is particular useful in interpersonal conversations, group meetings, or speeches where there is an active question and answer period. However, if you are in a situation where your primary role is listener only, there are still many techniques you can employ to improve the quality of your listening.

Activity 2: This time, let's focus on note-taking skills. Although there are many note-taking strategies, creating a **key word outline** is one of the most effective for actively listening to lectures and speeches. Put yourself in the place of an audience member and read the following speech excerpt. Do your best to create a key word outline based on the following informative speech:

Stress, we all seem to get it but often we simply "suck it up" not knowing how to better cope with it. Before I inform you how to handle stress, I want share with you what stress is, and the six stages of stress. After we have gained knowledge we can then gain control.

Webster's dictionary defines stress as a state of mental tension and worry or anxiety. Stress can have both physical and mental consequences. Marie Mosely, a business psychologist and top writer for *Business Communicator* magazine, claims that there are six-stages when dealing with stress that are similar to the stages of grief. The first stage is shock, when employees may experience a loss of focus on their work. The second is delusion, a psychological denial or a "this can't be happening" moment. The third stage is blame; people want to get angry with somebody else and search out potential targets for their anger. The fourth stage is depression, where one withdraws and productivity deteriorates. The fifth stage is letting go, where we make a conscious effort to release negativity. The sixth and final stage of dealing with *stress is exploring options, where we accept our past and current situations and explore alternative solutions.*

Conclusion

As we can see, although listening takes up a significant amount of our daily lives, there are many obstacles to listening effectively. By recognizing some of the common barriers to listening, as well as our own listening preferences, we become more aware of areas for improvement. Keeping in mind that listening is a skill we can improve upon, we can enhance our communication interactions with others—in the classroom, in our homes, and at work.

References

Barker, L. (1971). *Listening behavior.* Englewood Cliffs, New Jersey: Prentice Hall

Canpolat, M., Kuzu, S., Yıldırım, B., & Canpolat, S. (2015). Active listening strategies of academically successful university students. *Eurasian Journal of Educational Research,* 60,163-180Doi: 10.14689/ejer.2015.60.10

International Listening Association. (n.d.) Listening facts. Retrieved from http://d1025403.site.myhosting. com/files.listen.org/Facts.htm

Ripley, R. & Watson, K. (2014). We're learning—Are you listening? *Chief Learning Officer,* Retrieved from http://www.academia.edu/33001594/Were_Learning..._Are_you_Listening

Shwom, B. & Synder, L. *Business communication. Polishing your professional presence* (2nd edition). Boston: MA: Pearson, p. 11.

Watson, K. & Barker, L. (1995). *Listening styles profile.* Amsterdam, Netherlands: Pfeiffer & Company.

Zarefsky, D. (2016). *Public speaking: Strategies for success* (8th edition). Boston: MA: Pearson.

Janet Mock
January 2017 – Women's March

https://www.thecut.com/2017/01/read-janet-mocks-speech-at-the-womens-march-on-washington-trans-women-of-color-sex-workers.html

So we are here. We are here not merely to gather but to move, right? And our movements, our movements require us to do more than just show up and say the right words. It requires us to break out of our comfort zones and be confrontational. It requires us to defend one another when it is difficult and dangerous. It requires us to truly see ourselves and one another.

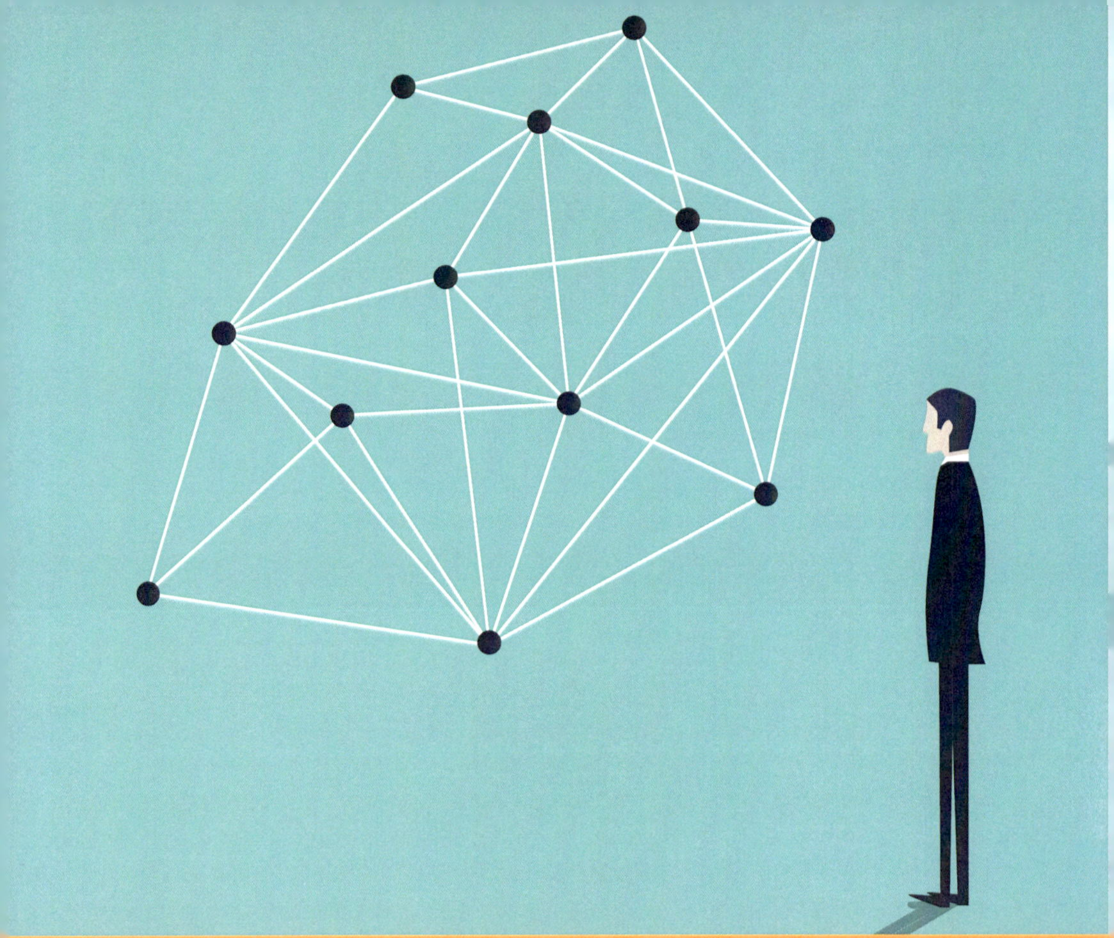

In this chapter, we will discuss the most common type of speech: the informative.

The purpose of an informative speech is to provide information to an audience, but it helps to think a little beyond what can sometimes seem like a dry recitation of facts and figures. Informative speeches at their best increase both the speaker's and the audience's understanding on a given topic. The facts and figures are selected, arranged, and shared in a way that provides context and relevance for the knowledge gained. Considering an informative speech from the perspective of increasing understanding can help you focus on a topic and on what to include to best reach that goal.

Informative Speaking

Dr. Matthew Jones
County College of Morris

The Function, Purpose, and Goal of the Informative Speech

Broadly considered, there are three types of speeches: **(1) Informative Speeches, (2) Persuasive Speeches, and (3) Commemorative Speeches.** The general purpose of a speech has traditionally fallen into one of three categories: **(1) Speeches to Inform, (2) Speeches to Persuade, and (3) Speeches to Eentertain.** The goal of the informative speech is to provide an audience with knowledge and understanding of a topic. An informative speech can also serve as a lesson, instructing the audience on a given subject.

Types of Informative Speeches

There are multiple ways to classify informative speeches. We will use the following categorization. Speeches to…

1. Describe
2. Explain
3. Report
4. Instruct

Description

Speeches of Description focus upon and seek to illuminate the features of an object, person (or animal/plant), place, region, period of time, experience, emotion, or anything else at all that's capable of being experienced through senses, thoughts, or feelings. Broadly stated, speeches of description attempt to answer questions that ask *"what"* (not how or why) insofar as inquiry centers on what features or aspects compose the thing that is being described. The objective of a descriptive speech, therefore, is to create a mental image in the mind of the listener of what is being described.

Imagine, for example, that you went on a camping trip with a group of friends. There would be a variety of ways to recount this trip descriptively. You might focus on the features of the campsite, the conversations and relationships among your friends, camping tasks or outdoor activities you participated in, your own subjective thoughts or feelings about being in nature, wildlife that you encountered, or any other aspect of the trip.

Once you've settled on a *specific purpose,* you can start to consider the *central idea* and *main points of your speech.* Let's say you want to focus on the "features of the campsite." The central idea of your speech could take the form of a lesson about the geography of the campsite. Phrased specifically, it might appear like this: ***"You can learn a lot about the local environment from a camping trip."*** From this point, you can start to identify features of the campsite that can be placed into categories and used as main points. In this example, where you are focusing on physical terrain, a spatial approach to organizing your main points might be used. Otherwise, a topical approach might be employed as in the following set of main points:

1. **Weather:** What is the climate like? (tropical, dry, temperate, continental, polar and alpine)
2. **Rock Formations:** What sort of bedrock, rock formations, or stones did you find? (igneous, sedimentary, metamorphic)
3. **Water:** Are there any nearby sources of water? (ocean, lake, river, stream, pond, etc.)
4. **Soil:** What kind of soil do you find? (silt, sand, gravel, clay, etc.)
5. **Plants:** What types of plants do you find? (types of trees, shrubs, vines, moss, algae, etc.)

Explanation

Rather than descriptions of features meant to develop mental images in the mind of the listener, a ***Speech of Explanation*** is concerned with meanings, origins, or correspondences. In short, a Speech of Explanation answers questions about "why" and "how" instead of "what" (i.e. when "what" refers to the thing being described). Keep in mind, though, that some level of description may be essential to a precise explanation, since explanation itself focuses on the correspondences between or among things. For example, if you are trying to explain how photosynthesis works, some description of plants, sunlight, carbon dioxide, water, chlorophyll, and oxygen will be necessary. In fact, as this example illustrates, an explanatory speech is primarily concerned with the relationships among things, particularly inasmuch as cause and effect are concerned.

Returning to the camping trip, what type of explanatory speeches might come out of such an example? The brief allusion to photosynthesis above could provide a useful starting point, especially since specific plant species might come in handy as examples for explaining the process. Additional possibilities might include explanations of moon phases, the food chain, the water cycle, fossils, or any other phenomenon that one might be exposed to in a wilderness setting.

Let us say for our present purposes that "moon phases" will serve as the topic of your explanatory speech. The central idea could be stated as follows: ***The spatial relationships among the earth, the moon, and the sun are responsible for what we perceive as moon phases.*** Once the central idea has been determined, it is then possible to identify main points and decide upon an organizational strategy that will inform the order of their presentation.

In this example, spatial and chronological strategies would be used to determine the order of main points. For example:

1. **Full Moon**
2. **Waning Gibbous**
3. **New Moon**
4. **Waxing Crescent**
5. **Waxing Gibbous**

Report Speeches

The purpose of a ***Report Speech*** is to share knowledge about facts, findings, or events. Accordingly, report speeches make use of both description and explanation to do this. In addition to questions of ***what, how, and why,*** which respectively characterize speeches of description and explanation, speeches of report may also center on questions of ***who, when, and where.*** Thus, a report speech may address any or all of these questions, to the extent that they are useful to the presentation of facts, findings, or events. More formally stated: A report speech uses description and explanation to share knowledge about facts, findings or events. For example, journalism often takes on the quality of a report because journalists report events and provide answers to questions of ***who, what, where, why, and how.***

Presenting an effective report speech requires storytelling skills. In the case of our camping trip example, it might be treated as a report if offered as a ***series of events that conclude with a climax.*** Understood in this context, an event is a ***continuous span of time and space that occurs in a setting, which may involve one or more characters and/or objects, but must feature one or more actions.*** Respectively, a setting is a physical place, a character is a person in the setting, an object is an inanimate entity (a "thing") within the setting, and an action is a physical occurrence (something that happens) within the setting. In short, an event is something that happens to someone, somewhere, and at some specific time.

A climax, on the other hand, is the culminating event that all the other events of the story lead up to. It gives the story its meaning and resolves the suspense that is built up through the series of preceding events. The art of telling an effective story comes in selecting the events and transitioning between them in such a way that the stage is set for an effective climax. Therefore, to report on your camping trip, you have to decide which events to include/exclude based on what you determine to be the climax of the trip. In the case of the literature review, you have to decide what research findings are included and what conclusion you can draw about the state of knowledge in that area. Obviously an element of subjectivity is involved in deciding what the climax is and which events or findings to include, but the story format is a much more compelling and effective means of presentation than a random list of events. You will also notice that reporting a story requires a chronological approach to the organization of events, while reporting research allows for a more topical organization.

In the context of our camping trip example it's impossible to provide a series of possible approaches, as in the previous types of informative speech, because everything is contingent upon the particulars of the trip itself. However, the following blueprint should provide some direction on how to craft an effective outline:

Central Idea: My friends and I survived a camping trip gone wrong by being resourceful.

Background: This past summer I, along with several friends, travelled into the mountains to go camping. Many miles into the wilderness as night was approaching our truck caught on fire and we lost much of our equipment. But, over the next five days, we managed to camp and hike our way out with what we had left.

Main Ideas:

Event A: Setting up camp in the dark without a flashlight.
Transition: The next day…

Event B: Finding a shortcut through the mountain.
Transition: Later that evening…

Event C: Making a fire without a flashlight.
Transition: The next morning…

Event D: Hunting and fishing for food.
Transition: That night…

Event E: A bear visits the camp.
Transition: The following day…

Climax: Arriving at the ranger's office.

For a literature review, an outline might look like this:
Central Idea: Digital communication, including social media and game studies, is a rapidly growing field of research.

Background: Just two decades ago, almost no research on social media or gaming was available. Now digital communication is one of the fastest growing areas of study.

Main Idea: The near-ubiquitous use of social media has drawn scholarly attention.
Support: Studies have been done on....

Main Idea: The huge numbers of people participating in gaming have also piqued the interest from scholars.

Support: Game studies include….

Conclusion: Although the research in digital communication has grown rapidly, there is still much work to be done on the how the shift to digital affects human interactions.

Other Types of Report Speech

It's important to recognize that stories and events are not the only possible subjects for report speeches. Though facts and findings may be presented in the context of a story, they do not have to be. Report speeches may take the form of a ***Literature Review,*** in which primary and secondary sources are reported on and document previous findings and widely accepted facts. In line with this type of report speech, new findings from original research may also be reported. Multiple organizational strategies may be applied to these tasks and the report need not be presented as a story, though an incremental historical narrative is often employed.

Speeches of Instruction

In their most basic sense, ***Speeches of Instruction*** are intended to teach, that is to transfer knowledge from speaker to listener. Like ***explanation,*** instruction is primarily aimed at answering questions of ***how,*** although, as in all informative speeches, other types of questions might be addressed along the way as well. This is especially true when aspects of description and reporting are applied to the task of instruction.

However, unlike any of the other types of informative speech described earlier, speeches of instruction are meant to develop competency in the listener. Consequently, understanding or comprehending the speech and remembering it are prerequisites for the development of other skills the speaker wishes to instill. However, it should also be acknowledged that comprehension and memory are skills in and of themselves.

According to Bloom's Taxonomy (a chart of verbs that describe different learning outcomes), other competencies fall under the following categories: ***knowledge, comprehension, application, analysis, synthesis, and evaluation.*** Particularly important among the many verbs that describe learning outcomes is demonstration. It goes without saying that to instruct effectively, one must possess the competencies necessary to demonstrate the skill being taught. For example, a math teacher needs to be able to demonstrate how to solve an algebra problem before expecting the student to solve it. The teacher's demonstration enables the student to modify his or her own approach to achieve competency in the skill being taught.

Going back once again to our camping trip example, a number of possibilities should come to mind when considering how camping might be instructed. Everything from choosing a campsite and setting up equipment to essential skills like building a fire and cooking could take the form of an instructional speech. Depending on how ambitious the trip is, other more advanced skills like hunting, fishing, rock climbing, rafting, etc. might come into play as well. For our purposes, let's pretend we're going to give an instructional speech on how to set up a practical campsite. The rough outline below demonstrates one approach that might be taken:

Specific Purpose: To inform my audience about the five important components of a well-assembled campsite.

Central Idea: There are five important components of a well-assembled campsite

Introduction

I. Attention Getter: It is sometimes said that camping is a leisure activity where you spend a fortune without getting any luxury… But it doesn't have to be that way, especially if you know how to set up your campsite correctly.

II. Central Idea: There are five important components of a well-assembled campsite.

III. Credibility & Importance: Based on my many experiences camping in the remote wilderness, I can't emphasize enough how important it is to incorporate these things into the layout of your campsite.

IV. Relate to the Audience: Many of you probably have not camped before: I know that it can be intimidating to think about all of the things you will need to be prepared for!

V. Preview of Main Points: They are as follows: Storage, Toilette, Kitchen, Tent, and Bonfire.

Transition: Let's discuss the first component.

Body

I. You need to prepare your storage.
   A. Storage should be centrally located as it will serve as a staging area for setting up and striking camp.
   B. You will need to rig a canopy over the storage area so that equipment stays as cool and dry as possible.
   C. In some cases, a tent will be needed to protect against animals as well.
      1. Once, I had to contend with red squirrels that were eating through rubber propane lines.

Transition: Let's move on to the second component.

II. You need to prepare your toilette accommodations.
   A. Toilette accommodations will vary based on where you are camping, but outhouses and portable toilettes are the most common arrangements for established campgrounds.
      1. Prior to use, you should inspect the facility for spiders, insects, and other creatures before cleaning all surfaces with disinfectant.
         a. Once, I had to remove a nest of very large wolf spiders from an outhouse before it could be used.

B. Toilette paper, a portable lantern, and a water-resistant case to store these items are the minimum necessities.

Transition: Next is the third component.

III. You need to prepare your kitchen.
  A. A kitchen area should contain coolers packed with ice for perishable food and secure containers for non-perishable items.
    1. It is important for all food containers to remain sealed when not in use to protect against hungry animals.
  B. Secure and efficient storage of cookware, plates, and utensils is also important to plan for.
    1. Cooking equipment varies widely, but it should be a primary consideration in setting up your kitchen.
      a. For example, you obviously don't want to build an open fire under a tent or canopy.
      b. The only acceptable cooking equipment to use in a sheltered area is a propane stove.
  C. Many established campsites provide picnic tables, but it may also be necessary to bring portable and collapsible chairs and tables to use in the kitchen if none are provided.
  D. Basins with water and detergent are necessary for washing cookware, plates, and silverware, unless you are using paper plates and plastic utensils.
    1. Reusable plates and utensils are better for the environment and produce less trash.
    2. Additionally, since cookware will need to be washed anyway, it doesn't pay to use disposable products.
  E. Finally, it's a good idea to cover the kitchen area with a screen tent to permit for protection against animals and the elements while, at the same time, allowing for ventilation of heat, odor, and fumes from cooking equipment.

Transition: Let's move on to the fourth component.

IV. You need to prepare your tent.
  A. Unless cabins are provided, it will be necessary to have a tent and know how to set it up.
  B. Some campsites offer wooden platforms for tents, but not all.
  C. If you must pitch your tent on the ground, be cognizant of drainage patterns during rainfall and other factors that may result in a flood.

D. Also be forewarned that most new tents are not completely waterproof.
   1. It's necessary to apply a solution to the seams of the tent to prevent leakage, and even then it's possible to have leakage in heavy rain storms.
   2. The best solution is to cover the tent with a waterproof tarp while making sure to still provide some ventilation.
E. You should place your sleeping bag on top of a cot so that you're elevated from the ground.
   1. Not only is this a more comfortable arrangement, it provides extra safety in the case of a flood.
F. Clothing should be stored in waterproof bags, and you should keep an extra bag for used clothing or clothing you intend to wash.
G. Finally, it's critical to remember flashlights and lanterns because it is difficult and dangerous to navigate in the wilderness while it's dark.
   1. A lantern can be used inside the tent the same way as a room light, and a flashlight can be used for venturing out at night.

Transition: Now that we have discussed setting up the storage, toilette accommodations, kitchen, and tent, let's move on to the fifth and final component.

V. You need to prepare your bonfire.

   a. A bonfire is normally constructed by digging a hole and encircling it with stones that are used to contain the flames.
   b. It's important to construct the bonfire pit at a distance from trees, brush, leaves and flammable liquids.
   c. Wood should be placed in the storage area or kept under a waterproof cover.

Conclusion

I. **Recap of Main Points:** So, remember: Storage, Toilette, Kitchen, Tent, and Bonfire.
II. **Restatement of Central Idea:** If you take these five points into consideration as you plan your next camping trip, you will be sure to have a well-constructed campsite that feels like home.
III. **Conclusive Statement:** *Good luck and happy camping!*

Methods of Organization

Organizing Your Informative Speech

The most important principle to consider when organizing your informative speech is *complexity*. The "Principle of Complexity" dictates that information be presented in an incremental, hierarchical fashion that proceeds from simple to complex. Ideally, an informative speaker should begin right about at the limits of the audience's knowledge and present new information in stages, consistently relating it to the audience's existing base of knowledge. Some more specific strategies include the following:

- **Chronological:** The chronological strategy is taken from storytelling, wherein events build upon each other successively, creating dramatic tension and resulting in a climax from which the moral of the story might be drawn. This strategy could be applied to a speech intended to inform about biographies, historical periods, technical procedures, or the subjective discovery process of the speaker.

- **Spatial:** The spatial strategy uses place, space, and/or geography as a tool of organization. Such a strategy could be applied, for example, to an informative speech identifying zip code as a predictor of poverty, wherein spatial relationships between cities were used to describe economic disparities in physical terms. Spatial strategies might also be employed to explain complex systems (such as a power grids or computers), communication patterns, and relationships between objects, ideas, or people.

- **Topical:** The topical strategy has no predetermined relationship among main ideas, rather it allows the speaker to impose his or her own logic on how the speech is organized. It is especially critical in the case of a topical strategy that the speaker be conscious of the principle of complexity, since it is very easy to introduce information out of context and confuse the audience.

Conclusion

The ability to effectively convey information is crucial to our personal and professional lives. Whether you are helping to teach an old friend to tie a bowtie or presenting a production plan to a board of directors, informative speaking skills are critical to successfully conveying your message. You will probably be asked to present or evaluate an informative speech at some point during your public speaking course. In this chapter you have learned about different types of informative speeches and about strategies for organizing an informative speech.

12 | INFORMATIVE SPEAKING

Informative speeches can come in a variety of types and patterns. While their principle goal is to impart information about a given topic, there are different ways that the goal can be achieved. As always, considerations of audience size and demographics, and of location and setting, can help to inform what organizational pattern and what type of informative speech will be most effective at communicating your message.

The Function, Purpose, and Goal of the Technical Speech

The purpose of a technical speech is to explain to an audience a complex topic that is technical in nature or has specific technical components. Technical speeches require that the speaker provide technical details in a way that can be easily understood by a general audience. Though often thought of as a scientific speech, technical speeches can be on a broad range of complex topics from many academic disciplines and aspects of life. For example, you could give a technical speech on the science behind the "scan and go" technology used in a grocery store checkout line. Or, you could explain the physics of a golf club swing. But you could just as easily explain how to prevent stress, the process of flower arranging, the components of a musical scale, or how to create a secure password online. In all cases a technical speech requires that the speaker has a strong organizational pattern, breaks down the information into digestible bites, uses nontechnical vocabulary and examples so that the audience comes away with a clear understanding of the object, process, or concept.

Technical Speaking

KAREN BRAGER, PATRICIA COUGHLAN, KATHERINE HARMAN, ALLISON S. WILLIAMS
Rowan University

Types of Technical Speeches
The three types of technical speeches are as follows:

1. an object speech
2. a process speech
3. a concept speech

Object: a technical speech where the speaker's specific purpose is to provide for a general audience a comprehensive, complex understanding of the materials and components that comprise an object.

> **Example:** smart wallpaper

Concept: a technical speech where the speaker's specific purpose is to break down and explain for a general audience the components of an idea, belief, attitude, principle, or theory.

> **Example:** Feminism

Process: a technical speech where the speaker's specific purpose is to describe to a general audience how something is made, done, or works.

> **Example:** the process of making chocolate

Is a technical speech a speech to inform?

Yes and no.

Yes, a technical speech at a simplistic level is a speech to inform. As previously stated in this text, "the goal of an informative speech is to provide an audience with knowledge and understanding of a topic. A speech to inform can also serve as a lesson, instructing an audience on a given subject" (171). So, on a very basic level a technical speech can be a speech of instruction. Yet, if we look closely, we can see that there are distinct differences between a technical speech and an informative speech with the purpose to instruct.

In today's world technical speaking is in demand. The 21st century is full of complex problems, issues, advancements, and changes that need to be explained to both workplace professionals and the general public. Consider the popularity of American astrophysicist, author, and science communicator, Neil deGrasse Tyson. Dr. Tyson's ability to take complex scientific ideas and make them understandable to the average person earned him the National Academy of Sciences 2015 Public Welfare Medal for "his extraordinary role in exciting the public about the wonders of science." As a science communicator, Dr. Tyson understands that complex technical ideas can be explained so that many different audiences can gain greater understanding. Dr. Tyson achieves audience understanding by providing concrete details, comprehendible vocabulary, strong organization, high-quality visuals, and a good sense of humor.

The ability to utilize strong organizational patterns, description, appropriate audience centered vocabulary, relevant analogies, and detailed visuals help an audience picture and understand technical complexity.

Technical speeches require more of the speaker. A technical speech must provide clear organization, concrete details, precise vocabulary, analogous thinking, and detailed visuals. An increased burden of explanation and instruction belongs to the speaker because a technical speech specifically describes how an object works, the mechanics of a process, or the underpinnings of a concept. Preparing a technical speech requires that the speaker conduct a thorough audience analysis which recognizes the audience's needs and expectations, the level of background on the chosen topic, with attentiveness to language, specifically technical jargon.

A technical speech requires that the speaker fully answer in understandable vocabulary the following key questions for the audience about the object, process, or concept being discussed.

The Key Questions of Technical Speaking:

What is it?
What does it look like?
What does it do and act like?
What is it made of?
How does it work?
How has it been put together?
What is its future/implications?

Technical speaking relies heavily on descriptive details and well-designed visuals. Word choice appeals to the 5 senses and attempts to create strong images. Overall, a technical speaker must determine how much specificity an audience requires to gain understanding. The speaker must choose a strong organizational pattern appropriate for the object, process, or concept being discussed. The speaker must take a very complex idea and explain it in a way that makes it easily understandable for all.

Is a technical speech a speech to inform? No. As you now understand, a technical speech is not an informative speech. It's so much more.

Activities:

A. Descriptive Detail:
Using an everyday, ordinary item (like your keys, pen, notebook, phone, watch, paperclip, mechanical pencil, etc.) Write a description of the object using sensory details (color, shape, size, materials, etc.). Begin by focus on describing the item, its parts and characteristics, not on its function/use. Orally share your descriptions with a partner or group.

B. Impromptu Speaking Function:
An analogy is a comparison between two things for the purpose of clarification and explanation. An analogy can help create description. Consider whether you can use an analogy to explain how the item you choose for activity A works or is used. For example, if you had chosen a paperclip you might make an analogy comparing it to a hair barrette or bobby-pin or a clamp. Make an impromptu speech explaining how your item works or is used.

Methods of Organization for Technical Speaking

As discussed in Chapter 8 on Speech Structure, careful consideration should be taken when arranging the speech's main points. The speaker should determine which method of organization will most effectively help his, her, their audience to follow, understand, and retain the information presented. For technical speeches, the following organizational strategies should be considered:

Chronological: this strategy is an effective method to organize the main points of a process speech by presenting the steps of a process.

Specific Purpose: To inform a general audience about how 3-D printers work.
Main Point I: First, the object must be designed for 3-D printing.
Main Point II: Next, the object is sent to the 3-D printer for creation.

Spatial: this strategy is an effective method to organize the main points of an object speech by presenting the main parts of the object according to their location/relationship/proximity to one another.

Specific Purpose: To inform a general audience about the V-2 Rocket.
Main Point I: First, the bottom of the rocket is the tail section.
Main Point II: Second, the section directly above the tail section is the midsection.
Main Point III: Third, the section above the midsection is the control section.
Main Point IV: Finally, the top of the rocket is the nose cone.

Comparison/Contrast: this strategy is an effective method to communicate a lesser known entity to the audience by comparing its similarities and contrasting its differences to an entity the audience is familiar with.

Specific Purpose: To inform a general audience about biodiesel fuel.
Main Point I: Biodiesel fuel has several similarities to standard diesel fuel.
Main Point II: There are several differences between biodiesel fuel and standard diesel fuel.

Problem-Solution: this strategy is effective when the technical speech highlights the solution or solutions to a problem.

Specific Purpose: To inform a general audience about smart wallpaper.
Main Point I: Traditional wallpapers are problematic in fires.
Main Point II: Naturally fire-retardant smart wallpaper can alert occupants to vacate a burning building.

Topical: this strategy is effective when the speech's main points are independent from one another, having no relationship determining the organization. The following is an example of a topical strategy for a concept speech:

Specific Purpose: To inform a general audience about the four fundamental interactions that make up string theory.
Main Point I: Gravity is one of the fundamental interactions of string theory.
Main Point II: Electromagnetism is also one of the fundamental interactions of string theory.
Main Point III: Strong nuclear force is another one of the four fundamental interactions that make up string theory.
Main Point IV: Weak nuclear force is the final fundamental interaction to make up string theory.

ELLIOT KRANE, MD
TED TALK - THE MYSTERY OF CHRONIC PAIN
https://www.ted.com/talks/elliot_krane_the_mystery_of_chronic_pain?language=en

Technical Language

Why do we want others to understand what we are saying?

Any time we deliver a speech or even just communicate with another person, we have a message that we are delivering. Clearly, we want that message to be understood. Think about a time where you tried to communicate with someone but weren't able to because of some type of barrier. Chapter One describes noise as "anything that interferes with the message transmission or receipt; it can be literal noise, distraction, lack of comprehension, or a host of other possibilities" (9). In this case, we will look at lack of comprehension due to little or no knowledge of the subject or content knowledge that can interfere with a message.

What makes language technical? What can we do to help to understand technical language? General Language, Plain Speak, or Layperson's Terms

Technical language, sometimes called jargon, is comprised of words that are usually very specific to a topic and often difficult to understand if your audience is not familiar with the topic. Jargon can range anywhere from a single medical term such as hypervolemia, meaning an abnormal increase in blood volume, to a specific process like brewing beer which involves milling, mashing, lautering, and fermenting, to a planogram which is a specific retail industry term. Unless your audience works in the medical, brewery, or retail industry, they most likely will not fully understand these technical terms. It is up to the speaker to break down the jargon barrier and define the words and the ideas to help the audience better understand the message. The best way to do this is to break the information down into general language or plain speak also known as "layperson's" terms. A layperson is defined as a person without knowledge or expertise in a particular area.

Jargon Examples:

Pedagogy – the method or practice of teaching, an educational philosophy;

Bovie – an instrument used for electrosurgical dissection and hemostasis. Used as a synonym for electrocautery, that is to "Bovie a blood vessel." Named after William Bovie, the inventor.

Roll Call – in business a mandatory team meeting to tell your forecast (how much business you expect to close this month) i.e. "I rolled a 6: = $60k.

Differentiated Instruction/RTI – response to intervention. Tiered system using data to instruct students based on individual needs.

S.O.A.P. (Subjective, Objective, Assessment, Plan) - Documentation method for Physical Therapy treatment plans.

Bowl Pick - cleaning the stadium after an event.

Analogies and Imagery

As mentioned earlier in this chapter, technical speaking relies heavily on descriptive details. Analogies and imagery are descriptive language devices that help make complex ideas understandable and relatable.

Analogies are key to making content relatable. An analogy is a comparison between two things. In this case, you want to compare the complex idea with something very simple. Using an analogy is an easy way to help someone understand what you are talking about. The TED Talk included in this chapter features Dr. Elliot Krane talking about chronic pain. Dr. Krane uses analogy most effectively when discussing a person's brain and its inability to interpret sensation correctly. In his demonstration Dr. Krane strokes his own arm with a feather. He shares the idea with the audience that while the sensation is coming from a feather, in the case of his chronic pain patient, her brain believed it to be the sensation of a blow torch.

Imagery – Write it out. Bring us there. Imagery is not just for written text. It is for spoken words too! What we say has the ability to create strong, vibrant, sensory images in the mind of the audience. Even in his TED Talk, Dr. Krane didn't need to show the feather and the blow torch.

He could have simply said, "Close your eyes and imagine a feather. Long and light yellow in color. Soft and supple. Imagine your forearm and that feather. Now imagine the flame of a mini blow torch. Light blue. An iridescent hissing flame shooting from a small canister. The feather strokes your arm and instead of feeling the slightest tickle of the individual hairs of that feather…you feel the hissing, screaming blow torch flame melting your skin. That blazing sensation is what it feels like to someone with chronic pain."

Be mindful of how you use language in your technical speech. Avoid jargon, use plain speak, incorporate analogies, and use strong imagery to engage your audience and clarify your content.

Tips for Technical Speeches

1. Ask yourself, "why should my audience care about this topic?" Your answer to this question will help you to formulate an audience relevance statement and to keep the audience engaged throughout the speech. If possible, present a benefit to the audience for knowing the information you are about to present.

   Audience Relevance Statement Example: "Understanding how a sneaker's design absorbs energy will help you pick the best footwear needed for your type of activity and help you to avoid agonizing foot pain."

2. Do not offend your audience by talking down to them. Your audience may not have the same technical expertise as you, but if you speak down to your audience, they may not want to listen.

3. Think of a family member or friend that does not share the same technical background as you. How would you explain your object, process, or concept to that family member or friend so that he, she, or they could follow along and understand the benefits to knowing the information you are sharing?

4. Focus! The main points of a technical speech should explain the object, process, or the concept and should not include main points explaining historical or anecdotal information associated with the topic. Background information about the topic could be included in the introduction as part of the attention-getter or audience relevance, but don't make it the focus of your speech.

5. Put emphasis on the key points that are critical for the audience to understand the object, process, or concept by using repetition, vocal variety, and visual aids.
6. Be prepared to answer questions. Anticipate questions that may be asked or practice the speech for friends or family that do not share your technical background. Encourage them to ask questions. Be open to all questions, and if you are unable to answer a question, instead of saying "no" or "I don't know," express interest in the audience member's question by saying, "that's something I would need to do more research on" or "I'd need to look into that further."

Purpose Statements for Technical Speeches

In Chapter 5 you learned about the difference between general and specific purpose statements. For a technical speech the general purpose statement is "to inform." Your specific purpose statement must include your general purpose, your audience, and the goal you wish to achieve through your speech. Remember your specific purpose statement needs to be focused on the technical content and not background information.

Incorrect Example:

Specific Purpose: To inform a general audience on how 3-D printers work.

Main Point I: First, I will discuss the history of 3-D printers

Main Point II: Next, I will discuss how 3-D printers work.

Correct Example:

Specific Purpose: To inform a general audience on how 3-D printers work.

Main Point I: First, I will discuss how to design a 3-D object for printing.

Main Point II: Next, I will discuss how a 3-D printer creates the object designed.

Technical Visuals

No matter the topic, length, or type of speech, a visual aid should always enhance your speech, not hinder it. Keep this in mind when deciding what you should or shouldn't use for a visual during a presentation.

What could help?

-Information that is clear, comprehensive, and straightforward

-Information that increases the audiences' understanding of and improves the quality of your topic

-Information that is well researched and interesting

What could hurt?

-Something that is unclear or hard to understand

-Something that explains your topic instead of enhancing what you've already told the audience

-Something put together haphazardly or sloppily

Overall, the visual aid for your technical speech should accomplish the following goals:

1. Make the components of your speech easier to understand
2. Support your main and subpoints
3. Improve upon the language included in your speech
4. Be used as supporting evidence
5. Convey a specific message

These goals can be attained no matter the type of visual aid you use— meaning that you should strive for these whether you create a slideshow, bring in a poster board with diagrams, or show your audience a video. Strong, professional visuals are especially vital for a technical speech, as these topics are often complicated, more difficult to explain, and can sometimes be less exciting for the audience.

Referring back to Dr. Elliot Krane's TED Talk about chronic pain, Dr. Krane's use of a blowtorch and a feather to demonstrate different sensations to the audience works because the audience can imagine what both a blowtorch and feather would feel like when used on the skin. Having each object with him on stage was an effective way for Dr. Krane to engage the viewers through visual props.

Other objects that could be productive for a technical speech include simple experiments or demonstrations. For example, you could:

- show the audience the concepts behind gravity by presenting how magnets work
- show water in its various forms to display the water cycle
- use different types of football helmets to display how changes in technology can impact player health.

Activities:

A. Think of an object (or objects) you could bring up with you to the front of the class to describe a process or concept. What would you do with the object? How would it engage the audience? How would it make your presentation easier to comprehend?

B. Think of a great speech you have witnessed - whether in person or online - how did the speech/speaker include visuals? Could you have improved upon them? If so, how? Now, relate this to your technical speech topic. How could a visual aid improve your material, while simultaneously keeping the audience interested and following along?

Multimedia:

Today's technology allows speakers to incorporate numerous visuals into a speech. Dr. Krane uses props but he also incorporates video, photos, and a slideshow element in his speech. All of these visuals do something for the viewer, while also making the information Dr. Krane is discussing seem less intimidating. While Dr. Krane incorporates many technical aspects in his presentation, the information is easier to digest because of the way he integrates the visuals throughout as a seamless multimedia presentation.

Visual Ideas:
- Charts, diagrams, or graphs (think science, medical, technology, or engineering fields)
- Graphics Interchange Format or GIFs (show how the gears in a manual transmission works, how a shutter on a camera works)
- Videos
- Slideshow presentation (incorporate pictures, graphics, diagrams, and/or videos within)
- Actual item (present to the audience the real item that they can touch)
- Images (best if used in concert with diagrams)

Remember technical visual aids can be used individually or together to make a cohesive multimedia presentation. As with everything, visual aids can be done well or poorly. When putting your visual aids together always think about what message is being conveyed to the audience and how the audience is going to interpret what you show them. Important things to remember include: the relationship between images and text, the size of the room, where the aid will be shown or projected in a room, and how easy or difficult it may be for your audience to see it clearly.

You also want to consider when to use images, as opposed to words, the size of the aids, and quantity vs quality. Videos can be effective visual aids but remember that your spoken descriptions and words should be what tell the audience how something works, not those encompassed in the video. Use a video clip to enhance understanding and provide further insight into what "you" are explaining. Tom Wujec's TED Talk on *How the Brain Creates* meaning offers some insight in how visuals can help your audience make meaning.

Tom Wujec

TED Talk – 3 Ways the Brain Creates Meaning
https://www.ted.com/talks/tom_wujec_on_3_ways_the_brain_creates_

Chapter Conclusion:

The ability to breakdown and translate complex ideas in a way that engages and educates an audience is a skill that is needed in the 21st century. Each day new objects, processes, and concepts are being developed which are changing our world and which need explaining to the general public. In this chapter you have learned about the different types of technical speeches, the methods utilized for organizing a technical speech, how to create an outline for a technical speech, the importance of language, analogy, example and visual to technical speaking, and the value of conducting research to ensure you are the expert. When you give a technical speech, remember to be audience centered and to translate your expert understanding into simplified everyday language that educates and informs. Remember even Albert Einstein understood the value of taking a complex idea and simplifying it. He reportedly said, "the definition of genius is taking the complex and making it simple."

Rupal Patel
TEDWomen 2013 – Synthetic Voices, as unique as fingerprints
https://www.ted.com/talks/rupal_patel_synthetic_voices_as_unique_as_fingerprints

TECHNICAL SPEECH OUTLINE SAMPLES:

Sample Outline – Object – MLA Format

Topic: Smart Wallpaper

Specific Purpose: To inform the audience about smart wallpaper.

Central Idea: Today, I would like to inform you about the life-saving technological advancement of smart wallpaper.

Introduction

I. If your home was on fire, how many minutes do you believe you would have to get out alive? According to the American Red Cross, over 60 percent of Americans surveyed believed they would have five or more minutes to exit their burning home; however, on average, they would have about two minutes ("New Red Cross Survey").

II. In addition, the American Red Cross reports that on average, 7 people in the U.S. die a day as a result of fires ("Sound the Alarm").

III. As the daughter of a volunteer firefighter, I have been taught various fire prevention and safety methods, and as a mechanical engineering student, developing technology that is safe is an important concern of mine. IV. Today, I would like t inform you about the life-saving technological advancement of smart wallpaper.

V. First, I will discuss the problems of traditional wallpaper in building fires, and then I will discuss a possible solution: smart wallpaper that is naturally fire resident and that can quickly alert occupants to vacate the building in a fire.

Body

I. Traditional wallpapers are problematic in fires.
  A. Traditional wallpapers, which are made mostly of cellulose or synthetic polymers, are highly flammable if not treated with a flame retardant.
    1. Cellulose polymers are plant-based chains of identically monomers, which are single molecules.
      a. According to physics blogger Quark Twain, "cellulose is like the cinder block of the plant world."
        i. "In tree leaves, cellulose gives the plant cell walls their structure" (Quark Twain).

2. Synthetic polymers are manmade chains of identical monomers.

   a. Rubber and plastics are types of synthetic polymers.

   b. According to a segment that aired on the Today show in 2016, newer homes burn five times faster than homes 30 years ago, when people had on average 17 minutes to escape, because today's homes are made of more synthetic materials (Rossen and Davis).

B. Some traditional wallpapers are treated with flame-retardants that can prevent or slow a fire, but concerns over their safety may not outweigh their benefits.

   1. According to the article, "How do Flame Retardants Work" there are three methods of flame retardance: vapor phase inhibition, solid phase char formation, and quench and cool systems.

      a. Vapor phase inhibition happens when additives, like the compound bromine, which is a halogen like chlorine and iodine, are heated, releasing atoms that disrupt the bonding needed to fuel a fire.

         i. imagine entering a crowded room with hundreds of strangers, the bromine atoms, and you, the heat source, must maneuver through the crowd to find your two friends, oxygen and flammable gas; of course, your night of fun, aka the fire, will be delayed until you can meet up with your friends among a sea of strangers.

      b. Solid phase char formation is when the top layer of the material is charred, reating a barrier that prevents additional flammable gases from emitting and protecting the non-charred substance below.

         i. It's like a force field that initiates from the initial burn that doesn't allow the necessary flammable gases needed to fuel a flame to escape, nor does it allow the layer below the char to be damaged by the intense heat.

      c. Quench and cool systems work with hydrated minerals that when heated release water molecules that dilute the flammable gases and are too cool to evaporate.

         i. The minerals work like tiny fire extinguishers.

   2. Although flame retardants can add some additional time to escape a burning home, there are some concerns that the benefits do not outweigh the risks.

      a. According to the National Institute of Environmental Health Sciences lame retardants in household materials have been linked to serious adverse health issues, which can include cancer, thyroid and immune system issues, reproductive problems, adverse fetal development, and eurological conditions ("Flame Retardants").

Transition: Now that I've discussed the problems of traditional wallpaper, let me discuss the **solution:** smart wallpaper.

II. Naturally fire retardant smart wallpaper can alert occupants to vacate a burning building.
   A. Unlike traditional wallpapers that are made of polymers, smart wallpaper is made of Hydroxyapatite, which is not very flammable.
      1. Hydroxyapatite is the mineral found in bones and teeth.
      2. According to Lisa Zyga, a writer with Phys.org, hydroxyapatite is typically not flexible; however, scientists found that hydroxyapatite is flexible when in nanowire form.
         a. According to Alexandra Taylor of Science News for Students, nanowires are about 10 nanometers wide.
            i. A nanometer is a unit of measurement equal to one billionth of a meter.
            ii. According to the National Nanotechnology Initiative, a human hair measures approximately 80,000 to 100,000 nanometers wide.
            iii. And a nanometer is the length your fingernail approximately grows in one second (National Nanotechnology Initiative).
      3. Materials composed of hydroxyapatite ignite and burn at different temperatures; however, the minimum temperature to ignite and burn materials composed of hydroxyapatite is much greater than the temperature needed to ignite and burn traditional wallpaper.
         a. It is well known that cellulose paper can ignite and burn at a temperature of approximately 451 degrees Fahrenheit.
            i. The dystopian novel turned popular movie about government book burning by Ray Bradbury, Fahrenheit 451, made this well known.
         b. Synthetic polymers ignite and burn at various temperatures and rates, but according to Tony Cafe, a fire scene forensic investigator, synthetic polymer ignition temperatures can range from 500 degrees Fahrenheit to 1058 degrees Fahrenheit.

c. In comparison, according to the article, "Plastics and Polymers: What Firefighters Need to Know," Kevlar, a form of nylon used to make protective gear for firefighters because it resists puncture and can withstand high heat, will start to melt in temperatures of 950 degrees Fahrenheit.

   d. And according to the National Funeral Directors Association, "the optimum temperature range is 1400 degrees Fahrenheit to 1800 degrees Fahrenheit" for a cremation chamber" (qtd in Barnett).

      i. Since human bone is mostly made up of hydroxyapatite, the material used in the making of smart wallpaper, similar high temperatures would be required for smart wall paper to ignite and burn.

   e. When the developers of smart wallpaper tested their product's heat resistance, they recorded tests where commercial wall paper made of plant cellulose burned completely through when exposed directly to an open flame in less than 10 seconds, and the smart wallpaper only sustained minor discoloration after a full minute of exposure to the same direct flame as the commercial wallpaper (Chen et al.).

  4. Unlike some traditional wallpapers that require potentially dangerous chemicals to be labeled flame retardant, the hydroxyapatite in smart wallpaper is nontoxic.

B. Smart wallpaper has a built-in fire alarm.

  1. According to Laurie L. Dove, a writer for How Stuff Works, after the nanowires are woven together and put into a papermaking machine, a special ink made of graphene oxide and water is printed on the backside of the wallpaper.

     a. Graphene oxide is made by oxidizing graphite, which is chemically combining graphite and oxygen.

     b. At room temperature, graphene oxide is in an electrically insulated state, meaning it does not allow the flow of electricity.

     c. According to Chen et al., when exposed to high temperatures, "the oxygen containing" groups are quickly removed within the graphene oxide, which then switches from an electrically insulated state to an electrically conductive state, meaning electricity flows freely.

  2. The graphene oxide ink printed on the back of the smart wallpaper works as a sensor.

a. The sensor will become electrically conductive at a temperature of 264 degrees Fahrenheit according to Chen et al.
   b. Once electrically conductive, the sensor activates a fire-alert light and sounds an alarm.
3. According to Zyga, an initial problem with early tests of the smart wallpaper was the sensor would only sound the alarm for about three seconds before burning out.
   a. To fix this problem, the researchers modified the graphene oxide with polydopamine (Zyga).
      i. Polydopamine is the oxidation (remember it's the combining of a substance with oxygen) of dopamine, which is a chemical found in the brain and is a neurotransmitter or a messenger service between brain cells.
      ii. According to Zyga, the polydopamine and graphene oxide mixture "has a much lower thermal responsive temperature than graphene oxide by itself, meaning that it not only responds to fire more quickly (in about two seconds), but also has a prolonged alarm time of more than five minutes."
      iii. In comparison, a study conducted in 2005 of two-story home smoke detectors by the National Institute of Standards and Technology found the home smoke detectors tested ranged in activation times of 78 seconds to 184 seconds.
4. The final step in producing a smart-wallpapered home that can alert its occupants to vacate a fire is the need for hydroxyapatite nanowire mass production.
   a. Professor Ying-Jie Zhu at the Shanghai Institute of Ceramics, Chinese Academy of Science, says his team is currently "striving to explore the low cost and environmentally friendly large-scale production technology for ultra-long hydroxyapatite nanowires" (qtd. in. Zyga).

Conclusion

I. In conclusion, today I spoke to you about the problems of traditional wallpaper in fires and a possible solution: smart wallpaper, which is naturally fire retardant and can quickly alert occupants to vacate a burning building.

II. Smart wallpaper is a life-saving technological breakthrough.

III. Perhaps with the incorporation of smart wallpaper in new buildings, those who believe they would have more than five minutes to exit a burning building would in fact be correct.

Works Cited

Cafe, Tony. "Physical Constants for Investigators." *T.C. Forensic,* 17 Jun. 2007, www.tcforensic.com.au/docs article10.html. Accessed 20 Aug. 2018.

Chen, Fei-Fei, et al. "Fire Alarm Wallpaper Based on Fire-Resistant Hydroxyapatite Nanowire

Inorganic Paper and Graphene Oxide Thermosensitive Sensor." *ACS Nano,* vol. 12, no. 4, 2018, pp. 3159-3171.

"Flame Retardants." *National Institute of Environmental Health Sciences,* www.niehs.nih.gov/health/topics/agents/flame_retardants/index.cfm. Accessed 20 Aug. 2018.

National Institute of Standards and Technology. "NIST Report of Test FR 4017." *US Department of Commerce,* Feb. 2005, www.nist.gov/el/nist-report-test-fr-4017. Accessed 20 Aug. 2018.

National Nanotechnology Initiative. "Size of a Nanoscale." *Nano.gov,* nano.gov/nanotech-101/what/nano-size. Assessed 21 Jul. 2018.

"New Red Cross Survey Shows Many Americans Overconfident and Underprepared for Home Fires." *American Red Cross,* 3 Apr. 2018, www.redcross.org/about-us/news-andevents/press-release New-Red-Cross-Survey-Shows-Many-Americans-Overconfidentand-Underprepared-for-Home-Fires html. Accessed 19 Aug. 2018.

"Plastics and Polymers: What Firefighters Need to Know," *Firehouse,* 28 Feb. 1999, www.firehouse.com/rescue/article/10544313/plastics-polymerization-what-firefightersneed-to-know. Accessed 20 Aug. 2018.

Quark Twain. "Recyclable Solar Cells: Green Energy Goes Green." *Physics Central*: Physics Buzz Blog, 27 Mar. 2013, physicscentral.com/buzz/blog/index.cfm?postid=20065197 61506511391. Accessed 21 Jul. 2018.

Rossen, Jeff and Josh Davis. "Newer Homes and Furniture Burn Faster, Giving You Less Time to Escape a Fire." Today. NBC Universal, 14 Jan. 2016. www.today.com/video/why-youhave-less-time to-escape-a-house-fire-today-than-30-years-ago-601680451516?v=railb. Accessed 19 Aug. 2018.

"Sound the Alarm. Save a Life." American Red Cross, 2018, https://www.redcross.org/soundthe-alarm.html

Taylor, Alexandra. "Hard-to-burn 'Smart' Wallpaper Even Triggers Alarm." Science News for Students, 9 May 2018, www.sciencenewsforstudents.org/article/hard-burn-smartwallpaper-even-triggers-alarms. Accessed 20 Aug. 2018.

Zyga, Lisa. "Fire Alarm Wallpaper Detects, Resists, and Warns of House Fires." Phys.org, 29 Mar. 2018, phys.org/news/2018-03-alarm-wallpaper-resists-house.html. Accessed 20 Aug. 2018.

Sample Outline – Concept – APA Format

Topic: Feminism

Specific Purpose: To inform the audience about a few types of feminism.

Central Idea: While the concept of feminism is commonly referred to as one specific entity, there are actually many different types that encompass different aspects of theory, movements, and activism.

Introduction

I. Beyoncé. Gloria Steinem. President Barack Obama. Malala. What do all of these people have in common? They identify as feminists.

II. As a consumer of feminist media, as well as someone who uses the moniker myself, this is a subject I am both passionate about but also feel is saddled with societal misconceptions.

III. You may not consider yourself a feminist but the general understanding of the term feminism is simply advocating for equality between men gand women.

IV. While that definition is clear and concise, the concept of feminism is not a monolithic entity. In fact, it can be understood through many different lenses and is often described as occurring in separate waves. For this speech we are going to look at what encompasses three specific types, the first of which is liberal feminism.

Body

I. Usually considered the most mainstream and prominent version of this ideology, liberal feminism is often identified with the first wave and women's suffrage but also encompasses many parts of the women's liberation movements of the 1960's and 1970's (Tong, 2009).

A. In this strand, equality for women is gained through political and legal reform because it is believed that women's subordination within society is tied to systemic restraints (Tong, 2009).

   1. An example of this is the fight for the right to vote.
      a. Liberal feminists say that women were looked at as inferior within the political sphere because they held no power in it. Once they earned the Right to vote in 1920 through the 19th Amendment, then, legally women held more political power.
         i. Women associated with the suffragist movement include Susan B. Anthony, Elizabeth Cady Stanton and Alice Paul.

ii. Although, women earned the right to vote, the political power liberal feminists imagined would appear did not, in part because of barriers at the polls. Literacy tests and poll taxes hampered women's attempts to vote (Corder & Wolbrecht, 2016).

B. Other policies that liberal feminists champion include equal pay for equal work, abortion rights, access to birth control, increased education, as well as fighting against sexual harassment, assault, and domestic violence (Tong, 2009).

C. The seminal literary works often associated with this type of ideology include The Second Sex by Simone de Beauvoir and The Feminine Mystique by Betty Friedan.

1. de Beauvoir's book was published in 1949 and considered by many to be the impetus for the second wave of feminism, while others have suggested it first determined the distinction between sex and gender (Butler, 1986)

2. Friedan built upon de Beauvoir's work in her 1963 book, The Feminine Mystique, in which she challenges the idea that women only find fulfilment as wives and mothers. This notion became the basis for the Women's Movement of the 1960's and 70's.

D. Perhaps the largest defeat the supporters of ideology faced is the failure to ratify the federal Equal Rights Amendment (ERA) - a piece of legislation stating, "Equality of rights under the law shall not be denied or abridged by the United States or by any State on account of sex." (Davis, 1999).

1. First proposed in 1920, it was passed with widespread - and bipartisan support - in 1972; however, it never received ratification from the required ¾ state legislatures (Davis 1999; Harrison, 1988).

E. A common critique of this type of feminism is that it focuses too much on the individual and not the group, as well as that it centers upon white, heterosexual, middle-class, cisgender women.

1. bell hooks (2000) argues that it has too strong a focus on equality within one's own class and does not consider group oppression, while also positing that the intricacies of race and class should be included within feminism.

2. Further, hooks (2000) argues for the inclusion of "men's liberation" within feminism by stating that men are harmed by traditional gender roles.

Transition: The next type of feminism we will discuss is one in complete opposition in both tenor and approach to liberal feminism.

II. While liberal feminism tends to work within existing legal structures, systems, and institutions, radical feminism stresses the complete reordering of society in order to eliminate male superiority and women's place as the other (Tong 2009; Willis, 1984; Atkinson, 1969)

   A. Think of it like the Founding Fathers when creating the framework for the United States of America. Instead of working within the system they were accustomed to, like making their own monarchy, they created their own system of government – a democratic republic.

   B. Radical feminists, then, believe in the eradication societal norms - especially ones that they feel oppress women – as well as the systems and institutions that thrive within them.

   1. An area of focus is the destruction of the patriarchy, a term Walby (1990) defines as "a system of social structures and practices in which men dominate, oppress, and exploit women."

   2. How does one accomplish this? Radical feminists believe that abolishing the sexual objectification of women, challenging traditional gender roles, and increasing the public's knowledge regarding violence against women is key in the fight against patriarchal systems and institutions.

   3. An example of this is outlined in Firestone's (1970) work, where she discusses cultural distinctions between men and women as having no power. For instance, if society no longer thought of women as the primary caregivers and men as the primary breadwinners, or if various jobs, clothing, or colors were no longer gendered.

   C. This ideology coincided with liberal feminism and therefore, was often at odds with the larger second wave movement.

   D. Some of the most prominent thinking within radical feminism deals with the sex industry, including pornography and prostitution.

   E. Catharine MacKinnon and Andrea Dworkin are the most famous radical feminists to argue against prostitution and pornography, asserting that both are inherently bad for women and are the result of a patriarchal society (MacKinnon, 1989; Dworkin and MacKinnon, 1985; Dworkin, 1981).

   1. *Sexual politics* by Kate Millet is a seminal work of this ideology, in which Millet examines the role patriarchy plays in sex.

   2. Criticisms to this form are similar to those lobbied against liberal feminism

– that it is not intersectional enough - it does not focus enough on race or class. Over the years, there has also been a split within the ideology whether or not to include transgender individuals.

Transition: While there are many other forms of feminism, including Marxist, socialist, and postmodern, one of the most influential theories that is still widely used today is black feminism)

III. At the center of black feminism is the notion that sex, gender, class, and race are bound together in ways that make them almost indistinguishable from one another.

   A. Crenshaw (1989) describes this as the theory of intersectionality.

      1. In her work, Crenshaw says that you cannot understand the experience of the black woman by looking at her as just black or just as a woman. Rather, she argues you can understand both identities as well as how those two identities interact with one another, reiterating and building upon one another.

      2. Due in large part to Crenshaw's significant work, many identify as intersectional feminists.

   B. Black feminists (as well as those who identify as intersectional feminists) posit that the experience of a black woman is drastically different than that of a white woman, due to the position of power - or lack of power - where she is placed in society's hierarchy.

      1. In this model, white women hold the most power in all realms of the public sphere, including education, business, politics, entertainment, law, medicine, etc.

      2. A few more tangible examples of this would be strangers deciding to touch a black woman's hair without asking first because of how the braids look, how their name at the top of a resume may make it less likely for them to get called back for an interview, and how the color of their skin may make an individual think they are less successful than their white counterpart.

   C. Prominent figures who furthered ideas within black feminism or greatly impacted it include Sojourner Truth, Ida B. Wells, Angela Davis, Alice Walker, Patricia Hill Collins, and Audre Lorde.

D. Collins' book, Black Feminist Thought, published in 1990, is largely considered one of the influential works in the discipline for her wide-ranging discussions of a variety of concepts, including the matrix of oppression, controlling images, and outsider-within.

E. Although it may seem like a new concept, the ideas behind black feminism have been around for almost two centuries, dating back to slavery, and are still prominent today, with many now understanding the need for - and importance of - its key terms, especially intersectionality.

Conclusion

I. In closing, I hope you are now better versed in the concept of feminism.

II. Today we discussed three types: liberal, radical, and black, all of which still resonate today, whether in Black Lives Matter, the #MeToo movement, or the Ask Her More Campaign. There are many other ways feminism impacts your daily life, too, whether through the media you consume, the friendships you have, or the academic research you do.

III. What type of feminist are you?

References

Atkinson, T. (1969). Radical feminism *The Feminists.*

Butler, J. (1986). Sex and gender in Simone de Beauvoir's second sex." *Yale French Studies*, No. 72, pp. 35–49.

Collins, P. H. (1990). *Black feminist thought: Knowledge, consciousness and the politics of empowerment.* Boston, MA: Unwin Hyman.

Corder, J. K., &Wolbrecht, C (2016). Counting women's ballots: Female voters from suffrage through the New Deal. Cambridge, England: Cambridge University Press.

Crenshaw, K. (1989). Demarginalizing the intersection of race and sex: A black feminist critique of antidiscrimination doctrine, feminist theory and antiracist politics. *The University of Chicago Legal Forum.* 140: 139–167.

Davis, F. (1999). *Moving the mountain*: The women's movement in America since 1960. Urbana and Chicago: University of Illinois Press.

Dworkin, A., & MacKinnon, C. A. (1988). *Pornography and civil rights:* A new day for women's equality. New York: Organizing Against Pornography.

Dworkin, A. (1981). *Pornography: Men possessing women.* London: Women's Press.

Evans, S. M. (2003). *Tidal wave: How women changed America at century's end.* New York, NY: The Free Press.

Firestone, S. (1970). *The dialectic of sex:* The case for feminist revolution. New York, NY: William Morrow and Company.

Harrison, C. (1988). *On account of sex: The politics of women's issues*, 1945-1968. Berkeley, Los Angeles and London: University of California Press.

Hooks, B. (2000). *Feminism is for everybody: Passionate politics*. Cambridge, MA:South End Press.

MacKinnon, C. A. (1989). T*oward a feminist theory of the state.* Cambridge, MA: Harvard University Press.

Tong, R. (2009). *Feminist thought.* Third edition. Boulder, CO: Westview Press.

Walby, S. (1990). *Theorizing patriarchy.* Cambridge, MA: Basil Blackwell.

Willis, E. (1984). Radical feminism and feminist radicalism. *Social Text.* 9/10: The 60's without Apology: 91–118.

Sample Outline – Process – MLA format

Topic: Chocolate

Specific Purpose: To inform the audience about the process of making chocolate.

Central Idea: There are many steps involved in the process of making chocolate and each step needs to be followed carefully to produce the sweet treat that many people enjoy worldwide.

Introduction

I. Hot chocolate. Chocolate bar. Chocolate fondue. Chocolate ice cream. Chocolate pudding. Chocolate mousse. And my all-time favorite… chocolate chip cookies fresh out of the oven with their ooey gooey chocolate chips just melting in your mouth.

II. These are just some of the ways that I, along with the rest of the world enjoy chocolate. For most of us, chocolate comes from the grocery store or as a dessert at a restaurant. Yet, very few of us have the opportunity to learn about the process of chocolate actually being made.

III. When tasked with looking into a process, I pondered a few ideas. How is something recycled? No. Solar Power and how it really energizes. Nah. How to make Make-Up. Maybe. Who am I kidding? Let's go with MY all-time favorite food. Chocolate! Let's look at the process of making chocolate from the bean to the bar.

Body

I. It all begins with a bean. But where does one get this bean? And what is this bean called? The bean comes from the cacao tree which is found in over 50 tropical countries according to the Equal Exchange Company, which specializes in chocolate, tea and coffee ("Building a Vibrant Community").

   A. The site also shares that there are approximately 2 million producers of the cacao bean and the majority of the farms have less than 12 acres where they grow the trees that give us the beginning stage ingredient of chocolate ("Building a Vibrant Community").

   B. A program from the United Kingdom's Discovery UKTV channel's informational video "The Whole Process of Making Chocolate", explains further how the cacao tree is planted and grows to produce the beans. Farmers plant a tiny seed in coarse damp soil bags. The seeds sprout shortly after planting.

1. Within four weeks, the sprout grows to about a foot high. It will take about three years before the tree produces any viable seeds.
2. The tree can grow to 30 feet, but farmers will often prune them to make the harvesting more manageable according to the same article from Equal Exchange's website ("Building a Vibrant Community").
3. The tree grows many flowers all over the branches and trunk but only a small percentage develops a cacao pod.
   a. The pod is essentially the fruit from the tree.
   b. It resembles a football in shape and size.
   c. It will be ready to pick after about 6 months of flowering.
   d. Insects are a danger to the pods; however, some growers will wra the pods in a plastic sleeve according to the Discovery UK video.
   e. Within the pod, there are between 30 and 50 beans.
   i. Those beans will be processed into either cocoa powder or chocolate.

C. Now that the pods have matured, they need to be taken from the trees for the next step which is harvesting.
  1. Each pod is carefully cut from the cacao tree by hand.
     a. The harvesters must be sure that they do not damage the stalk so that the spot can bear fruit again the following year.
  2. Ecole Chocolat, an online professional Chocolate school, describes on their website, "The pods are carefully broken open to release the cacao beans, which are embedded in a moist, fibrous, white pulp" ("Lesson – How Chocolate is Made").
     a. The pod is cracked open and the beans and pulp are put into a box with a lid.
        i. This process is done by hand.
        ii. The bean itself is hard and not sweet.

D. Once the beans are harvested and, in the box, it is time for fermentation.
  1. Andy George of the YouTube series, How to Make Everything, says "In the container, microorganisms grow and begin the fermenting process. Yeast turn the cacao sugars into alcohol and other bacteria's produce lactic acid and acidic acid. Together these all help produce a distinct chocolate flavor in the cacao beans."

2. He goes on to say that during the fermenting process, the beans will change color and begin to smell (George).
   a. One of the keys is that the beans will begin to smell like alcohol.
   b. As they finish fermenting, the pulp around the bean dissolves and that gets drained off through openings in the container.
   c. The temperature in the box of beans is also key to stop the beans from germinating or sprouting. It can rise up to 120 C to 140 C degrees.
   d. Depending on the type of cacao tree, the fermenting process can take anywhere from five to eight days.
E. Now that the fermentation has taken place, it is time to dry out the cocoa beans. This must happen before they can be stored or sent on to the next step.
   1. The typical drying process is simply laying the beans out to dry naturally in the sun.
      a. If the area has daily rainfall, which is common in the tropics, they can be dried in sheds.
         i. A key to successful drying in sheds, according to Ecole Chocolat, is keeping air circulating throughout ("Lesson – How Chocolate is Made").
   2. Another step is to continually rake the beans in order to have an even drying process.
   1. Equal Exchange mentions on their website that the drying process takes up to a week but it is a delicate process ("Building a Vibrant Community").
      a. Drying too long causes beans to become brittle and not drying long enough can create a moldy bean. When dried, the cacao bean can be stored for four to five years.

Transition: Now that we've discussed the bean, let's move on.
II. The next step finds the beans leaving their farm and moving to a facility to go through the next process of roasting, winnowing, grinding and conching.
   A. The beans go through a cleaning process, and after cleaning and removal of any beans that have been compromised by insects or mold, they go into the roaster.
      1. The length of time and temperature will vary depending on the bean and the environment.

2. The roasting will darken the color and bring out more flavor of the cacao.
3. During the roasting process, the shell of the bean will separate out from the kernel and is removed.
   a. They call this cracking or fanning according to Ecole Chocolat ("Lesson– How Chocolate is Made").
4. The beans pass through serrated cones which cracks them, and they become cocoa nibs.

B. Winnowing is the next step. The Merriam-Webster Dictionary defines the word "winnow" with "to remove something by a current of air. In the case of the cacao, exposing the bean to an air current will allow the shells to be separated from the bean.
   1. The nibs are about 50% cocoa butter depending on the species of the cacao.

C. The nibs now go through the grinding process.
   1. They will be put through a grinding machine which liquefies the cocoa butter and it becomes chocolate liquor.
      a. While it is called liquor, there is zero alcohol in it.
      b. This can be used in the production of chocolate bars or it can be refined more to separate the fat also known as cocoa butter, from the cocoa solid.
      c. Equal Exchange's article tells us that the cocoa butter is used in chocolate bars as well and also, beauty products ("Building a Vibrant Community").
   2. Cocoa presscake is what is left behind.
      a. The presscake will be milled into a powder, and that powder will be used for baking cocoa and hot cocoa.
   3. Let's take a look at the refining process a little more in depth.
      a. The roll refiner or a ball mill is usually used.
      b. There are two functions to these: the first is to reduce the particle size of the cocoa mass even further and second, to create an even distribution of cocoa butter throughout the mass thus coating all the particles.
      c. Ecole Chocolat describes the rolling process as one that will create heat that will melt and distribute the cocoa butter ("Lesson – How Chocolate is Made").
      d. The manufacturers of the chocolate will also determine the particle size of each chocolate, and this will help to develop a smooth and creamy feel.

i. As an example, Equal Exchange chocolate refine the particles so small that the human tongue cannot feel them; this gives the chocolate the smooth texture ("Building a Vibrant Community").
   e. Manufactures will also add or remove cocoa butter to the chocolate liquor.
   f. The flavor of chocolate is carried in the cocoa butter and will produce what Ecole Chocolat describes as a cooling effect on your tongue that is noticeable when eating dark chocolate ("Lesson – How Chocolate is Made").
   g. Other ingredients such as milk, lecithin, sugar and many others including spices like vanilla.
   h. The individual formulas create the unique taste of different chocolate varieties.
D. The next step is called conching.
   1. This is where the finished products of the chocolate truly begin.
   2. It is, however, important to know that manufacturers can take the refining and conching steps and complete them all at once with machinery.
   3. We will visit that idea in a bit but let's go back to conching.
   4. The Grenada Chocolate Company describes this on their website: "Conching is a long process of intense mixing, agitating, and aerating of heated liquid chocolate. During this long process various off-flavored, bitter substances as well as water vapor evaporate away from the chocolate. The long intense mixing action assures complete coating of every solid particle with cocoa butter, giving the chocolate a well-developed and delicious flavor and texture" ("Refining and Conching").
      a. Grenada uses a machine which allows both processes to take place at once.

Transition: Now that we've discussed the roasting, winnowing, grinding and conching, let's move on to the final steps.

III. The last part of this process is tempering and molding.
   A. The chocolate now is "tempered" by slowly and deliberately lowering the temperature.
      1. It will be cooled, then warmed, then cooled further and then warmed again.

2. It will continue the process until it gets to the desired temperature.
   3. This will create even crystallization throughout the chocolate.
   4. One of the outcomes should be a smooth texture and the chocolate should snap when broken in two.
      a. Weis Market bakery manager, Courtney McCafferty, shares her insight on chocolate: "Chocolate is very sensitive. You have to melt it a certain way, to a certain temperature, so that when it is hardened, it's shiny and has a snap to it. The temperature or humidity in the room can affect it as well. It can also burn very easily."
   5. Additional ingredients such as sea salt or nuts can be added to the chocolate at this point.
B. The chocolate is now poured into the appropriate mold, usually to form the shape of a chocolate bar.
   1. It will cool until it solidifies.
   2. After removing it from the mold, it will be cooled and wrapped.
      a. The wrapper will keep the chocolate fresh for up to 24 months.
   3. The bars are then wrapped in an outer wrapper and shipped to stores to be purchased and enjoyed.

Conclusion

I. And there you have it; chocolate from the bean to the bar. As you have heard, there are many steps and it is imperative to complete each one with care. From the farmer to the manufacturer to the retailer, they all take their jobs very seriously and go to great lengths for the public to enjoy this divine treat.

II. So whether you prefer your chocolate in a bar or in a drink, from Hershey's or from Godiva, just know the next time that you sink your teeth into a delicious piece of chocolate, great care has been taken so that you enjoy every last bite.

Works Cited

"Building a Vibrant Community." *Equal Exchange:* Fairly Traded, equalexchange.coop/.

Discovery UK. "The Whole Process of Making Chocolate | How Do They Do It?" *YouTube*, 23 Mar. 2018, www.youtube.com/watch?v=P_JuQCiKWUc.

George, Andy. "Fermenting & Roasting | How to Make Everything: Chocolate Bar." *YouTube*, 11 Feb. 2016, www.youtube.com/watch?v=mUJ0heMcE-g.

"Lesson – How Chocolate is Made." *Ecole chocolate*, www.ecolechocolat.com/en/howchocolate-is-made.html

McCafferty, Courtney. Personal interview. 2 Feb. 2019.

"Refining and Conching." *The Grenada Chocolate Company*, 30 Aug. 2015, www.grenadachocolate.com/tour/refining-and-conching/.

"Winnow." *Merriam-Webster*, www.merriamwebster.com/dictionary/winnow.

Evan Rachel Wood
2017 – Human Rights Campaign

2017 HRC North Carolina Gala

https://www.youtube.com/watch?v=6xLYTun4KaU

'I write for those women who do not speak, for those who do not have a voice because they were so terrified because we are taught to respect fear more than ourselves. We've been taught that silence would save us, but it won't.

13 | TECHNICAL SPEAKING

Persuasion is the double-edged sword of public speaking.

Persuasion is the double-edged sword of public speaking; it can bring together the very best in effective communication, and it can demonstrate the very worst.

At its best, excellent persuasive speaking can move audiences and speakers toward the highest ideals and efforts of human ability. At its worst, persuasive speaking can twist and manipulate ideas and push us toward evil actions. Persuasive speech is intended to influence the audience toward the speaker's desired response. In some situations, that response is an action by the audience. In others, that response is acceptance of an idea or a change in attitudes toward a given subject. It is sometimes claimed that all communication is persuasive, because all communication seeks to influence the audience in some way.

There is some truth in that perspective, but here we will focus on persuasion that is explicitly intended to move an audience to mental or physical change desired by the speaker.

Persuasive Speaking

Dr. Matthew Jones
County College of Morris

In a persuasive speech, the ***central idea*** is always a ***proposition,*** which can be defined as the ***statement of an idea that may be accepted or rejected by an audience and is potentially subject to debate.*** Moreover, a persuasive speech is intended to try to move the opinion of the audience in some direction along the spectrum of agreement or opposition. Therefore, we may define the general purpose of a persuasive speech as to **convince or reinforce** a proposition in the mind of the audience.

Ethos/Pathos/Logos/Mythos

In addition to presenting perhaps the oldest model of communication, Aristotle was also the first to closely analyze the art of persuasion *(rhetoric)* by dividing it into three qualities: ***ethos, pathos, and logos.*** Ancient as these principles are, they still describe the three major variables that contribute to or detract from the effectiveness of a persuasive appeal.

Ethos

Ethos refers to spirit or character. A large part of the persuasive effectiveness of a message comes from the person who is presenting it. To test this idea, think about how you would respond to surprising information shared by a close friend whom you trust versus an acquaintance with a hidden agenda who has lied to you in the past. The very same words would likely be treated seriously in the first case and with great skepticism in the second. We know, therefore, that the reputation of the communicator plays an important role in the persuasive effectiveness of the message.

Credibility

Credibility refers to the trust an audience places in the speaker, and it plays an important role in developing the sort of character audiences find persuasive. In practice, credibility is an evolving mixture of reputation and performance: what you've done in the past and what you're doing now. Every performance is simultaneously a risk and opportunity to one's reputation. Some theorists, therefore, divide credibility into three categories: *initial* (reputation), *derived* (earned during the performance), and *terminal* (the final impression of the speaker).

So what makes you trust a speaker? There are seven primary qualities that enhance credibility: sameness, reputation, personal stakes, empathy, knowledge, intelligence, and personal experience.

Characteristics

- **Sameness:** For many reasons people tend to place more credibility in those who are similar to themselves. Noted communication theorist Wilbur Schramm also pointed out that we can only communicate to the extent that we share similar *fields of experience.*
- **Reputation:** As referenced above, reputation is a critical factor in establishing credibility, but it's not just about performance. Collective evaluation also plays an important role in shaping reputation. In other words, it's not just your performance, but how the audience collectively interprets and evaluates your performance that counts. Thus, it's especially important to consider the audience when crafting a persuasive speech.
- **Personal Stakes:** What do you have to gain or lose with the success or failure of your persuasive appeal? The more clearly and obviously your personal stakes overlap with the collective stakes of your audience, the better your credibility will be. Think about how you would feel, for instance, if a stranger gave you a gift. You might be grateful, but also skeptical about what they expect in return or could potentially gain from it.
- **Empathy:** The ability to relate emotionally to your audience is important to establishing trust and credibility. Do you care about the things they care about? If you do, they will put their faith in you and your credibility will increase.

- **Knowledge:** Your awareness of the facts related to your persuasive appeal increase credibility. If it becomes apparent that you lack important knowledge of information associated with your topic, audiences will have reason to doubt you. For example, someone giving a speech about the history of the alphabet would lose all credibility if they attributed the first alphabet to a language like English or Russian. This is why it's important to choose a topic that you are interested in and willing to study carefully.
- **Intelligence:** Intelligence refers to the ability to manipulate knowledge to achieve specific outcomes. Without intelligence, knowledge is meaningless and without knowledge, intelligence is vacuous. The audience will judge your intelligence on many factors, but foremost among them are the way you use language, your logic and reasoning, and your conclusions.
- **Personal Experience:** As discussed in the chapter on informative speech, science has changed how we have come to know the world; increasingly, we use specialized methods to overcome the natural limitations of personal knowledge. However, we still place great importance on individual personal experience, and for good reason. Personal experience is the intimate testing ground for all theory. If something lacks the resonance of truth in our own experience (or in someone else's) we're less likely to buy into the persuasive message.

Pathos

Pathos refers to the use of emotional appeals in persuasion. Even when logic, reasoning, evidence, and research are lacking, audiences may be moved by a speaker's passion. A ***demagogue***, for example, is a speaker who makes use of emotion, prejudice, and fear to persuade an audience. Other examples of emotional appeals are appeals to compassion such as the case of abused animals or children with leukemia, appeals to anger towards oppressive forces in society, or appeals to guilt about not being environmentally conscious. To some extent, pathos is also dependent upon ethos. For an audience to be persuaded by a speaker's emotional appeals, they must on some level trust in the character of that speaker.

How are emotions manipulated through speech? Topic choice, verbal cues, nonverbal cues, and presentation aids can all play a role in the manipulation of emotion in a speech.

Topic Choice
Some topics lend themselves particularly well to emotional manipulation, while others do not. For example, the time-worn debate over abortion is so predisposed to emotional appeals that even when speakers attempt to approach it objectively the results are often clouded by pathos. Other topics like recycling are relatively less controversial on the surface, but they can lend themselves to the use of emotion in the right context. Generally speaking, when you approach your topic from the perspective of ***values*** (deeply held personal judgments about right and wrong), pathos has a much greater chance of coming into play. ***Attitudes*** (liking or disliking) and ***beliefs*** (truth or falsehood) tend to be less volatile when challenged, though they can still provoke strong emotions to the extent that they support value systems.

Verbal Cues
We have a visceral reaction to some words based on their repeated use in prior contexts; therefore, it's possible to touch on an audience's emotions simply through language. Consider the differences between words like "ecstatic" vs. "glad" to describe happiness, "dejected" vs. "glum" to describe sadness, "terrified" vs. "anxious" to describe fear, and "tortured" vs. "hurt" to describe pain. In each of these pairs, the first word has more emotional impact than the second. Another example of creating or reframing words to create an emotional response would be referring to a "dog breeding operation" as a "puppy mill".

Nonverbal Cues

Delivery is a holistic concept, and therefore all aspects of nonverbal communication play a role in emotional persuasion. But there are still several key features that stand out: facial expressions, eye contact, and paralanguage.

- *Facial Expressions:* Beneath the skin of our face, a layer of delicate interconnected muscles conveys happiness, sadness, pain, anxiety, anger, surprise, and a host of other more subtle emotions. Even when we don't want to show our emotions, they often betray us through facial expressions. In psychology, "emotional contagion theory" even suggests that looking at a face with a particular emotion on display transmits that emotion to the viewer. In other words, looking at happy faces makes us happy, and looking at sad faces makes us sad.
- *Eye Contact:* Looking at audiences directly and (in most cases) providing sustained, individualized eye-contact is vital to emotional persuasion. As noted above, pathos is somewhat dependent upon ethos, and we tend not to trust other people and their emotional appeals when they don't look at us in the eyes.
- *Paralanguage:* In addition to being your primary means of communication in public speech, the voice is also a very sensitive conductor of emotion. Every subtlety of our present emotional state is broadcast through the voice. Absence of emotion in the voice is referred to as being monotone and that is to be avoided. The emotional tone of your voice should mirror the content of your speech and remain consistent throughout. For example, tragedy should be treated with a somber tone.

Nonverbal Consistency Theory suggests that trust and credibility will be vastly diminished if nonverbal cues don't match the verbal message. For example, smiling and having an upbeat tone of voice when reporting bad news would be greeted with obvious skepticism.

Logos

Logos refers to the use of logic to persuade an audience and stands in direct opposition to "common sense." Though usually defined as "good judgment," common sense is actually nothing more than a combination of hearsay (unsubstantiated information) and popular opinion and is used primarily for reasons related to political ideology. For example, "It's common sense that we need to lower taxes right now!" or "We need a 'common sense' approach to immigration reform!" Whereas common sense implies that no further explanation is necessary, logic demands a formal description of the thought process employed to come to specific conclusions. In other words, ***logic*** is a system of reasoning based on the internally consistent application of rules. The most fundamental distinction in logic exists between inductive reasoning and deductive reasoning.

Deduction

Deductive Logic: When we apply general rules to specific instances, we use deductive logic. The principles of deductive logic are demonstrated in a structure of the syllogism (a logical statement where a conclusion is drawn based on two premises that share a common term).

Premise 1: Jim's favorite carbonated beverage contains 300 calories per serving.

Premise 2: On average, Jim drinks 3 servings of his favorite carbonated beverage per day.

Conclusion: Therefore, if Jim were to substitute a non-caloric drink like water for each serving of his favorite carbonated beverage, he can eliminate, on average, 900 calories from his daily diet.

Induction

Inductive Logic: When we come to a general rule of understanding based on a collection of specific instances, we are using inductive logic.

Premise 1: 50 individuals took a new diet pill once a day for a 2-week trial.

Premise 2: During the two weeks, 38 out of the 50 individuals taking the diet pills reported having nausea and other gastro-intestinal ailments that they did not suffer before or after the trial.

Conclusion: Therefore, the new diet pills should not be approved by the FDA because they will likely result in stomach and/or gastro-intestinal discomfort.

Mythos

The appeal to mythos is often overlooked by both instructors and speakers, but it can be a powerful addition to a speech. Aristotle explained logos, ethos, and pathos in *The Rhetoric*, but left mythos to his book on *Poetics*. Mythos is the use of narratives tied to cultural understanding as persuasion; in simpler terms, it's using stories or fragments of stories to persuade. For example, Oprah Winfrey's or Steve Job's stories, as they are so deeply tied to our broader American narrative of "individual achievement through hard work," could add persuasive power to a number of topics. Think about a speech encouraging young women or children of immigrants to pursue high goals that used short stories from the lives of Jobs or Winfrey. A more classic example of a speaker using mythos is John F. Kennedy's speech at Rice University in 1962. Kennedy set the goal of putting an American on the moon by the end of the decade - at the time, a goal seen as nearly impossible to achieve.

The famous quote from the speech invokes the American cultural narratives of manifest destiny, exceptionalism, and achievement with these words: "We choose to go to the moon in this decade and do the other things, not because they are easy, but because they are hard, because that goal will serve to organize and measure the best of our energies and skills, because that challenge is one that we are willing to accept, one we are unwilling to postpone, and one which we intend to win." Mythos is powerful because it links in narrative (story) form something deeply familiar to something new. A powerful short story, or even an allusion to a strong cultural narrative helps the listener understand and readily accept the new idea as a natural extension of what they already know.

Informal Fallacies

Ad Hominem

This fallacy occurs when an author attacks his opponent instead of his opponent's argument.

Example: Dr. Richard Lindzen at MIT has argued for years that climate science does not support mainstream alarmist views concerning climate change. He urges us not to worry so much. But Lindzen smokes cigarettes. Who can take seriously the views of a "scientist" who smokes cigarettes?

Example: Al Gore argues convincingly for addressing climate change in his film An *Inconvenient Truth* and elsewhere. But I've seen Internet posts alleging that he owns a palatial house where he leaves all the lights on and that he drives gas-guzzling cars. Surely we must dismiss Gore's arguments if these allegations are true.

Ad Populum

Example: Everyone I know thinks it is wrong to require a business owner to provide their service to gay people if being gay is against the business owner's religious beliefs. Therefore, requiring them to do so is wrong.

Example: 90% of people eat meat. Therefore, being a vegetarian is unhealthy.

Appeal to Authority: In this fallacy, the author bases the validity of his argument on the premise that the argument is supported by someone famous or powerful.

Example: My pastor was quite clear in a recent sermon saying that drinking alcohol is physically and morally degrading. Therefore, I believe alcohol consumption is unhealthy and wrong.

Begging the Question

Example: Camouflage is important for soldiers because it is important for them to be outfitted to blend in with the background.

Example: The Bible tells us that God exists. As God's word, the Bible must be true. Therefore, God exists.

Appeal to Emotion
A popular tactic among demagogues and dictators, this fallacy manipulates the emotional states of an audience to support an argument.

Example: Yes your honor. But while I may have taken that money… at gunpoint… you must understand. My reasons were completely compelling. My mother is very sick, and I have hungry mouths at home to feed. I've been trying to find work every day for months. You must appreciate, your honor, how serious my circumstances were.

You are my employee. This is the political position we take at this company. If you would like to take another political position, then perhaps you would like to find another job.

Begging the Question
This occurs when the premise of an argument contains or assumes its conclusion. Another name for this fallacy is "circular reasoning."

Example: Gracie: Gentlemen prefer blondes.
George: How do you know that?

Gracie: A gentleman told me so.
George: How did you know he was a gentleman?
Gracie: Because he preferred blondes.
(George Burns and Gracie Allen, quoted by Ronald J. Waicukauski et al. in "The Winning Argument." American Bar Association, 2001)

False Dichotomy/False Dilemma
A fallacy that relies on the assumption that only two possible solutions exist, so that disproving one solution means the other solution appears to be the only logical conclusion. However, other options exist.

Example: Help our group save the planet by reducing carbon and methane emissions, or else you show that all you care about is consumption and personal satisfaction.

Hasty Generalization

When the proponent uses insufficient evidence to support a sweeping generalization.

Example: Jeff and Lucy couldn't find any cool comics at the comic book store, so the comic book store doesn't have any cool comics.

Post Hoc/False Cause

This fallacy confuses correlation and causation, that is, if one event precedes another event, it is concluded that it must also be the cause of that event. However, it is false that a correlation always indicates a causal relation.

Example: When President XYZ took office, unemployment dropped to historically low rates. Clearly his policies caused the economic improvements that created so many jobs.

Example:
A: "I've had a fever since arriving in England."
B: "You must feel terrible."
A: "Actually no. I feel fine. But I take my temperature everyday a 4 o'clock, and it's clearly elevated."
B: "I say, isn't that just when you are having tea? Wouldn't your mouth be quite warm?"
A: "Hmm. Rather."

Missing the Point

This fallacy occurs when one draws an irrelevant (invalid) conclusion from an argument or other evidence.

Example: Our country is as politically divided as it has ever been. The search for common ground upon which various parties can come together has never been more pressing. Therefore, my party's views should be used as that common ground, since they are the most rational.

Straw Man

The author distorts or misrepresents his opponent's argument because it is easier to dispute than the opponent's true stance.

Example: Darwin argued that humans are descendent from apes. So if that were true, I guess I would still have some ape relatives out in the jungle or in the zoo. But no matter how far I go out or back in my family tree I find no apes. All my relatives were and are humans; therefore, Darwin was wrong.

Example: People who are for gun control want to take away your second amendment.

Red Herring
This is an attempt to distract the audience by straying from the topic at hand through introducing a separate argument the speaker feels is easier to speak to.

Example: We cannot worry about reducing the use of plastic straws and utensils when we have an immigration crisis at our nation's border.

Example: The overall federal debt is of crucial importance to the nation's economic health, and it must be attended to closely. And we've lowered the deficit significantly since I've taken office. This is the kind of fiscal responsibility I campaigned on. Deficit levels are down and will continue to drop.

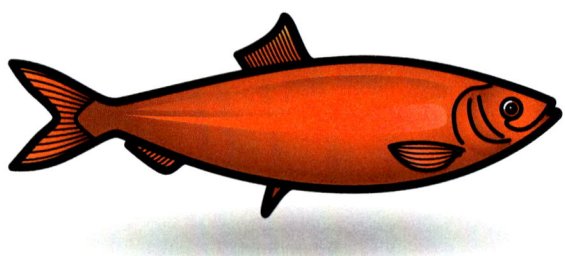

Slippery Slope (the edge of the wedge, camel's nose)
This fallacy is the assertion that a relatively small first step will inevitably lead to a chain reaction of subsequent events culminating in some significant and disastrous impact/event that would inevitably occur. Hence the very first step should not occur.

Example: If we don't build a wall, more immigrants will come in. If more immigrants come in, more crimes will be committed. The inevitable increase in crime means more stealing and murdering until, eventually, our entire way of life is destroyed.

The Appeal to Closure
This fallacy makes the case that an argument, viewpoint, or conclusion must be accepted as final no matter how dubious it is, or else the issue will remain unresolved, which is inconceivable since those involved would be denied "closure".

Example: Look, you see wisdom in how the President is handling Russia and North Korea. But you and I have been going around and around in our discussion, and I still can't agree with anything you say on this matter. Let's agree that we each want the best for our country and go down to dinner.

Types of Persuasive Speech

The structure described above can be molded into several different forms based upon the nature of the persuasive claim (the "type" of persuasive speech) and the method of organization. As with informative speeches, persuasive speeches come in a variety of different types, but based on a proposition rather than a lesson. These include the following:

Proposition of Fact: A statement asserting something about some aspect of reality. A statement such as: "Humans evolved from primates," is a good example of a proposition of fact because it clearly asserts something about an aspect of reality. Keep in mind, however, that propositions of fact must be supported by evidence and are vulnerable to critique based on their premises and conclusions. In this particular example, there are three premises that I will focus on.

Premise #1 is the theory of evolution. If the audience doesn't accept the theory of evolution and the speaker fails to demonstrate it through logic, evidence, and reasoning, the persuasive appeal is unlikely to be accepted. To support this premise, a summary of Darwin's theory along with more recent evidence should be presented.

Premise #2 is the idea that humans are subject to evolution. Even if the audience accepts evolution as a theory, it is still necessary for them to accept that premise that humans are organisms that evolve. Supporting this premise means arguing that humans are a particular species of mammal which lack any distinguishing characteristics suggesting they are exceptions to the theory of evolution.

Premise #3 is the proposition itself: "Humans evolved from primates." This is to say that even if the audience accepts evolution and is open to the idea that humans evolve, there may be disagreement about the origins of human evolution. For this premise, recourse to fossil records and other anthropological or physiological evidence is necessary for support.

Other examples of a *Proposition of Fact* include the following:
a. "Intelligent life exists on other planets."
b. "Greenhouse gasses produced by human industry have resulted in climate change."
c. "Spiritual life persists after the death of the organic body."
Notice that among these examples, truth or falsehood is quite irrelevant. A proposition of fact must be supported with evidence, reasoning, and logic.

Proposition of Value: In line with our previous description of value, this is an ethical statement about good vs. bad characteristics.

"Honesty is the best policy" provides us with a simple example of a proposition of value statement. Unlike the proposition of fact, it's not always possible to argue directly for a value using specific evidence. Instead, the speaker must identify a characteristic that is generally associated with worthwhile or positive outcomes and argue from there. In this case, one could argue for the value of honesty based on its relationship to other positive values and desirable outcomes.

To begin with, other basic human values such as "equality," "justice" or "fairness" imply a need for honesty. Examples of how dishonesty corrupts justice and prevents fairness are plentiful since people generally lie in order to protect or extend their own personal interests at the expense of justice, fair play, and equality.

Less abstractly, dishonesty hinders personal relationships, obscures the truth, and leads to a communication breakdown. That is to say, when people lie about their perceptions, thoughts, and emotions they do so in order to hide information from others or to present false realities that confer personal advantages. In so doing, misunderstanding, mistrust, and animosity tend to develop as a consequence and it is more difficult to understand each other and the world around us.

One may also investigate ethics or moral philosophy as a resource when arguing a proposition of value. For example, German philosopher Immanuel Kant famously argued for honesty as a "categorical imperative," and his reasoning would be useful to any speech concerned with the absolute moral value of honesty.

Specific cases that illustrate the value of honesty through an analogy (or an allegory) may also be effectively employed in a proposition of value speech. Individual stories where the truth prevailed with positive consequences can be powerful if well told with convincing ethos and pathos. However, remember that it's also important to address counterexamples. For example, someone may ask if lying to protect an innocent person from harm would demonstrate a problem with the universal application of the value of honesty.

Other examples of a *Proposition of Value* **include the following:**
A. Adopting from an animal shelter is better than adopting from a breeder.
B. You should donate your time to Habitat to Humanity.
C. Investing in a hybrid car is good for the environment.

Propositions of Policy: A statement urging or recommending new regulations, the elimination of old regulations, or the modification of existing regulations.

To develop a proposition of policy, it is first necessary to identify a social problem. The very purpose of policy is to resolve or mitigate social problems by legislative action (e.g. government or bureaucracy). A very simple example of a proposition of policy would be the requirement of a driver's license to operate a motor vehicle. Though this policy has long been in place, it hasn't always. As motor vehicles became more common at the turn of the 20th century, it also became necessary to regulate their use to manage traffic flow and to reduce property damage, injuries, and deaths related to traffic accidents.

You should also take notice of the fact that *propositions of policy* are always premised upon a combination of propositions of fact and value. In the case of the driver's license policy, facts related to traffic accidents need to be established. For example, young children lack the sense of responsibility and sensorimotor coordination necessary to

handle an automobile, therefore a minimum age for obtaining a driver's license should be put into place. In other words, if one can establish underage drivers as a cause of traffic accidents, this proposition of fact can be used to support the policy being proposed. Other elements of the policy, such as testing and license renewal, should (ideally) be based on propositions of fact that address the causes of the problem at hand (i.e. traffic accidents). Policies related to driving "under the influence," or "while intoxicated" as well as certain health conditions (e.g. seizures, vision impairment, narcolepsy) are also being enforced through the regulation of driver's licenses. In all of these cases, the cause/effect relationship between the social problem and these causal factors should be made apparent.

On the other hand, we interpret facts through our personal and collective values. To the extent that we value human life, want to reduce injury and pain, and avoid damage to property we will consider regulating the operation of motor vehicles through issuing driver's licenses. To the extent that driver's licenses are denied or restricted to certain groups, however, we are also reducing personal freedom since those driving without a license are restricted to punishment by law. Therefore, in arguing a proposition of policy, one must always be aware of the balance between the relative benefits and disadvantages of the freedom being forfeited and the potential gain to civil society. For example, few people would argue on behalf of a drunk driver's freedom to drive drunk, but many would argue on behalf of a competent senior citizen who was losing his or her license due to age restrictions.

Other examples of a *Proposition of Policy* include the following:

a. "Recipients of public assistance between ages 18 and 65 should be required to work in order to be eligible for their benefits."
b. "Citizens of the United States should be entitled to comprehensive health care coverage regardless of their ability to pay."
c. "Business owners should not be permitted to limit their financial liability through incorporation."

Methods of Organization

Generally speaking, the structure of the introduction and conclusion of the persuasive speech follow the guidelines discussed in Chapter 8. The introduction serves to get the audience's attention, establish credibility, relate to the audience, state the central idea, and preview the main points of the speech. The conclusion should summarize the main points, refer back to the introduction, motivate the audience, restate the central idea, and provide a closing statement.

All the methods for organizing a speech covered under informative speaking are applicable here, as well. In addition, however, there are some valuable strategies for ordering main points that apply directly to persuasive speaking. These include the following:

1. **Recency:** The main points of the speech are organized so that the best arguments and evidence come last. This leaves the audience with the strongest possible impression of your persuasive message.
2. **Primacy:** The opposite of recency. The main points of the speech are organized so that the best arguments and evidence are presented up front. This is especially useful with skeptical or hostile audiences. Initially impressive arguments may capture their attention and give you a chance to make your case.
3. **Problem/Solution:** This strategy divides the body of the speech into main points based on problem and solution. In some cases, multiple problems and solutions are presented and, through the process of elimination, the proposal offered by the speaker is ultimately recommended.
4. **Monroe's Motivated Sequence:** This strategy is a variation of problem/solution. The first step is to gain the 'attention' of your audience. The audience is then offered a "need" (a problem that needs solving), a "satisfaction" (a solution to the problem), "visualization" scenarios where the problem is solved and/or not solved, and "action" where the audience is called upon to do something to enact the satisfaction/solution.

Referring back to the organizational strategies offered for the informative speech, you may notice that *reorganization* (deliberately choosing the order of your events or main points) plays an important role in persuasion. Main points must be ordered according to the *principle of complexity* (simpler information is presented before more complex information), but can be further organized to achieve a recency or primacy effect, or in a problem/solution strategy.

Conclusion

In order to persuade an audience, you must be authentic, your reasoning must be sound, and your audience must believe you to be credible on the topic on which you are speaking. Remember the responsibility that you have as a speaker and always consider ethics when attempting to sway the attitudes, values, and beliefs of your listeners.

AL GORE
TED TALK—15 THINGS THAT WE CAN DO TO AVERT CLIMATE CRISIS

https://www.ted.com/talks/al_gore_on_averting_climate_crisis

14 | PERSUASIVE SPEAKING

Public speaking is often associated with formal presentations to a large audience.

Ceremonial Speeches: An Overview

Public speaking is often associated with formal presentations to a large audience.

If you google "public speeches" you will find information on the Roman orator Cicero, as well as lists of greatest historical speeches and lists of all-time great speeches. These results illustrate the power of public speaking to cultivate public discourse, especially during important events.

Previous chapters focused on the skills you need to succeed as a citizen and in your professional life. In this chapter, we focus on ceremonial speeches. One of the most common speech types, ceremonial speeches commemorate or celebrate special events in a person's life. Ceremonial speeches are so common that Aristotle in *On Rhetoric* devotes a section to what the Greek's called **epideictic** speeches. An **epideictic** speech either praises a person for virtuous actions or blames them for bad deeds. While we see fewer speeches of blame today than in Ancient Greece, the importance of the epideictic or ceremonial speech of praise has changed little over the past 2,400 years. Our modern lives are punctuated with special celebrations and events that provide opportunities for you to "say a few words." For example, you may have given an acceptance speech to an organization that gave you a scholarship. Or perhaps you gave a toast at your brother's wedding. In the future, you may be asked to present an award to honor a co-worker or a community leader. In each of these situations, you use your public speaking skills to celebrate an event, a person, or a group.

Speaking on Special Occasions or Ceremonial Speaking

Dr. Thomas S. Wright
Temple University

Dr. Maxine Gesualdi
West Chester University

The purpose of a ceremonial speech is to **express the importance of the moment and the people involved.** It is given to publicly celebrate or commemorate a special occasion. A **special occasion** is a time set apart from both everyday life and its events to reflect on and publicly state what we value most. Since the time of the Greeks, ceremonial speeches have had a ritualistic quality, which means they elevate and transcend our everyday lives but in a way that is familiar. In other words, social and cultural expectations often determine how you should perform ceremonial speeches.

What does an audience expect when they hear a *eulogy* (a speech given at a funeral or memorial service) Based on cultural expectations, a eulogy must express sadness at the loss of a loved one and joyfully celebrate her life. What should you do when you accept an award? A speech of acceptance must include a thank you to the organization or person who presented the award.

What do wedding guests think is an appropriate story in a toast? A toast should be cheerful and reflect on the special nature of the occasion. In this sense, all of these speeches are ritualistic. Each type of ceremonial speech reflects a set of cultural values governed by a set of situational requirements. In the following sections, we will walk you through the process of applying your existing public speaking skills to the process of constructing several types of ceremonial speeches.

In this chapter, you will learn:

- **How to apply the public speaking skills you already learned to ceremonial speaking.**
- **The preliminary rules for preparing a ceremonial speech.**
- **Detailed insights and advice for constructing six common types of ceremonial speeches which are as follows:**
  - Toast
  - Speech of Introduction
  - Speech of Presentation
  - Speech of Acceptance
  - Speech of Commemoration
  - Eulogy

Public Speaking Skills Application

Preparing a ceremonial speech will involve the same public speaking skills you have learned up to this point but you will apply them for a different purpose. An effective ceremonial speech requires that you use an organizational pattern that fits your personal style, helps the audience follow the flow of the presentation, and meets the criteria for the specific type of ceremonial presentation. For example, the chronological **organizational** pattern used for many informative speeches is used often for speeches of introduction, and eulogies. However, many times ceremonial speeches use creative organizational patterns and themes.

An effective ceremonial speech requires you to use many of the same **delivery** techniques and skills that you use in informative and persuasive speaking. The delivery skills of maintaining eye contact, using nonverbals, speaking clearly at an appropriate volume, using dynamic vocal range, and avoiding distracting gestures or movements are also important in ceremonial speeches. In addition, you will use the same modes of presentation. Most ceremonial speeches use the extemporaneous mode of presentation. One key difference you will find is that ceremonial speeches are often less formal or more conversational than informative or persuasive professional presentations. For example, when speaking to introduce someone to an audience, you may be upbeat and speak with greater range because your purpose is to enliven the crowd and raise their expectations for the featured guest.

Finally, the process for **selecting** content for a ceremonial speech is not so different from your preparation for an informative or persuasive speech. In each case, your goal is to find the most accurate sources and use them effectively. For a ceremonial presentation, as discussed later in the chapter, you must include accurate details and up-to-date information. While it is important to note who said a famous quote or where the passage in the Quran it can be found, no one expects you to cite the source of personal information included in the speech.

When considering the purpose of your ceremonial speech, our advice is as follows:
- Apply the research, organization, and content selection skills discussed in previous chapters.
- Review the criteria for each type of ceremonial speech discussed later in this chapter.
- Determine whether your speech will be memorized, extemporaneous, or scripted.

A Distinct Audience

The audience for a ceremonial speech is different from those at an informative or persuasive presentation. Specifically, the audience for a ceremonial speech connects more intimately to the content of the speech than an audience for an informational or persuasive presentation. Toasts and eulogies are the perfect examples of this difference. A toast, as you will learn, is not for a generic audience. Its purpose is to celebrate a person or event that connects directly to that specific audience at that exact time. When you are called on to deliver a toast at your best friend's wedding, the audience is there to celebrate that specific couple in a very personal way. In contrast, consider how the toast at your friend's wedding is different from a speech to the city council about adding bike lanes. While the citizens at the council meeting have an interest in the topic, their connection to it is on a much less personal level.

When considering the audience for your ceremonial speech, our advice is as follows:
- Find out as much as you can about the audience using techniques you learned in the previous chapter on audience analysis. Knowing who may attend will affect content selection and delivery.
- Think of yourself as a surrogate or representative for the audience. For example, not everyone will make a toast, so you are speaking for everyone in attendance.
- Consider the emotional needs of the audience. How do you want them to feel and what content and language selections can you make to reflect that feeling?

Reducing Apprehension

You also need to practice the techniques you learned for managing **public speaking apprehension.** Almost everyone feels nervous in public speaking situations. Whichever term you choose to apply, apprehension, "stage fright," or "nervousness," all show that you care about the situation and the audience. It is natural to want to perform well and meet the needs of the audience. What makes you different is that you have learned a set of techniques for managing your apprehension and those are just as important when giving a ceremonial speech as they are when presenting in class or at work. The setting, purpose, and time requirements for ceremonial speeches also influence any apprehension you feel about your speech.

The settings for ceremonial speeches are often less formal than those in professional presentations. For example, you can treat a speech of introduction for a new manager to the office or a guest pastor at church less formally and more relaxed than a report over annual sales or a proposal to build a new adult care facility in town. As we discussed, the purpose of a ceremonial speech is to mark a special occasion that reflects how you feel about the person or event. Because the purpose of the speech is less formal and more about creating connections and positive feelings, you should approach the situation as one in which the expectations for your performance are different.

Unlike a work presentation, the purpose of a ceremonial speech is not to demonstrate your mastery of the topic. Instead, in a ceremonial speech you want to connect with an audience that is already prepared to embrace you with feelings of good will. The purpose of the ceremony, of that moment in time, ties to the emotions of the audience. The audience wants you to succeed. Remember, you are their surrogate. You represent them. They are not there to find fault but to support you. Finally, you will see later in the chapter that the time expectations for a ceremonial speech are generally much shorter than a traditional informative or persuasive presentation. The relatively short time you have to speak may lessen any apprehension you experience. For example, a speech of introduction is usually only two to three minutes.

When managing your public speaking apprehension, our advice is as follows:
- Practice the techniques for reducing public speaking apprehension
- To reduce your apprehension and prepare yourself for the occasion, find out as much as you can about the setting. For example: ***When will you speak in the ceremony's agenda? Will you have a microphone? Will you be on a dais? Will there be a podium to hold notes? Knowing these details will help you prepare and be confident in your delivery.***

Rules for Preparing a Ceremonial Speech

While every type of ceremonial speech has its own requirements, there are standard rules you should follow in preparing your presentation. These rules include keeping your speech brief, doing your research, using specific details, using pathos or making an emotional connection, and making figurative language choices.

Rule 1: Keep Your Speech Brief
Ceremonial speeches are brief and reflect their specific purpose or event. Remember, ceremonial speeches are often included as a part of a large and elaborate ceremony that may include a number of speakers, officials, dignitaries, executives, religious figures, or honorees. It is more important to leave a lasting impression with the audience through brevity rather than thoroughness. Because you are the surrogate for the audience, you should keep in mind that your speech is not why they are attending the event. Therefore, your brevity will help the ceremony or event progress smoothly. You must practice your speech with a timer to ensure that you keep the speech short.

When timing your speech, our advice is as follows:
- Find out from the event organizers how long they would like you to speak.
- Practice for time a few times to ensure you are staying within time limits.
- Respect the audience, the occasion, and the other speakers by using your allotted time and no more.

Rule 2: Do Your Research

Informative and persuasive speeches require extensive research. You use books, newspaper articles, websites, government documents, and interviews to provide credible information or to create persuasive appeals. Ceremonial speeches do not require as much research. However, a good ceremonial speech will need specific information that will personalize the speech and accurately reflect the event and people you are honoring. As the speaker, you are responsible for giving the audience accurate and timely information.

When conducting your research, our advice is as follows:
- If your speech is about a person (introduction or eulogy), check all available web resources and talk to people who know the person being celebrated. You may include anecdotes or stories from friends, colleagues, and loved ones.
- If your speech involves a specific event or award, find out the purpose and history of the event/award.
- Ask the event sponsors who will be attending the event and how many people they expect to attend. You do not want to be surprised by your audience size.
- Talk to previous presenters. Do they have any useful tips or advice?
- Look for sample speeches or examples. There are many excellent examples available on youtube.com or via a simple Google search. These examples will help you set the tone for your speech and better understand the type of information you need to include.

Rule 3: Fact Check Your Details

Although ceremonial speeches require less research than informative or persuasive speeches, the research you conduct for ceremonial speeches should focus on detailed pieces of information that demonstrate your understanding of the person, event, or award. Using detailed, factual information also helps you meet your responsibility as a knowledgeable and conscientious speaker.

When fact checking the content for your speech, our advice is as follows':
- Double-check the accuracy of all of your facts, quotes, readings, and anecdote/stories. If you are speaking to an organization, giving a speech of introduction, or commemorating an event, be sure to check with the event organizers if you are unsure of any details.

- Double-check the names of everyone mentioned in your speech for both accuracy and pronunciation.
- Double-check the titles used in the organization (President, CFO) or in the family (uncle or second cousin, grand-mother or grandma).
- Ensure all chronological and biographical information is correct.
- Practice your speech so that you are familiar with the quotes, dates, and names you will be using.

Rule 4: Create Emotional Connections and Express Shared Values

Ceremonial speeches evoke a broader range of emotions than informative and persuasive speeches. They will sometimes mix humor and sadness, joy and sorrow, pride and happiness. While informative speeches rarely include emotional language, the purpose of some ceremonial speeches is to create an emotional response for its own sake. Eulogies are the clearest example of the emotional focus and range of ceremonial speeches. Other ceremonial speeches including a toast or speech of acceptance demonstrate the emotional connection every speaker hopes to achieve. For example, when you give a toast, you are making a public proclamation of joy. In a speech of acceptance, you would be providing a public "thank you" to the organization or person who bestowed the award on you.

In addition, creating an emotional connection exemplifies the special role that audiences play in ceremonial speeches. We can see that creating a feeling of identification is one of the central purposes of ceremonial speaking. Commemorative speeches, like those given in the U.S. on the 4th of July to honor the founding of the United States, lean heavily on the use of identification around patriotism and American ideals to generate a sense of togetherness among all members of the audience.

To bring emotional focus to your speech, our advice is as follows:
- Consider the purpose of your speech. Some ceremonial speeches (introduction, presentation, acceptance) are about shared values while other types (eulogies, ceremonial) are about the public expression of private emotions. We will review each of these speech types later in the chapter.
- Before outlining and writing your speech, reflect on and write out one or two specific emotions or values you want your speech to evoke.
- When you write or outline your speech, note which emotion(s) or values you want each section of your speech to create. This will bring focus to your speech and delivery.
- Before writing and practicing your speech, reflect on how you feel and what you believe the audience feels or values. As a surrogate for the audience, you are responsible for representing how they feel or what they value.
- In order to build toward the emotional release you have planned, determine the best content to expresses these emotions (such as anecdotes, quotes, or visual aids) and which organizational pattern (topical, chronological, cause-effect or creative pattern you develop) will build toward an emotional release.
- If your speech is on a particularly emotional topic or situation, consider how to best control your own emotions when you are practicing your delivery.
- Consider how you can create a sense of identification. Why are all the audience members at the event? What values, beliefs, or attitudes do they all share? What are some key things that everyone would agree on?
- Search for sample speeches or examples. There are many excellent examples available on youtube.com or via a simple Google search. These examples will help you set the tone for your speech and better understand the type of information you need to include.

Rule 5: Use Figurative Language
One of the unique and exciting characteristics of ceremonial speeches is that you can use more figurative language in your delivery than in informative or persuasive speeches. Figurative language is language that moves beyond the literal meanings of words or phrases found in the dictionary. **Figurative language** is more poetic, embellished, visual, emotive, and exaggerated than everyday language. Think of this when considering the use of language: ceremonial speeches do not happen every day so they should not use everyday language. The language should paint a picture in the audience members' minds to help them see what you are saying.

Because the purpose of ceremonial speeches is to evoke an emotional response or create a sense of identification, your choice of words or phrases should reflect that purpose. Unlike the straightforward language used in an informative speech, the words and phrases in a ceremonial speech serve a different purpose. For example, if you were to eulogize your grandma, you would not describe her cookies as just "good" would you? You might use a *metaphor, or a comparison using two unlike concepts,* and call them "heavenly"! You might use *hyperbole, or exaggeration,* and say, "grandma's cookies were the best cookies in the world!" It is easy to see how using figurative language relates closely to rule #4, creating an emotional connection. Remember, ceremonial speeches aspire to create a strong connection to the audience and painting a picture helps reach this goal.

When selecting the figurative language for your speech, our advice is as follows:
- Use metaphors, similes, hyperbole, alliteration, repetition, and imagery or sensory details.
- Use a thesaurus. While you never want to rely too much on a thesaurus or choose words you are not comfortable saying, finding just the right word or phrase to express how you feel is worth a few extra minutes.
- Use resources to find inspirational or famous quotes, poems, or religious verses. A well-chosen quote or religious verse can express how you feel and create identification for the audience.
- Consider using song lyrics. Depending on the type of speech you are giving, lyrics are an easy way to enliven your speech, reflect an emotion you are trying to evoke, and create a sense of identification.
- Avoid clichés or overused phrases. If it does not express exactly how you feel or seems like it is said in everyday conversation, look for a different word or phrase.

Rules for Preparing a Ceremonial Speech

> Keep Your Speech Brief
>
> Do Your Research
>
> Check Your Facts
>
> Create Emotional Connection and Express Shared Values
>
> Use Figurative Language

Common Types of Ceremonial Speeches
The Toast

A toast is a short ceremonial speech that celebrates a person or group and is a custom in Western cultures. During a toast, the speaker holds a filled drinking glass. At the end of the speech, the speaker ritualistically raises her or his glass into the air as a gesture of good will and asks the audience members to raise their glasses as well. Then, everyone takes a drink. Toasts are often common at events that celebrate family milestones (an engagement, wedding or anniversary party) or mark achievements in organizations (retirement, award ceremonies, or reunions).

Delivery Tips

- Keep your toast brief. A toast is rarely more than one to three minutes (200-300 words). There are often more than one or two people giving a toast.
- Get everyone's attention before you begin. Your goal is to honor those being toasted and bring an emotional focus to the event.
- Encourage everyone in the audience to be prepared to toast. Everyone should have a glass and be prepared to raise it as a symbolic gesture.
- Keep your remarks informal and relaxed to match the tone and expectations of a celebration.

Organization Suggestions

- A toast usually follows a simple organizational pattern:
  - welcome the guests and thank them for attending,
  - acknowledge those responsible for the event (parents, organization),
  - state who or what you are toasting,
  - state your relationship to person(s) or the event,
  - provide detail to personalize the toast and make an emotional connection to the person being toasted and the audience (an anecdote, example, quote, religious reading/quote),
  - add a look toward the future (e.g. "many years to come"),
  - and end with a thank you. You should add a reminder to the audience to raise their glasses at the end of your toast.

Content Guidelines

- Do research to make sure that you know all the names you need to mention and how to pronounce them.
- Toasts often include humorous quotes or anecdotes about the person(s) being toasted or the event. Be sure that your humor is in "good taste" and does not involve inside jokes that many in the audience will not understand.
- Toasts should make it clear why the person(s) or the event are special. What makes this event toast-worthy?

- The tone of a toast should almost always be positive and optimistic. You are either wishing someone good luck for the future (wedding, retirement) or reflecting on the importance of an event and what it means to the audience (holiday celebration, work event).
- A toast is not a roast. While humor is often used when giving a toast, your goal is not to embarrass, make fun of, or humiliate anyone in attendance. Save any questionable or potentially embarrassing stories for another time.

Speech of Introduction

A speech of introduction is a general term used to refer to any speech that is announcing or previewing another speaker or event. It is given in preparation for something more to come. There is a wide variety of speeches of introduction including welcoming a new employee, introducing a keynote speaker or special guest, or an event.

Delivery Tips

- A speech of introduction should be two to three minutes long (300-400 words). Because your remarks are preparing the audience for a longer speech, you should keep them brief.
- An important goal for the speech of introduction is to focus the audience's attention. It is your responsibility to use your delivery to engage the audience and hold their attention. You want to shift their attention from interaction to listening.
- The speaking style for a speech of introduction should be professional. Because speeches of introduction are used most often in a professional or organizational setting, you should be prepared, make consistent eye contact, and speak with authority.

Organization Suggestions

- A speech of introduction follows a standard organizational pattern:
    - thank everyone for attending or welcome the audience to the event,
    - remind them of the purpose of the event,
    - provide information about the next speaker or agenda item of the event,
    - build anticipation,
    - and welcome the speaker (with applause) or kick off the event.

Content Guidelines

- Do your research and double-check that you have all of the information correct about the speaker or event. It is a best practice to review your information with the person you are introducing and the event coordinators. Oftentimes, a speaker will give you a biography of information you can include.
- State the purpose or relevance of the event. Why is the audience in attendance? Why is the speaker in attendance? What will the audience learn or take away from attending?
- Briefly thank those who organized or sponsored the event.
- Establish the credibility and credentials of the speaker. You may include any of the following types of professionally appropriate information: degree(s) or certifications, schools attended, experience, previous awards, prior presentations, grants received, and title(s).
- Depending on the event, you may be asked to include basic pertinent personal information. You do not have to provide a complete biography but sometimes you may include a speaker's hometown, hobbies, family status, and travel experiences. The person you are introducing and/or the event coordinator can help you determine if personal information should be included for the purpose of the event.
- One way to build anticipation is to preview the speaker's topic with a teaser. You are not responsible for providing a summary but offering a glimpse of what the audience will be hearing may motivate them to pay better attention. This can also be done as an attention getter.

Speech of Presentation

A speech of presentation occurs when a speaker gives an award, honor, or commendation to a recipient or organization. Similar to the speech of introduction, this type of speech leads into the main focus of the occasion. You may be asked to announce the winner of a scholarship, a local leader who is receiving an award for public service, or presenting a trophy to the local girls' softball team. In each case, your responsibilities are like those for the speech of introduction. You need to highlight the accomplishment of the recipient.

Delivery Tips

- A speech of presentation should be one to two minutes long (200-300 words). Your remarks prepare the audience to celebrate achievement so keep them brief.
- Do research to make sure that you know all the names you need to mention and how to pronounce them.
- An important goal for the speech of presentation is to focus the audience's attention. You want to shift their attention from interaction to listening.
- The speaking style for a speech of presentation should be enthusiastic but respectful. You should be prepared, make consistent eye contact and use open and engaging language while speaking with passion.

Organization Suggestions

- A speech of presentation follows a simple organizational pattern:
    - thank everyone for attending or welcome them to the event,
    - provide background information or context for the award, honor, or commendation,
    - briefly thank everyone who participated in the process or who were nominated,
    - and reveal the name of the person or organization.

Content Guidelines

- Do your research and double-check that you have all of the information correct about the award and the person or organization receiving it. It is a best practice to review your information with the event coordinators.
- Briefly, explain the purpose of the award, honor, or commendation. You may include a brief history, who sponsors it and why, the ideals it represents, or the criteria used during the selection process. While there is no perfect combination of information, your goal is to provide context for the audience so they can appreciate the importance of the award.
- Depending on the award, you may need to explain why the person or organization was chosen as the recipient.
- Depending on the award, you may also convey what the award means to you as a person, a member of the community, or as a representative of an organization.

15 | SPEAKING ON SPECIAL OCCASIONS OR CEREMONIAL SPEAKING

Speech of Acceptance

A speech of acceptance is a short speech you would give when receiving an award, honor, or commendation. You might be asked to say a few words after receiving an award for yourself or as a representative of an organization. An important characteristic of a speech of acceptance is that while you are receiving recognition, the purpose of the award is to link to a larger social good or shared value. For example, a scholarship from a local club is not just about awarding money to you but is also about publicly recognizing the importance of hard work and the value of higher education.

Delivery Tips

- A speech of acceptance is rarely more than one to two minutes (100-200 words). There is often more than one person accepting an award or there may be multiple awards given out, so you do not want to dominate the proceedings.
- Your delivery should demonstrate humility and enthusiasm for being chosen. It is important to use open and engaging body language, vocal range and variety, and make consistent eye contact. You need to show the audience that you are thankful and worthy of the award.
- Whether or not you know in advance that you will be receiving the award, be prepared to accept it. Even outlining a few remarks will make you less nervous and will help you avoid veering off the subject and taking too much time.

Organization Suggestions

- A speech of acceptance follows a standard organizational pattern:
  - thank the presenter and the organization or person who bestowed the award,
  - give credit or recognize other people or organizations that could have received the award,
  - and briefly state what the award means to you.

Content Guidelines

- Thank those giving the award. Do your research so that you know who (person, organization) is giving the award and its significance. How long has it been awarded? Who else has received it? What values, beliefs, or ideals does it represent?
- Be prepared to state what the award means to you. If you are accepting a scholarship, you will want to state how it will help you meet your expenses (and have more time to study). If you are receiving a civic or organizational award, you will want to convey how you connect to the community or organization.
- Briefly mention other people or organizations that could have also been given the award.
- Thank those who helped you or your path to accepting the award. This may include your parents, siblings, coach, co-workers, boss, etc.

Speech of Commemoration

A speech of commemoration honors, pays tribute to, or celebrates an event, place, or person. Three key characteristics of these speeches are that they take place in public ceremonies, represent widely held beliefs or values, and deal with something in the past. For example, a speech given before a 4th of July parade commemorates the founding of the United States and will mention widely held American values such as freedom, liberty, and unity. Speeches of commemoration are often given on historic anniversaries (e.g. December 7th) or holidays (e.g. Memorial Day) and to celebrate important people (e.g. Susan B. Anthony).

Delivery Tips

- A speech of commemoration may be either one to two minutes or five to six minutes, depending on the occasion and precedent. You should ask the organizers how long speeches have been in the past or how long they would like you to speak.
- Your delivery should be well practiced, formal, and fit the tone or mood of the occasion. Some commemorative speeches are focused on memorializing a tragic event (e.g. 9/11) while others are celebrating the life of an important public figure (Dr. Martin Luther King).

Organization Suggestions

- A speech of commemoration follows a standard organizational pattern:
  - thank everyone for attending or welcome them to the event,
  - thank the event organizers,
  - provide background information or context for the commemoration,
  - and discuss how the event or person is relevant today (this often includes the audience's shared values or beliefs). You may also discuss how the events of the past or how the celebrated person's life relates to the future.

Content Guidelines

- Do your research and double-check that you have all of the information correct about the event or the person being commemorated.
- Establish why the event or person is being celebrated. What about the event or the person elevates them to a place of honor?
- Provide specific details about the event or the person being commemorated. In this way, the speech of commemoration is similar to an informative speech. You cannot assume that everyone in attendance is familiar with the basic information about the event or the biographical details of the person you are celebrating.
- Use quotes or readings from significant individuals to highlight the importance of the event or person being celebrated.
- Perhaps more so than any other type of ceremonial speech, a speech of commemoration uses stories or a narrative format. Because you are recounting a historical event or the life of a person, consider what details are necessary to construct the narrative of what happened or the important events of a person's life.
- Some commemorative events will be attended by those who were directly involved in the event or know the person being honored. It is important to mention their presence and allow the crowd to applaud.
- Provide image-rich examples that focus on values (courage, sacrifice, hard work).

Eulogy

A eulogy is a speech given to celebrate the life of a person who is now deceased. They are often given at a memorial service and the audience includes family members, friends, and coworkers. A eulogy must walk a complicated path between recognizing the emotional pain caused by the person's death and celebrating her or his life. This complicated path highlights how eulogies are distinct from the other types of ceremonial speeches we have discussed. The content or purpose is more emotional than other types of speeches and the speaker is allowed to be more emotional. Additionally, you are responsible for representing the feelings of the audience. Because not everyone in attendance will be asked to give a eulogy, the selected speakers should reflect the thoughts and feelings of the audience. Your goal is to get the audience to transcend their sorrow and see how fortunate they were to have known the deceased.

15 | SPEAKING ON SPECIAL OCCASIONS OR CEREMONIAL SPEAKING

Delivery Tips

- Eulogies range in length but are usually three to five minutes long (300-500 words). It is common for there to be a number of speakers or religious figures scheduled to speak, so be sure to find out how much time you have to speak.
- Your delivery should be well practiced, formal, and fit the tone or mood of the occasion. As discussed above, it is important to recognize the solemnity of the occasion but also show the joy that a person brought to your life.
- One of the more challenging aspects of delivering a eulogy is managing your emotions. Practicing your speech will often help because you will be better prepared for emotional moments in your speech.

Organization Guidelines

- There are many excellent resources available for organizing a eulogy. You should not be embarrassed to use templates or premade organizational patterns. It is an emotional time and anything that may help reduce your stress or anxiety is important.
- A common organizational pattern is to do the following:
  - thank those in attendance,
  - state your relationship to the deceased (if it is not obvious or already known),
  - provide a brief biographical overview of the person's life,
  - mention those things in life that she or he loved most,
  - show how her or his life affected those in the audience,
  - and how the audience members can honor her or his passing.

- You can also use a thematic approach that centers on her or his life (biographical, chronological), accomplishments, roles they played (mother, wife, dancer), or personality characteristics.

Content Guidelines

- One of the more challenging aspects of giving a eulogy is managing the amount of content available with the amount of time you are allotted. Imagine the challenge of summarizing a person's life and what she or he meant to you (and everyone in the audience) in just a few minutes.
- Acknowledge the loss to the family, friends, and colleagues but recognize how the deceased person's spirit will live on in everyday events and actions.
- Use quotes (either famous or from family members), a poem, song lyrics, or religious readings to bring focus to the person's life or impact the person had on the lives of those in attendance.
- Use anecdotes or stories to illustrate aspects of the person's life, personality, or important relationships.
- Recognize the person's uniqueness. How was she or he different or special? Be sure to use an example or anecdote to highlight this.
- Use your personal relationship to focus on the particular role the person played in life. For example, if you were the person's colleague, you should focus on that particular aspect of her or his life. You are representative of all of her or his work relationships.
- Ask friends, family, and colleagues what they will remember most about the deceased. Do they have a favorite anecdote? What are three words they would use to describe her or him? What is the funniest thing he or she ever said or did? This allows you to meet your goal of honoring the person's life but it also allows you to include the audience.

Conclusion

The purpose of a ceremonial speech is to **express the importance of a milestone moment and the people involved.** It is given to publicly celebrate or commemorate a **special occasion.** In your personal and professional life, you will at some point be asked to deliver a ceremonial speech. In this chapter, we have provided you with advice, rules, and guideline for preparing for six distinct types of ceremonial speeches: Toast, Speech of Introduction, Speech of Presentation, Speech of Acceptance, Speech of Commemoration, and Eulogy.

Small group presentations are common in schools, workplaces, and civic forums.

Small group presentations are common in schools, workplaces, and civic forums. At this point in your education, you have probably participated in numerous small group presentations. Teachers and professors often use small group presentations to distribute class workload and cover a wide range of content in a short time. While some students find small group work challenging, they may not realize how common small group presentations are in the contemporary workplace. Whether your employer calls it a committee, team or working group, they will expect you to collaborate with other employees and make presentations. Our everyday lives are populated with group presentations that center on civic responsibilities. For example, when you join your neighborhood association, members of the association may have to address the city council concerning the development of a new golf course.

We also have seen the emergence of virtual small groups in which the members are dispersed across the world, work on varied schedules, and represent different parts of the organization (marketing, distribution, production).

These groups are connected via technology (Skype, shared documents) but are responsible for the same outcomes as groups that physically meet. In the following sections, we will walk you through the process of applying your existing public speaking skills to the construction of several types of small group presentations.

In this chapter, you will learn

- Characteristics of a small group.
- Types of small group presentations:
  - Symposiums
  - Panel Discussions
  - Working group Presentations
- Do's and Don'ts for preparing and planning a working group presentation.
- How to apply your existing public speaking skills (content selection, organizational patterns, dynamic delivery) to working group presentations.
- How to apply public speaking apprehension management techniques in working group presentations.

Small Group Presentations

Dr. Thomas S. Wright
(Temple University)

Dr. Maxine Gesualdi
(West Chester University)

Characteristics of a Small Group

Communication in small groups is a distinct area of communication theory and research. People who study small group communication examine group dynamics and individual contributions that lead to effective small group interaction. Small groups are defined as having between three and 12 members. These groups have unique challenges related to effective communication between members. The scope of small group theory and research is too broad to discuss in a book about public speaking. Therefore, this section describes unique characteristics and challenges of a small group that has been assigned with putting together a presentation.

The main challenge of working in a small group is communication between members. Sharing information, research, documents, and plans for a presentation require coordination among all group members. The failure of members to communicate with each other is one of the primary causes of groups failing to meet deadlines and achieve goals. As a group's size increases, so do the challenges of communicating effectively and efficiently. However, the benefits of group work often outweigh the challenges. The main benefit of group work is shared responsibility and workload. Distributing the workload among members makes every member's work easier. Shared workload also means that multiple group members may participate in the presentation.

Second, small groups have a clear set of goals or objectives for developing the presentation. Your group will have a higher likelihood of succeeding when working toward a clear goal or objective. Every group member should understand what constitutes "success" for the group or know the criteria being used to evaluate what counts as a good presentation.

A third characteristic is that members of a small group interact and influence each other. As you will see later in the chapter, professional working group presentations require each member to participate and provide feedback throughout the entire process from finding the initial information needed for the presentation to reflecting on ways to improve after the presentation is delivered. In addition, fellow group members can help you manage your public speaking apprehension. Whether you are in a small group for a class project or at work, everyone in the group will be held responsible for the final product or presentation. Groups are grounded in shared work and responsibility.

Another key component of a successful small group is the establishment of trust among the group members. When all of the members of a small group trust that each other is working hard, contributing and upholding a high standard of professionalism, higher levels of productivity are be reached. In fact, trust between small group members is essential to functionality. In a work setting, adherence to professional norms helps to further this trust. There is an expectation that fellow small group members will comport themselves in a professional way and further group goals.

Finally, small groups use structured decision-making processes to develop a presentation. Each group member participates in either selecting specific members to make decisions (e.g. representatives, leader, or chair) or they directly participate in the decision-making process. Group presentations require a lot of decision making. Some of these decisions include the following: who should conduct the research or information gathering? how should that information be shared? what information is important (and what is not)? how should the presentation be structured? what type of visual aids will be needed (and who will create the visual aids)? who will present the content? and who will answer questions from the audience? Whatever decision-making process your small group employs, it should help you meet the goal or objective of your group.

Small Group Characteristics

Shared Workload

Clear Set of Goals

Members interact and influence each other

Structured Decision Making Processes

Types of Small Group Presentations

Small group presentations are categorized by their purpose or format. The purpose of a small group presentation, much like many individual speeches, may be to persuade or inform.

Persuasive Small Group Presentations
Persuasive small group presentations are common in professional and civic settings. An example of a persuasive small group presentation is a **sales pitch** or **sales proposal** in which the group is trying to convince a prospective client to buy a product or service. Another example of a persuasive small group presentation is one involving civic **engagement**. In this instance, the group makes a proposal to a representative body about making a change in public policy. For example, a civic group may propose that a school board provide more funds for an elementary school theatre program. In each of these scenarios, members of the small group have a singular purpose: persuading an audience to act. As we will discuss in the next section, **symposiums** and **panel discussions** are persuasive small group presentations that include multiple presenters.

Informative Small Group Presentations
Informative small group presentations are ever-present in college classrooms, professional situations, and civic settings. Many students in high school and college are required to work in small groups to present assigned content to a class. Some common criteria for these informative presentations are that each student must participate, the group must cover the assigned content, and the group should use visual aids. The purpose of the presentation is for students to present information in an interesting or engaging way. The larger purpose of classroom presentations is to prepare students for professional situations in which teams and committees regularly present their work or findings. While these informative small group presentations may include some persuasive elements, the purpose of these presentations is to provide information.

Small groups are an effective way for organizations to delegate and distribute work. Some examples of informative professional small group presentations are staff reports, progress reports, marketing plans, **orientation** and **training seminars**. Orientation and training is a common, reoccurring example of an informative small group presentation. Management's goal is to ensure that each new employee understands the organization's policies and procedures as well as to introduce hires to the organization's culture. To accomplish this task, a team or group must present information to the new employees related to policies and rules of conduct. For maximum efficiency, the group or team members want to avoid providing redundant information or incongruous messages about the organization.

Professional Interactions

Two common types of professional interactions that do not fit the standard small group presentation format are **conference calls** and **group interviews**. A **conference call** is a telephone call in which someone speaks to several people at the same time. For example, a representative for an organization may need to provide information concerning an upcoming event to stakeholders of the organization. The stakeholders will then have the opportunity to ask questions or respond to the representative. A **group interview** is when a person is one among many people, generally job candidates, who are interviewed simultaneously. For example, an organization may use a group interview for an entry level position with many applicants. Group interviews are a cost effective and efficient way to conduct a job interview with multiple candidates. It is also a way to compare different job candidates' social skills or assess how they perform under pressure.

Best practices for conducting a conference call include the following:

- Make a list of all of the participants including their names, organizational affiliation, and title.
- Provide participants with the specific time the call will occur and how long it will last.
- Prepare your remarks or talking points before initiating the call. Since you are providing information or trying to persuade your audience, you should prepare for a conference call the same way you prepare for any other presentation.
- Create and share an agenda before making the call. Review the agenda at the start of the call.
- Create and share any media (PowerPoint, documents, websites, etc.) before making the call.
- Check the equipment and make sure it works before initiating the call. This is particularly important if you are using a computer or web based software.
- Leave time for feedback or answering questions.
- Let the participants know who else will be included in the conference call.
- Ask everyone to mute their phones/mics when they are not participating.

The best practices for participating in a group interview are as follows:

- The most important part of any interview is to come prepared. If you want to stand out from the other applicants, you have to demonstrate that you are more knowledgeable about the organization.
- Before the interview, introduce yourself to the other candidates. You may have to participate in group or team building activities.
- Come prepared to participate in team or group activities. Group interviews are often used not only to assess how knowledgeable candidates are about the organization but how well they function in group or team building activities.
- Come prepared to differentiate yourself from other candidates. Organizations often ask candidates questions like "What makes you unique?" or "Describe a situation in which you challenged the status quo?"
- Come prepared to answer questions that link you to other candidates. Organizations often ask questions that highlight cooperation or team orientation. For example, the interviewer may ask you "What is something you all have in common?"
- Express yourself and participate but never dominate the discussion or time.
- Never interject or cut off another applicant while they are speaking.
- Listen to the other applicants while they are speaking. It is polite and respectful, it shows that you are a team player, and it allows you to answer questions more effectively.

Small Group Presentation Formats

Another way to categorize small group presentations is by format. There are three basic formats used for small group presentations; **symposium, panel discussion, and working group.** The first two, the **symposium** and the **panel discussion,** are less common than the **working group presentation.**

A symposium is a small group of speakers who provide commentary, analysis, or information on a single topic or theme or provide contrasting viewpoints on the same topic or theme.

Characteristics of a symposium include the following:
- Speakers who are experts in the symposium's subject area or who have long-term experience relevant to the subject matter;
- A **moderator** who is tasked with introducing each speaker, providing an overview of the topic or theme, managing speakers' time, transitioning between speakers, providing closing remarks, and regulating audience interaction (taking questions, comments, etc.);
- Equal speaking time for each participant;
- An audience whose members offer questions or comments for the speakers.

Best practices of a symposium include the following:
- The moderator is responsible for ensuring a sense of cohesiveness between the speakers. If the relationship between the speakers' presentations is not obvious, the moderator should draw connections between them during the symposium.
- The moderator and the symposium sponsors are responsible for communicating time limit expectations to every speaker before the symposium begins. It is important to plan for an introduction, transitions, and questions from the audience in addition to symposium speakers.
- The sponsor of the symposium should decide or discuss with the participants what mode of presentation each speaker is expected to use. Should each participant speak extemporaneously or use a manuscript? Different modes of delivery by the speakers may lead to confusion among the speakers and the audience. In either case, the speakers should know well in advance the preferred mode of delivery.

- While it is less common to use visual aids in a symposium, the sponsor of the symposium should decide or discuss with the participants whether they are expected to use visual aids and what type of visual aids are appropriate for the setting.
- If you are the moderator or sponsor, you are responsible for making appropriate physical arrangements. For example: seating arrangements so that the speakers can see the audience and each other, microphones (if necessary), water or other beverages (if necessary), pens and paper, and name cards.
- If the participants are expected to take different sides or positions on the same topic with the purpose of persuading the audience, the moderator may need to regulate the number of questions taken for each speaker, to ensure decorum and a civil discussion.
- If you are a speaker, you should state your name, organizational affiliation (if necessary), and your credentials before you speak, if you were not introduced by the moderator.

A panel discussion is a small-group of speakers (panelists) who present a diversity of viewpoints on the same topic or theme and actively engage one another. The topic of a panel discussion may be political or professional. For example, a political panel discussion may consider whether drone strikes are an appropriate way to conduct the "war on terror." On the other hand, professional panel discussions may consider changes in the newspaper industry, advice for job hunting, or the best use of social media in the healthcare industry.

Characteristics of a panel discussion include the following:
- Panelists who are experts in the subject area being discussed or have long-term experience relevant to the subject matter. Selecting participants for a panel can be less strict than a symposium because the purpose is engagement or interaction and not always sharing information with the audience.
- Interaction between the panelists and the audience. The panelists are conducting a public conversation about a topic or theme in front of an audience. The goal is for their interaction (debate, deliberation, discussion) to enlighten the audience or sway audience member's beliefs or opinions.

A moderator is tasked with introducing each panelist, providing an overview of the topic or theme, asking questions for the panelists to answer, providing closing remarks, and regulating audience interaction (taking questions, comments, etc.).

Best practices of a panel discussion include:

- If you are the moderator or sponsor, you are responsible for making appropriate physical arrangements. For example: seating arrangements so that each panelist can see the audience and each other, microphones (if necessary), water or other beverages (if necessary), pens and paper, and name cards.

- The moderator should ensure active engagement between the panelists by beginning with a question or scenario, prompting responses from each panelist, and asking panelists to respond to other panelists.

- The moderator should ensure that no one panelist dominates the conversation.

- The mode of delivery used in a panel discussion is often more informal than those used in a symposium or working group presentation. However, like a symposium, the sponsor should decide or discuss with the participants what mode of presentation each panelist is expected to use. For example, should the panelists speak extemporaneously or use a manuscript? In either case, the panelists should know well in advance the preferred mode of delivery.

- While it is less common to use visual aids in a panel discussion, the sponsor of the panel should decide or discuss with the participants whether they are expected to use visual aids and what type of visual aids are appropriate for the setting.

- If the panel is discussing a politically charged topic or theme, the moderator should ensure that each panelist is respectful when engaging another panelist. While the topic may be contentious, the discussion should be civil.

- If you are a panelist, you need to state your name, organizational affiliation (if necessary), and your credentials if you were not introduced by the moderator.

A working group presentation is a small group of speakers who present information on a single topic for a specific audience.

Characteristics of a working group presentation include the following:

- One or more speakers who are responsible for presenting. A single group member, multiple group members, or every group member could present information to an audience.
- A smaller audience than for a symposium or panel discussion. Professional and educational small group presentations are often for a much smaller audience than those in a public symposium or panel discussion.
- A specified amount of time to present the group's work. Presentations take more time than individual speeches (but no more time than a symposium or panel discussion).
- An audience that can make decisions and act on the information provided. Professional and educational small group presentations are often given for an audience that can use the information to make decisions or for the teacher to provide a grade.
- The use of visual aids to present the working group's information. Visual aids are less common in symposiums and panel discussions.

Best practices of a working group presenting its findings include the following:

- Speakers should state the group's credentials and references/citations for the information being presented.
- Group members should be prepared to answer questions about the subject matter presented. Group members should spend time preparing for these questions in advance by anticipating what the audience may want to know.
- Group members should collaborate with each other before, during, and after the presentation. Unlike a symposium or panel discussion, the whole working group is responsible for the planning process and preparation, the presentation, critique and improvement, and a follow up with the audience (if necessary). In a symposium or panel discussion, the participants are not necessarily responsible for each other or accountable to each other.
- Visual aids should help show the audience something that enhances your message. Use charts, graphs, diagrams, and pictures instead of lists and paragraphs.

Of the three types of small group presentations we discussed, the symposium and the panel discussion are less common than the working group presentation. One reason for this is that symposiums and panel discussion are often used to present a diversity of information or opinions on a topic whereas the working group presentation are often used as an efficient and effective means for providing information in a professional setting. For example, a university political science department may sponsor a campus-wide symposium on race relations in the United States. On the other hand, your boss may ask you and your coworkers to provide a project overview using the group presentation format. Because working group presentation are common, we focus most of our attention in this chapter on working group presentations.

Understanding the difference between the two types of small group presentations (informative and persuasive) and the three formats (symposium, panel discussion, and working group), provides your group with an opportunity to consider which format is best for your small group presentation. Each format can be adapted to suit the specific purpose or goal of your group.

The rest of the chapter focuses on the working group format because it is the most common used for educational and professional presentations.

Working Group Presentation: Preparation and Planning

The process of preparing and planning a working group presentation is similar to the stages used for an individual informative, persuasive, or special occasion speech. Having a detailed list of guidelines and a plan of action will help your group maximize your potential and ensure an effective presentation. A consistent problem with working groups is that they begin the process by focusing too much on the final product without taking the important and necessary first steps to ensure a high functioning group. At every stage of preparation and planning, group members must place a premium on good communication between all the group members, on meeting deadlines and goals, and on conducting practices or rehearsals. The key to a successful presentation is collaboration.

To ensure a highly efficient and functional working environment, our advice is:
- Ensure that everyone knows everyone else in the group (including her/his title or position in the organization).
- Establish when, where, and for how long you will be meeting. Does everyone need to be present at every planning meeting? Will there be any virtual meetings? Will the meetings always last the same amount of time?

- Establish clear lines of communication. Choose one form of communication everyone will commit to using and check regularly (text message, email, conference calls).
- Establish the format group members will use to share documents (Word, .pdf, Google docs).
- Collect, communicate, and organize all the basic information about your presentation. This information will include the following:
  - Who is asking for the presentation and what is the purpose?
  - Where and when will the group be delivering the presentation?
  - Who will be in attendance?
  - What resources will be available to the group when presenting? Will the group have easy access to a computer and projector? Will the group need to bring any presentation technology?
  - What criteria will be used to evaluate the presentation?
- Commit to a schedule and stick to it. The benefits of a group schedule are that it creates expectations and criteria for progress, allows individual members to manage their personal schedules, helps to ensure accountability, and encourages each member to stay on track. Your schedule should break up the tasks into a timeline that includes specific milestones and responsibilities including the following:
  - When is the research to be completed and who is responsible for it?
  - When are drafts or outlines due and who is typing and distributing them?
  - When are the visual aids to be completed and who is designing them?
  - What are the specific dates, times, and locations for practice or rehearsal?

Once your group has established the basic functional processes necessary for small group work, you can begin creating content, choosing an appropriate organizational pattern, and practicing your delivery.

Working Group Decision Making

One challenge every working group will encounter is decision making. One widely used process for decision making was developed by the American philosopher and educator John Dewey. Dewey outlines a six-step process that working groups can follow. One reason Dewey's approach is widely used is that it can be used for making both major and minor decisions. For example, a working group may be formed to address a specific issues or problem an organization has encountered. This is a major decision. If there was no problem, there would be no need for a working group. On the other hand, Dewey's approach can also be used for minor decisions within a working group. For example, selecting the best font or background to use when presenting the group's findings. From the outset, it may be helpful to discuss whether your group will use a **consensus** model of decision making, in which there is agreement in the group, whether you will be **voting** throughout the process, or whether there is one **executive** who will make decisions. No matter what model of decision making a working group employs, group work is a **collaborative** process. Everyone in the group should be working together to ensure the highest quality presentation.

Dewey's Six Steps for Decision Making

1. Identify or Select the Problem: In the normal process of group work, problems or issues will arise regarding the nature of the goal of the group's presentation: how to select content, how to organize the material, and how best to present it to an audience. In this step group members, should identify one problem to focus on first, making sure to only work on one problem at a time.

2. Analyze the Problem: What do we know about the problem? In some instances, analyzing a problem may involve outside research and a presentation of those findings. Other times, a problem can be solved with knowledge already within the group. In these cases, the analysis may only consist of making sure every group member understands the nature of the problem and why it needs to be addressed.

3. Criteria Selection: What are the goals of a final decision or what are the parameters for that decision? A clear set of criteria provide the group with a means for evaluating what is an appropriate or inappropriate outcome to solve the problem.

4. Solution Generation: What are all the possible solutions that fit the criteria? A popular method used in working groups is **brainstorming** during which everyone offers possible solutions without judging the solutions

5. Selection: Which decision or solution best meets the criteria? Oftentimes picking the best solution is not unanimous within the group, so the group members may have to discuss further to reach a consensus.

6. Solution Implementation: In this stage, the working group may be implement the solution. With working groups, it is also likely the group will present their solution to others within the larger organization, and the implementation is left to these other people.

Some discussion of Dewey's decision making process include an additional step and that is **evaluating** the decision after it has been implemented. This step includes evaluating how the solution was implemented to gain knowledge about future problems and solutions and about the decision-making process within the organization.

Working Group Presentations: Content Selection, Organization, and Dynamic Delivery

In this section, we discuss the challenges working groups face when selecting the appropriate content, applying an organizational pattern, and practicing a dynamic mode of delivery. Working in a group will involve adapting and applying your public speaking skills in a more dynamic and complex presentation context than in individual presentations. To reduce or overcome these challenges, we offer a set of specific guidelines to ensure an effective presentation. Unlike a single speaker addressing an audience, group presentations depend on a high degree of collaboration and teamwork.

Selecting the Appropriate Content for a Working Group Presentation

An effective working group presentation requires that your group select the appropriate content and ensure that every group member is familiar with it. Because the goal of a group presentation often is to inform or persuade, the group's goal is to find the most accurate sources and use them effectively. There are some challenges to reaching this goal. First, working groups often distribute the responsibility for finding information which can lead to confusion. Your group may break up the research so that each member may be assigned different research topics, tasks, or sections. For example, if your group is presenting on new gun regulations in your city, one member may be responsible for researching legal precedent and existing laws while another member is responsible for researching current public opinion. Distributing the workload is highly efficient but it also means that group members may not be aware of all the information gathered for the presentation. Group members need to make sure they agree on an organized way of storing the information gathered from each member so that any member can access the research if needed.

In addition, every group member needs to thoroughly understand and know the content of the presentation including the sources used to create it. Even if the group's research is conducted by one group member, everyone in the group is responsible for the accuracy of the information. As we discussed earlier in the chapter, having processes in place for sharing information, checking each other's work, and preparing and practicing together will ensure both adequate content selection and the accurate presentation of the content.

When selecting the content for your working group findings, our advice is to do the following:

- Delegate the research process. Agree on specific tasks for each member of the group.
- Conduct an audience analysis. What does the audience already know about the topic? Who will be attendance? What are their expectations?
- Once each member has assembled information, establish a process for sharing and reviewing the information. This process would include setting deadlines for reviews, requiring an overview at each meeting, or using digital tracking software to see who has viewed each document.
- Some ways your group can keep everyone informed are:
  - Provide updates at every meeting.
  - Share all the research, outlines, and visual aids.
  - Discuss how everyone is meeting their due dates (from the agreed-upon schedule)
- Focus on content synchronization.
- Collaborate to ensure that everyone is using the same terminology, jargon, and tone throughout. When your group practices, it is helpful to record the practice and check for consistency.
- Collaborate to ensure that your visual aids are consistent. Have one person in charge of the visual aids create a template and share it with the group. The template should have a fixed background, font, and style of graphics.
- Avoid having too many sections in your presentation. Each additional section increases the time spent practicing, adds to the possibility of confusion, and increases the number of transitions.
- Allow time for every group member to review the final documents (outline, PowerPoint, etc.) before practicing.

Applying an Organizational Pattern for a Working group Presentation
An effective working group presentation requires that your group use an organizational pattern that works for each group member, helps the audience follow the flow of the presentation, and meets the goal of the presentation (to inform or to persuade). Similar to an individual speech, a chronological, cause-effect, or topical organizational pattern can be used for an effective group presentation. One challenge working group members face is ensuring coherence and consistency.

The key difference from a single speaker using these organizational patterns and a working group using these patterns is not the specific organizational pattern itself but how a working group works together. It is often obvious and embarrassing when a group member is unsure or confused during the presentation to the audience. Each group member needs to agree on the appropriate organizational pattern and understand how the different parts of the presentation relate to one another to ensure a smooth presentation. For example, if your group is using a cause-effect organizational pattern, each group member needs to understand and be able to present the information in a way that demonstrates their knowledge of each cause and the related effect (e.g. gentrification results in higher home prices)

When organizing for your working group findings, our advice is to do the following:

- Gather all your research and supporting materials and as a group decide which information must be covered versus which information you would like to cover. Beginning with only the necessary (or "must be covered") information, the group will decide which organizational pattern is most effective.
- Determine if one group member will be presenting all the content, if separate sections will be covered by different members, or if everyone in the group must present.
  - You then will need to assign specific members to specific sections (if having multiple speakers).
  - Some groups have the same person present the introduction and conclusion.
  - Remember: the more members you have speaking, the more time you need for transitions.
  - Remember: the more members you have speaking, the more time you need for rehearsal.

- Structure your group presentation like an individual presentation with an introduction, body, and conclusion. You should adapt each section to the requirements of a working group presentation.
- The Introduction may include the following::
  - An attention getting device (if appropriate for the presentation)
  - Statement of the purpose of presentation (if appropriate based on your audience analysis)
  - Preview the presentation (what will be covered, who will cover what content, etc.)
  - Introduction of everyone in the group. This is done either individually, round robin style, or using a visual aid/slide for each member.
  - An explanation of which member(s) performed specific roles or tasks (optional). For example, who completed the research, who gathered the data, who conducted the focus groups, etc. This can also be done for each individual section.
  - A discussion of the nature of your project. For example, who commissioned the group's work, how long the group has been working together, etc.
  - A statement informing the audience how long you will be presenting.
  - A statement informing the audience if you are taking questions during or after the presentation.
- The body of a working group presentation is like those found in an informative or persuasive individual speech. Your body should have identifiable main points supported by key information and include transitions. In addition, your group should do the following:
  - Ensure that the content achieves the agreed-upon goals you were given for the presentation.
  - Ensure that content being presented is coherent (everyone is using the same terminology, examples, etc.) and cohesive (each section clearly relates or they build on one another).
  - Discuss expectations regarding audience interaction during or after the presentation. If your group expects ongoing interaction, you will need to consider the time it may take and who will be responding.

- Discuss how the group will handle transitions between different sections. Will each member introduce or preview the next section or is each group member responsible for previewing her own section?
- Find out whether the group is expected to provide citations or references during the presentation. Should these be stated during the presentation? Should citations be listed on a slide at the end of the presentation?
- Recognize the work each group member put into the presentation. This is especially true if one member is presenting all the content.

- The conclusion of a working group presentation is also like those found in an individual speech. Just like in an individual speech, you should leave the audience with a strong impression. In addition, your group should do the following:
    - Provide a concise summary. Use a visual aid to reinforce key messages or talking points.
    - Consider what actions or steps you expect the audience to take. How can you facilitate the audience taking action? Is the audience supposed to visit a website (have it up on the screen and email a link), use a smartphone or tablet app, or receive a handout?
    - Consider your group's next steps for interacting with the audience. Is your group expected to follow up with the audience? Will your group be contacting audience members? How and when? Should the audience members be contacting you?
    - Recognize the sponsors or host of the event (if necessary) and thank the audience.
    - Indicate if you are taking questions, how much time you have for questions, and who in the group will be responding.

Delivering Working Group Findings

An effective working group presentation requires that each group member uses the same **delivery** techniques and skills that a single speaker uses in an informative or persuasive speech. For the purposes of this section, let us assume that your working group has opted to have multiple members present to the audience. If you are in a working group for a class, this is often a requirement. The delivery skills of maintaining eye contact, using nonverbal communication, speaking clearly at an appropriate volume, using dynamic vocal range, and avoiding distracting gestures or movements are important for each individual speaker during the presentation.

What are some of the challenges faced by working groups in delivering their presentation? One challenge you will face is consistency. Speakers often have personal styles based on their experiences or their personalities. There is nothing inherently wrong with some variation in group members' delivery but your group needs to be aware of how that may affect timing, transitions, audience perception, and engagement. Another challenge is that your group will need to allow additional time for practice as a group. One of the most common pitfalls for a working group presentation is not practicing together and hoping that things will "just work out" if everyone knows his or her part. A lack of practice will ensure that everyone in the group will be more nervous and that each member is unfamiliar with the content of the entire presentation. Lack of preparation is most apparent in transitions. Groups that are not adequately prepared often have disjointed, time-consuming transitions that do not link the sections together in a coherent way. And audiences can often tell when a group is not prepared. Finally, remember that when a group fails, every group member's credibility is harmed. Even group members who did not present are responsible for the final product.

Before rehearsing as a group, our advice is as follows:
- Remember that practice and rehearsal are more important for a group presentation than an individual speech. Every aspect of a group presentation presents additional potential problems that do not exist when only one person is speaking. Collaborating with one another at the outset will reduce the likelihood of a poor performance and increase the likelihood of success.
- Remember that a group presentation reflects on every person in the group whether she or he is presenting or not.
- Commit to practicing and rehearsing more than one time. There is no magic number for how many times a group should rehearse, but a lack of rehearsal creates greater stress and a higher probability for delivery problems.

- As discussed previously, commit to a rehearsal schedule and have agreed upon dates, times, and locations.

- If a single or only select members are presenting for the group, have an honest discussion during the rehearsal period about which group members are the best public speakers, who are the most qualified, and who has the most authority, credibility, or experience? In other words, who will your audience respond to and respect?

- Discuss the mode of presentation everyone will be using. Is everyone speaking extemporaneously? Is everyone using a manuscript? Is everyone using the PowerPoint or visual aids for prompts? Different modes of delivery among presenters leads to an inconsistent and sometimes confusing presentation. Different modes can also make it seem like some members are not prepared.

- Discuss the dress code. Is everyone expected to dress professionally? Is it business casual? You do not want one person over or under dressed.

When delivering the group's findings, our advice to your group is as follows:

- Monitor each member's nonverbal communication. Everyone should be paying attention, nodding along, smiling, or in some way indicating interest throughout the presentation. Do not expect the audience to be interested if the group members do not seem interested.

- Use inclusive language. Every group member should be using "we," "our," or "us" when discussing the group's work.

- Do not talk over one another. Practice and rehearsal will often eliminate this issue but be aware of it when you have questions from the audience.

- Use smooth and coherent transitions from one member to the next. Remember: each transition should explicitly and clearly indicate a change in topic and speaker.

- Be aware of the physical space the group is using during the presentation. Practice and rehearsal should eliminate any problems but remember that multiple speakers translate into more people occupying the physical space. If you will be presenting in a room, consider where each speaker needs to be positioned to quickly reach the speaking area, and whether they will sit or stand when not speaking.

- Use a Google or Youtube.com search to find examples of good presentations and watch them as a group.

Working Group Presentations: Reducing Apprehension

For a working group presentation, use the same techniques you learned for managing **public speaking apprehension** when giving an informative, persuasive, or ceremonial speech. As we discussed in the chapter on ceremonial speaking, apprehension, "stage fright," or "nervousness," are common terms that are used describe the feelings we have before a presentation. There are two unique aspects to managing apprehension when delivering a working group presentation. First, it is safe to assume that everyone in your group has at one time or another been nervous about public speaking. Everyone is your group cares about performing well for the audience and meeting the group's goal(s). You can find comfort in the fact that everyone in your group will live through the same experience. When working in a group, you have a valuable new resource: the experience of your group members. You should ask them how they manage their apprehension and provide them with the techniques you use.

Another unique aspect of apprehension when giving a working group presentation is that your group is also an audience. You are not just performing for those in the audience but also for the other group members. Your group members are your **compatriot audience.** A compatriot audience is one that participates in the group presentation preparation process and supports your success. A compatriot audience gives your group a distinct advantage when preparing your presentation. They help you before your presentation by assuring that you know the content, guaranteeing that everyone is well practiced, and providing constructive feedback in advance. You should consider your team members' feedback and thank them for their help. A compatriot audience helps during a presentation by ensuring that everyone meets the same high standards for delivery that you have agreed on and providing support (by nodding, paying attention, using visual aids). After your presentation, your group members can provide feedback on those elements of the presentation that worked well and those that need improvement. While we assume from our classroom experience that group presentations are given only one time, in the professional setting your working group may give the same presentation several times. Sometimes multiple times during the same day. Presenting in front of an audience, as well as your group, may seem at first to be more of a challenge but it is in fact an opportunity for you to reduce your apprehension and improve your public speaking skills. In the long run, knowing the strengths and weaknesses of every group member will allow your group to grow and improve.

To manage your public speaking apprehension when presenting a working group's findings, our advice is as follows:

- Practice your most effective techniques for reducing public speaking apprehension.
- Use your working group as a resource for apprehension management techniques.
- Consider the benefits of your compatriot audience (before, during, and after speaking).

Conclusion

Small groups are defined as having between three and 12 members. These groups have unique challenges related to effective communication between members. In your personal and professional life, you will participate in making small group presentations. In this chapter, we described the characteristics of a small group, the three most common types of small group presentations (symposiums, panel discussions, and working group presentations.)We also provided guidelines for preparing and planning a working group presentation, decision making, the best ways to apply your existing public speaking skills (content selection, organizational patterns, dynamic delivery), and advice for managing your public speaking apprehension in working group presentations.